Mastering SQL Queries for SAP Business One

Utilize the power of SQL queries to bring Business Intelligence to your small to medium-sized business

Gordon Du

BIRMINGHAM - MUMBAI

Mastering SQL Queries for SAP Business One

First published: May 2011

Production Reference: 3010711

Published by Packt Publishing Ltd.
32 Lincoln Road
Olton
Birmingham, B27 6PA, UK.

ISBN 978-1-849682-36-7

www.packtpub.com

Cover Image by David Guettirrez (bilbaorocker@yahoo.co.uk)

Credits

Author
Gordon Du

Reviewers
Zal Parchem

Muddassar Imran

Wolfgang Niefert

Navneet Dhami

Acquisition Editor
Stephanie Moss

Development Editor
Susmita Panda

Technical Editor
Pallavi Kachare

Copy Editor
Laxmi Subramanian

Project Coordinator
Vishal Bodwani

Proofreader
Aaron Nash

Indexer
Monica Ajmera

Graphics
Geetanjali Sawant

Production Coordinator
Arvindkumar Gupta

Cover Work
Arvindkumar Gupta

About the Author

Gordon Du studied System Engineering and Computer Science at the Nankai University in Tianjin, China. He has over 28 years of experience in diversified information technology fields. His experience with SQL goes back to 1987.

Gordon was the first person in China to successfully implement an international software package for a Chinese investment-only company in 1995.

Gordon has been the top contributor on the SAP Business One forum since August 2008. He has been awarded 45,000 points as of January 16, 2011. This is the highest lifetime points recorded by SAP Community Network for a non-SAP employee since 2004. Over 25 percent of Gordon's points are related to solving SQL query questions and problems posted by other forum members. Here are some links demonstrating this.

His SCN profile link for reference:

`http://forums.sdn.sap.com/profile.jspa?userID=4130357`

His first blog on SCN:

`http://www.sdn.sap.com/irj/scn/weblogs?blog=/pub/wlg/17099`

The congratulations and thanks thread to his 35,000 points from forum users:

`http://forums.sdn.sap.com/thread.jspa?threadID=1718298&tstart=0`

Gordon has worked and trained extensively in China, Singapore, USA, and Canada. He also holds the following certificates: a Microsoft Certified System Administrator, Microsoft Certified System Engineer, and a Microsoft Certified Database Administrator.

Gordon is planning to write a series of books related to SAP Business One in response to the demand from many SAP Business One users and consultants.

Acknowledgement

Special thanks goes to my wife, Lisa, whose love and encouragement helped me to complete this book. Thank you, my son Mason and his fiancée, Ava, for your support and reviews. Thank you to Zal Parchem, who not only inspired me from the beginning, but also provided a professional technical review. Thanks to the staff at Packt Publishing and all my friends who supported me in writing this book. Among all my friends, MS Christine Malone has given me the greatest support by her excellent final proof reading and editing.

Last but not least, thank you to everyone who posted on the SAP Business One forum providing me the opportunity to solve so many SQL query problems.

About the Reviewers

Zal Parchem has been in the business world working in the Information Systems area for over 31 years. For the past 10 years, he has been working as an Independent Consultant, concentrating on helping small to midsize companies install and customize their ERP (Enterprise Resource Planning) systems. He has restricted his work efforts to the SAP Business One (SAP B1) ERP system and is actively involved in many SAP Forums, SAP Blogging areas, and the Wiki sections for SAP B1. He works with SAP, SAP B1 Partners, and Customers around the world. For the past three years, Zal Parchem has been using SQL extensively in SAP B1 for reporting and customization purposes in SAP B1.

He has been employed in a variety of industries, with company sizes ranging from six personnel to over 250,000 employees. Having retired from The Home Depot in 2001, he started his career as an Independent Consultant.

He has also written a "guerrilla handbook" titled *Project Methodology and Documentation for SAP Business One Implementations*. He actively reviews all SAP B1 books available in print; his reviews can be seen online at Amazon.

> I would like to thank Gordon Du for this opportunity to do the technical aspect of his work in SQL. Gordon is the most active participant in the SAP B1 forums where he helps dozens of people daily. I am honored to know Gordon as a Fellow Forum Friend (FFF) and to have been asked to work with PacktPub on this publication, which is certainly going to extend Gordon's ability to help even more individuals to be productive and effective in the use of SQL inside SAP Business One.

Muddassar Imran is a passionate Web Developer. He is the Web Developer at Page and Moy, UK. He is a First Class Graduate from DMU (De Montfort University, Leicester UK) and was awarded the best final year project award from BCS (British Computer Society). Moreover, he is a Professional Member of BCS. He is enthusiastic about modern expert system and database administration. He has aesthetic skills in writing complex SQL Queries, ASP.NET, VB.NET and AJAX.

Imran was born in Gujranwala, a small city famous for its peaceful atmosphere. He attended Suffa Secondary School at 10th Grade and achieved the highest scores in his city. He got admission at the Government College University, Lahore for further education in Computer Science. He went to Malaysia for higher education and finished a Higher Diploma in Computing Studies from KDU College Malaysia. Then he went back to Pakistan and worked with Wateen Telecom Pvt. Ltd. and Telenor for two years, primarily developing web-based applications and working on automation projects.

Muddassar then traveled to the United Kingdom to attend the De Montfort University. In 2010, he received his Bachelors in Computer Science. While studying at DMU, he was working with Venus Packaging Solutions Ltd. As a VB.NET Developer until March 2011 and then joined Page & Moy in April 2011.

Further, Imran writes on his blog (www.blog.mudasar.co.uk) and his personal website is www.mudasar.com. For relaxation, he likes to workout at the gym and travel.

Wolfgang Niefert has more than 15 years experience with international SAP implementations. A certification for the SAP Production Planning (PP) module with the SAP academy in London allows him to relate larger SAP solutions to SAP Business ONE. Wolfgang has worked in Germany, Switzerland, UK, U.S., Poland, Russia and Saudi Arabia. He is the managing director of NIEFERT Certified Solutions (NCS, LLC) in San Diego, CA. NCS LLC is an SAP Channel Partner and recognized Software Solutions Partner (SSP) for SAP. He designed the N2ONE Portal Solution that integrates with SAP Systems in Real-Time. The N2ONE Portal solution is a hosted eCommerce platform that that works with SAP Business ONE and SAP All-In-ONE.

In Europe his work with NIEFERT GmbH has led to multiple project solutions including quality control systems with SAP integration. These systems are live today with 24x7 operations worldwide. As part of high-availability projects he acquired certifications in Hewlett-Packard Cluster Design.

Wolfgang provided training for cluster systems with Oracle Failsafe in Europe and the US.

NCS LLC is also a Microsoft Certified Gold Partner and publishes the Momentum Reporter for Excel. This solution allows the visual design of database queries and retrieves query results directly in Excel. In addition NIEFERT published the N2ONE Forecast Manager (SAP Edition). This solution manages SAP data for KPI reporting and web based dashboard publishing.

As a true renaissance consultant with a broad knowledge and skill set in multiple fields, Wolfgang provides a 360 perspective on modern business solutions. Orchestrating project areas and translating visions into realities is his core competency.

In his spare time Wolfgang has established a recognized portfolio of Black and White Large Format landscape and portrait photography.

After passing B-Tech in Computer Science and Engineering **Navneet Dhami** joined ITSL Technologies as a .Net developer in June 2007. He worked on ERSys (ERP Systems) and internal CRM product of ITSL Technologies. He then moved to SAP as TechnoFunctional consultant, and also provided training on TB1000, TB1100, TB1200 books. After that he joined Sapphire systems in June 2010 as SAP SDK Support consultant.

He is an active contributor to the SAP sdn community. He got gold contribution status in the year 2010 in sdn community.

I would like to thank my family and my team for helping and supporting me.

www.PacktPub.com

Support files, eBooks, discount offers and more

You might want to visit www.PacktPub.com for support files and downloads related to your book.

Did you know that Packt offers eBook versions of every book published, with PDF and ePub files available? You can upgrade to the eBook version at www.PacktPub.com and as a print book customer, you are entitled to a discount on the eBook copy. Get in touch with us at service@packtpub.com for more details.

At www.PacktPub.com, you can also read a collection of free technical articles, sign up for a range of free newsletters and receive exclusive discounts and offers on Packt books and eBooks.

http://PacktLib.PacktPub.com

Do you need instant solutions to your IT questions? PacktLib is Packt's online digital book library. Here, you can access, read and search across Packt's entire library of books.

Why Subscribe?

- Fully searchable across every book published by Packt
- Copy and paste, print and bookmark content
- On demand and accessible via web browser

Free Access for Packt account holders

If you have an account with Packt at www.PacktPub.com, you can use this to access PacktLib today and view nine entirely free books. Simply use your login credentials for immediate access.

Instant Updates on New Packt Books

Get notified! Find out when new books are published by following @PacktEnterprise on Twitter, or the *Packt Enterprise* Facebook page.

Table of Contents

Section 2 – SQL Query in Action

Preface

This book has been created to serve the needs of many SAP Business One users. If you have a chance to browse the SAP business One website between mid-2008 and mid-2011, you will find that my name is always on the top contributor's list. I have solved many SQL Query related problems faced by many users, and some such users have asked me to write a blog or wiki page on the topic. However, the subject is too big to fit into any of those information holders. That is why this book came into being.

Business Intelligence (BI)

This is a buzz word nowadays. Usually, only big companies use this term very often. However, from the strict definition from Wikipedia, we can understand the following:

BI refers to computer-based techniques used in spotting, digging-out, and analyzing business data, such as sales revenue by products and/or departments or associated costs and incomes. BI technologies provide historical, current, and predictive views of business operations. BI often aims to support better business decision-making.

That means BI can be used in any type of solution as long as the technology allows the supporting business decision making process. In this book, you will learn why BI could be a perfect fit for SAP Business One. Hence, it will benefit small-to-midsized businesses. SQL Query is one of the most powerful tools in SAP Business One that is related to BI.

 SAP Business One is usually abbreviated as B1 by many users. It could be easily confused with BI. In this book, B1 is not used. Full names of SAP Business One can be found throughout.

What this book covers

There are two sections present in this book.

Section 1: SQL Query Basic

The first section is mainly for beginners who have limited knowledge of SQL Query but want to use this tool as soon as possible. You will learn basic tools to start writing your query quickly. Upon completion, you could jump to the next section to further your skills to complete more. Section 1, *SQL Query Basic* comprises three chapters:

Chapter 1, *SAP Business One Query Users and Query Basics*, discusses the basic concepts and knowledge needed to use SQL query in SAP Business One. You will learn a clear definition of SQL query, the data dictionary, and table links.

Chapter 2, *Query Generator and Query Wizard*, introduces two basic tools for SAP Business One. Query Generator and Query Wizard will teach you to create SQL query in SAP Business One quickly to get the job done.

Chapter 3, *Query Manager*, illustrates the most important business intelligence tool for SAP Business One. Query Manager will help you write query freely. This chapter covers the most frequently used query statements one by one. All statements are explained with concrete examples.

Through these three chapters, you will gain the basic knowledge to jump to the next section and have to use SQL query in more areas. Even experienced readers may find some value in going through this section.

Section 2: SQL Query in Action

The second part of the book will jump to a higher level of complex SQL queries. You will learn different skills for different categories. This section is more closely related to Business Intelligence more closely because it can retrieve more business required data at the right time by the right people. Section 2, *SQL Query in Action* comprises six chapters:

Chapter 4, *Query Examples*, shows the most widely used query examples. You will learn more query features first. By showing query examples from three primary usage categories, you will be able to build the queries to meet your specific need. The alert query examples are discussed especially for those important on-demand situation.

Chapter 5, Securities and Approval, describes the security for query by SAP Business One and also the query associated with approval processes. You will learn how to handle query security by utilizing query groups. You will also learn user query for approval procedures with query examples.

Chapter 6, SQL Query for Formatted Search (FMS), emphasizes one of the most frequently used and error-prone processes to create SQL Query for Formatted Search (FMS). You will learn everything needed in FMS query and the associated Auto Refresh functionality.

Chapter 7, SQL Query for Other Reporting Tools, focuses on SQL query usage in some other reporting tools. You will learn Query Print Layout Designer as well as the SQL query usage within Crystal Reports. The latter focuses on Command in the database expert selection of Crystal Reports.

Chapter 8, SQL Query for Stored Procedure (SP), is about one of the very special cases for query usage. You will learn query that is used in a special Stored Procedure: SBO_SP_TransactionNotification. By giving a clear overview of the SP, the last section shows some kernel SQL query examples for this SP.

Chapter 9, More Complicated SQL Query Topics, extends the scope of basic SQL query to more complicated cases. You will get in depth query knowledge to bring more Business Intelligence into SAP Business One. At the end of the book, you will get some good advices about query writing.

Through these six chapters, you will gain more knowledge regarding SQL query for SAP Business One. If you have specific questions in mind, you may jump to the chapter that most attracts you and go from there.

Each chapter contains specific query examples. For ease of reference in Chapters 4 and 9, each example refers to the chapter number, along with a letter code denoting the subject of the query. Please refer to the following key:

Letter code	Query subject
R	Variables
D	Data function
O	Orange arrow
T	Subtotal
M	Marketing documents
I	Inventory transactions
F	Financial transactions
A	Alerts
X	Miscellaneous

Letter code	Query subject
C	Case expression usage
S	Subquery
P	PIVOT

What you need for this book

- SAP Business One installation or trial system
- An eagerness to get more pertinent information from your database
- A table reference from help file REFDB.CHM in SAP Business One SDK Help Center

Who this book is for

This book is written for every kind of SAP Business One user who needs to obtain information, which is not available in the standard reports. SQL query is also the tool to provide specific solutions and alternatives to SAP Business One authorizations and standard business Processes. The audience for this book includes Consultant, Programmer, Administrator, and many other end users. In fact, every SAP Business One customer could benefit from this book. To get the right information at the right time is one of the most important tasks to bring SAP Business One's power to small and midsize businesses. This is the main goal of the book.

If you have started to use SQL Query already, the book will help you to use this tool more efficiently. If you are a beginner with very limited SQL knowledge, you will find the book easy to follow to solve your SQL query problems quickly. You may also find the book helpful if you are not a SAP Business One user, but have interest in learning SQL query skills. However, to run example queries in the book, SAP Business One installation or trial system is required. There are many examples in the book that are "Ready to Go". They cover many areas that may be similar to what you need.

Conventions

In this book, you will find a number of styles of text that distinguish between different kinds of information. Here are some examples of these styles, and an explanation of their meaning.

Code words in text are shown as follows: "Although, you could link any fields between tables, if the field is not NULL, you should try to use key link wherever possible."

A block of code is set as follows:

```
DECLARE @Factor as numeric(1,0)

SELECT @Factor =
CASE (SELECT TOP 1 DispPosDeb FROM OADM)
 WHEN 'N' THEN 1 ELSE -1
END
```

New terms and **important words** are shown in bold. Words that you see on the screen, in menus or dialog boxes for example, appear in the text like this: "Under **Select**, three fields are selected from two tables".

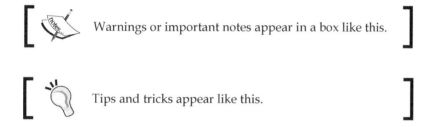

Warnings or important notes appear in a box like this.

Tips and tricks appear like this.

Reader feedback

Feedback from our readers is always welcome. Let us know what you think about this book—what you liked or may have disliked. Reader feedback is important for us to develop titles that you really get the most out of.

To send us general feedback, simply send an e-mail to feedback@packtpub.com, and mention the book title via the subject of your message.

If there is a book that you need and would like to see us publish, please send us a note in the **SUGGEST A TITLE** form on www.packtpub.com or e-mail suggest@packtpub.com.

If there is a topic that you have expertise in and you are interested in either writing or contributing to a book, see our author guide on www.packtpub.com/authors.

Customer support

Now that you are the proud owner of a Packt book, we have a number of things to help you to get the most from your purchase.

Downloading the example code

You can download the example code files for all Packt books you have purchased from your account at http://www.PacktPub.com. If you purchased this book elsewhere, you can visit http://www.PacktPub.com/support and register to have the files e-mailed directly to you.

Errata

Although we have taken every care to ensure the accuracy of our content, mistakes do happen. If you find a mistake in one of our books—maybe a mistake in the text or the code—we would be grateful if you would report this to us. By doing so, you can save other readers from frustration and help us improve subsequent versions of this book. If you find any errata, please report them by visiting http://www.packtpub.com/support, selecting your book, clicking on the **errata submission form** link, and entering the details of your errata. Once your errata are verified, your submission will be accepted and the errata will be uploaded on our website, or added to any list of existing errata, under the Errata section of that title. Any existing errata can be viewed by selecting your title from http://www.packtpub.com/support.

Piracy

Piracy of copyright material on the Internet is an ongoing problem across all media. At Packt, we take the protection of our copyright and licenses very seriously. If you come across any illegal copies of our works, in any form, on the Internet, please provide us with the location address or website name immediately so that we can pursue a remedy.

Please contact us at copyright@packtpub.com with a link to the suspected pirated material.

We appreciate your help in protecting our authors, and our ability to bring you valuable content.

Questions

You can contact us at questions@packtpub.com if you are having a problem with any aspect of the book, and we will do our best to address it.

Section 1

SQL Query Basic

*SAP Business One Query Users
and Query Basics*

Query Generator and Query Wizard

Query Manager

1

SAP Business One Query Users and Query Basics

This chapter will begin by identifying the target audience of this book, and will then go on to discuss the basic concepts and knowledge needed to use SQL query in SAP Business One. In the first section, you will be given a clear definition of the specific scope of the **SQL** and **Query** used in this book. The following section discusses the Data Dictionary and table links such as base tables versus target tables. The last section gives you a key concept to remember for building a good query by keeping it simple.

Who can benefit from using SQL Queries in SAP Business One?

It may not be easy to deduce the ideal reader of this book. In fact, there are many different groups of SAP Business One users who may need this tool.

To my knowledge, there is no standard organization chart for Small and Midsized enterprises. Most of them are different. You may often find one person that handles more than one role. In this sense all users, especially end users, may need this book as long as they can use SQL query with the basic knowledge required.

You may check the following list to see if anything applies to you:

- Do you need to check specific sales results over certain time periods, for certain areas or certain customers?
- Do you want to know who the top vendors from certain locations for certain materials are?

- Do you have dynamic updated version of your sales force performance in real time?
- Do you often check if approval procedures are exactly matching your expectations?
- Have you tried to start building your SQL query but could not get it done properly?
- Have you experienced writing SQL query but the results are not always correct or up to your expectations?

If the answer to any of the questions mentioned earlier is "yes", then you can certainly benefit from reading this book. It will answer each and every question mentioned earlier and give you the power to solve complicated problems.

Consultant

If you are an SAP Business One consultant, you have probably mastered SQL query already. However, if that is not the case, this book would be a great help to extend your consulting power. It will probably become a mandatory skill in the future that any SAP Business One consultant should be able to use SQL query.

Developer

If you are an SAP Business One add-on developer, these skills will be good additions to your capabilities. You may find this book useful even in some other development work like coding or programming. Very often you need to embed SQL query to your codes to complete your **Software Development Kit (SDK)** project.

SAP Business One end user

If you are simply a normal SAP Business One end user, you may need this book more. This is because SQL query usage is best applied for the companies who have SAP Business One live data. Only you as the end users know better than anyone else what you are looking for to make Business Intelligence a daily routine job. It is very important for you to have an ability to create a query report so that you can map your requirement by query in a timely manner.

Non-SAP Business One users

To the other readers who are not SAP Business One users, you could still get some hints and tips from this book because the working and the problematic queries are both shown. Even without an SAP Business One user interface, you may still gain some useful concepts. In one query example of this book, I will show you that even without the actual data from my database to test the query due to localization limitation, the correct answer to the questioner can still be deduced.

No matter what your background is, you will find this book useful whenever you need to get certain data quickly and accurately.

SQL query and related terms

Before going into the details of SQL query, I would like to briefly introduce some basic database concepts because SQL is a database language for managing data in **Relational Database Management Systems (RDBMS)**.

RDBMS

RDBMS is a Database Management System that is based on the relation model. **Relational** here is a key word for RDBMS. You will find that data is stored in the form of **Tables** and the relationship among the data is also stored in the form of tables for RDBMS.

Table

Table is a key component within a database. One table or a group of tables represent one kind of data. For example, table OSLP within SAP Business One holds all Sales Employee Data. Tables are two-dimensional data storage place holders. You need to be familiar with their usage and their relationships with each other. If you are familiar with Microsoft Excel, the worksheet in Excel is a kind of two-dimensional table.

Table is also one of the most often used concepts in the book. Relationships between each table may be more important than tables themselves because without relation, nothing could be of any value. One important function within SAP Business One is allowing **User Defined Table (UDT)**. All UDTs start with "@".

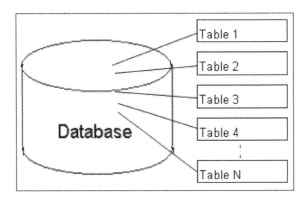

Field

A field is the lowest unit holding data within a table. A table can have many fields. It is also called a **column.** Field and column are interchangeable. A table is comprised of records, and all records have the same structure with specific fields. One important concept in SAP Business One is **User Defined Field (UDF).** All UDFs start with **U_**.

SQL

SQL is often referred to as Structured Query Language. It is pronounced as S-Q-L or as the word "Sequel". There are many different revisions and extensions of SQL. The current revision is SQL: 2008, and the first major revision is SQL-92. Most of SQL extensions are built on top of SQL-92.

This book has very specific scope for the terms "SQL" and "query". Please read through this section carefully first if you find that the scope of the book is not right for your needs.

T-SQL

We have to limit the scope of the term SQL in this book. First of all, since SAP Business One is built on Microsoft SQL Server database, SQL here means Transact-SQL or **T-SQL** in brief. It is a Microsoft's/Sybase's extension of general meaning for SQL. Because we only use T-SQL throughout the book, SQL in this book will mean T-SQL unless it is clearly mentioned otherwise.

Subsets of SQL

There are three main subsets of the SQL language:

- Data Control Language (DCL)
- Data Definition Language (DDL)
- Data Manipulation Language (DML)

Each set of the SQL language has a special purpose:

- **DCL** is used to control access to data in a database such as to *grant* or *revoke* specified users' rights to perform specified tasks.
- **DDL** is used to define data structures such as to *create*, *alter*, or *drop* tables.
- **DML** is used to retrieve and manipulate data in the table such as to *insert*, *delete*, and *update* data. *Select*, however, becomes a special statement belonging to this subset even though it is a read-only command that will not manipulate data at all.

Query

Query is the most common operation in SQL. It could refer to all three SQL subsets. In this book, however, you will only learn the read-only part of the query. No *Add*, *Delete*, or *Update* SQL statement in DML will be discussed in the book since it is prohibited from SAP support policy for SAP Business One database integrity. All DCL or DDL SQL will also not be included because we neither control access to data in a database, nor define data structure for a database. You will find SELECT leading query only within the book. Read-only query SELECT has powerful functionality for finding useful information to meet your specific needs.

You have to understand the risks of running any Add, Delete, or Update queries that could potentially alter system tables even if they are User Defined Fields. Only SELECT query is legitimate for SAP Business One system table.

Data dictionary

In order to create working SQL queries, you not only need to know how to write it, but also need to have a clear view regarding the relationship between tables and where to find the information required. As you know, SAP Business One is built on Microsoft SQL Server. Data dictionary is a great tool for creating SQL queries. Before we start, a good Data Dictionary is essential for the database. Fortunately, there is a very good reference called *SAP Business One Database Tables Reference* readily available through SAP Business One SDK help Centre. You can find the details in the following section.

SAP Business One—Database tables reference

The database tables reference file named REFDB.CHM is the one we are looking for. SDK is usually installed on the same server as the SAP Business One database server. Normally, the file path is: X:\Program Files\SAP\SAP Business One SDK\Help. Here, "X" means the drive where your SAP Business One SDK is installed. The help file looks like this:

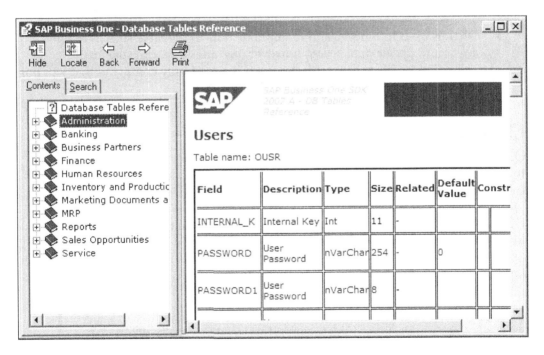

In this help file, we will find the same categories as the SAP Business One menu with all 11 modules. The tables related to each module are listed one by one. There are tree structures in the help file if the header tables have row tables. Each table provides a list of all the fields in the table along with their description, type, size, related tables, default value, and constraints.

Naming convention of tables for SAP Business One

To help you understand the previous mentioned data dictionary quickly, we will be going through the naming conventions for the table in SAP Business One.

Three letter words

Most tables for SAP Business One have four letters. The only exceptions are number-ending tables, if the numbers are greater than nine. Those tables will have five letters. To understand table names easily, there is a three letter abbreviation in SAP Business One. Some of the commonly used abbreviations are listed as follows:

- ADM: Administration
- ATC: Attachments
- CPR: Contact Persons
- CRD: Business Partners
- DLN: Delivery Notes
- HEM: Employees
- INV: Sales Invoices
- ITM: Items
- ITT: Product Trees (Bill of Materials)
- OPR: Sales Opportunities
- PCH: Purchase Invoices
- PDN: Goods Receipt PO
- POR: Purchase Orders
- QUT: Sales Quotations
- RDR: Sales Orders
- RIN: Sales Credit Notes
- RPC: Purchase Credit Notes

- SLP: Sales Employees
- USR: Users
- WOR: Production Orders
- WTR: Stock Transfers

"O" tables

All tables starting with "O" refer to **master tables**. O here represents **Object**. For example:

- OITM: Items Master
- OCRD: Business Partners Master
- OSLP: Sales Employee

"A" tables

Most tables starting with "A" may mean historical log tables. A here represents **Archive**. For example:

- AITM: Items — History
- ACRD: Business Partners — History
- AUSR: Archive Users — History

Document header tables

These are special O tables with the exact same structure. They can be tables related to Sales or Purchase. These are called Marketing Documents. These also include most Inventory transaction tables. Some examples are:

- OINV: A/R Invoice Header
- OPCH: A/P Invoice Header
- OIGN: Goods Receipt Header

Document line tables

All tables ending with a number refer to document line detail tables or subtables for the master table. Numbers here could refer to different properties of the header tables.

- INV1: A/R Invoice Row
- PCH1: A/P Invoice Row

- IGN1: Goods Receipt Row
- INV2: A/R Invoice—Row Expense

Important table examples

Some specific tables very important for query building are listed here:

- **OJDT-Journal Entry**: This table includes all financial journal entries no matter whether they are automatically posted or manually posted.

- **OINM-Warehouse Journal**: This table includes all inventory-related transactions. It is a single point to check everything in relation to your inventory (or stock). It becomes a view in the new version. This view must be queried very carefully.

- **ADOC-Document History**: This table includes all document history. However, it is wrongly named in the documentation, "Invoice History" table in the help file.

Table links—the key for the right query

Table links are fundamental for query building. You will see some different links in this section, but the most common links will be discussed in the next section because there are too many and they are used too often.

To understand table links, you need to know more about table structures.

Primary key

Every table has a primary key. Some of the tables have foreign keys too. All those keys are used for the index. Docentry is a typical primary key to link OXXX with XXXn document tables. For example, Docentry is a common key field to link OPOR with POR1, POR2 to POR12.

A primary key can be one or more fields. For a simple table one key field would be good enough. For a complicated table, two or more fields for primary key are not rare.

A primary key has to be unique within the same table. This key will not allow NULL value—that is, an empty field or a field with no data.

Foreign key

A foreign key is usually used to link to some other table's primary key. This field will be updated whenever the other table record has changed.

Although, you could link any fields between tables, if the field is not NULL, you should try to use key link wherever possible in order to increase the database performance.

Example of table links within SAP Business One

To be clearer about the link, here are a few table link examples:

- **OITM-Items table and ITM1-Items Prices table**:

  These two tables are linked through ItemCode field. Both tables have the same field name to link. It is not one-to-one but one-to-many relationships. One Item Code in item master may have more than one item price associated.

- **OITT-Product Tree table and ITT1-Product Tree Child Items**:

  These two tables are linked through **Code** field in OITT and **Father** field in ITT1. These tables are used for Bill of Materials.

- **OCRD-Business Partner table and OSLP-Sales Employee table**:

  These two tables are linked through the same name field SlpCode. In the second table, SlpCode is the primary key for OSLP. On the other hand, it is a foreign key in the first table OCRD.

Base tables versus target tables

Base tables and **target tables** are special linked tables within SAP Business One. They are the most often used linked tables for SQL queries too.

You may find most of them related to "Sales-A/R" and "Purchase-A/P" documents or so-called "Marketing Documents".

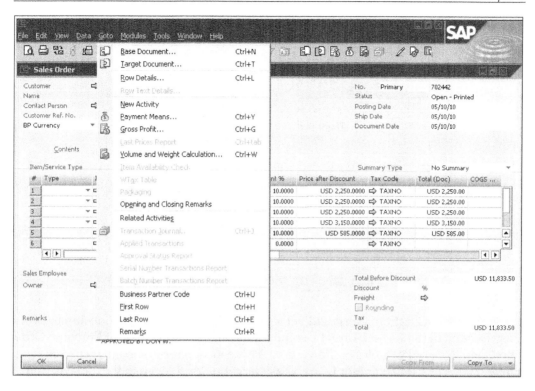

Marketing documents may not have base tables or target tables. From the previous screenshot, you could clearly find that the **Base Document** and **Target Document** are available to this Sales Order. To get the Base Document, you may click on the "left arrow icon" or use the shortcut key *Ctrl+N*. To get the Target Document, you may click on the "right arrow icon" or use the shortcut key *Ctrl+T*. Only when the base table or target table is available to the current document, will you find the menu items and icons in active status. Otherwise, both icons and menu items are grayed out.

From the terms "Base" and "Target", it is clear that the target table can be based upon the base table.

One table could be based on different types of tables:

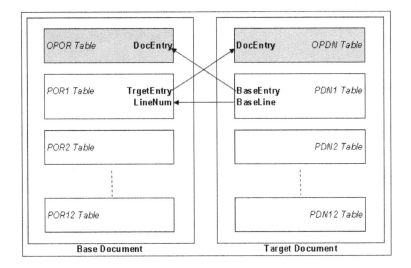

From this demonstration, you could get a clear picture about the relationship between Base Document (table) and Target Document (table). A specific pair of Purchase Order and Good Receipt PO tables is shown here. This concept applies to all document type tables. Here is a list of commonly used base-target pairs; they are not inclusive. You may find more, but the following are the most frequently used ones:

Base Table	Target Table
OQUT – Sales Quotation	ORDR – Sales Order
OQUT – Sales Quotation	ODLN – Delivery
OQUT – Sales Quotation	OINV – A/R Invoice
ORDR – Sales Order	ODLN – Delivery
ORDR – Sales Order	OINV – A/R Invoice
ODLN – Delivery	ORDN – Returns
ODLN – Delivery	OINV – A/R Invoice
ORDN – Returns	ORIN – A/R Credit Note
ODLN – A/R Invoice	ORIN – A/R Credit Note
OPOR – Purchase Order	OPDN – Goods Receipt PO
OPOR – Purchase Order	OPCH – A/P Invoice
OPDN – Goods Receipt PO	ORPD – Goods return
OPDN – Goods Receipt PO	OPCH – A/P Invoice
ORPD – Goods return	ORPC – A/P Credit Note
OPCH – A/P Invoice	ORPC – A/P Credit Note

I have omitted the details for the link. Actually, you will find that all the links exist on the first child table or so-called **row table** for the header table, such as QUT1 instead of OQUT.

The linking fields are very clear. For example:

- BaseEntry in the target table refers to the base table's DocEntry
- BaseType refers to the types of the base table
- BaseRef is usually linked to DocNum field in the base table
- BaseLine will be the line number in the base line table
- TargetEntry in the base table refers to the target table's DocEntry
- TargetType refers to the types of the target table

Keeping it simple—The key to build a good query

Before you go on to the next chapter, an important concept needs to be kept in mind:

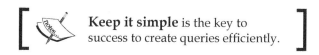

Keep it simple is the key to success to create queries efficiently.

Simplicity is in need everywhere in the current changing world. Wherever you make things complicated, you may find yourself in an awkward position to compete with others.

My slogan is: simple, simpler, the simplest.

I have a habit in query building: the last step for any new query would be checking to see if it is the simplest one. In this way, "keep it simple" would not only be kept in the already built query, but also helps new queries to be the simplest in the beginning.

By keeping a query as simple as possible, it will ensure that the system performance is not affected. It will also be a great help to the troubleshooting process. A short checklist for simplicity is as follows:

- **Other queries**: Are there any other queries doing a similar job, and if yes, why does the new query need to be built?
- **Tables**: Are there any tables that have not been used for the query?
- **Fields**: Are there any fields that have not been used for the query?
- **Conditions**: Are there any condition overlaps?

The list can be much longer. The meaning behind it is clear: there is a never ending battle to get rid of complications.

When you try this method and it becomes a routine, you will find that query building becomes an enjoyable process.

Summary

In this chapter, you have been identified to be an appropriate reader who needs this information, supposing that you read through the beginning chapter and still want to read more.

You have been given all the basic concepts such as RDBMS, Table, SQL, T-SQL, SQL Subsets, and Query. You also get the idea of what the strict meanings of "SQL" and "Query" are within this book.

By going deeper into discussing table relationships, you gained a bigger picture of SAP Business One's database structure and tables' naming conventions. You also learned about base tables versus target tables in SAP Business One.

The "Keep it simple" principle has been emphasized in the last section of the chapter. You are advised to use it whenever you practice your own queries.

The next chapter will introduce you to the Query Generator and Query Wizard tools, so that you can start hands-on in building SQL query as soon as possible, if you have not yet done so.

2
Query Generator and Query Wizard

In the previous chapter, you learned basic concepts regarding certain terminologies used in this book. You also know that tables and table relationships are important for SQL Query. What are all of these concepts about? You will better understand when you start your own journey to create a SQL Query report.

How do I start? That is a good question. I have learned this the hard way. Even though the tools to create queries are readily available from the SAP Business One menu, I myself had never gone through most of these tools before I planned to write this book to show *you* how to start. I have kept using only Query Manager and system queries until now. To be honest, I just found out too late that I took such a longer route than necessary. What a pity! If I had started with Query Generator and Query Wizard, it would have saved me a tremendous amount of time.

These tools are quite convenient and efficient for everyone to use, especially for starters to write their first query for SAP Business One. These tools will help you to omit this process of writing every single statement, tables' names, or fields' names, etc.

This chapter will introduce you to two basic SQL Query tools for SAP Business One:

- **Query generator**
- **Query wizard**

Both tools are for starters to get to know SQL query in SAP Business One quickly. After you have learned these tools, you could get a simple job done just with a few mouse clicks. The introduction gives you detailed steps so that you can have step-by-step advice.

In the next section, the differences between these tools are discussed. You can decide which one is more suitable for you when you read through all their features and benefits.

If you are a more experienced reader, you may find that these tools are no longer necessary. Otherwise, you are strongly encouraged to go through the chapter to refresh yourself.

The last section introduces **System Queries** built-in to SAP Business One. Those system queries are another good start for readers whose SQL Query level is above average. You could then customize them and create your own queries quickly. For a beginner, you may just learn how to run those queries first to save time.

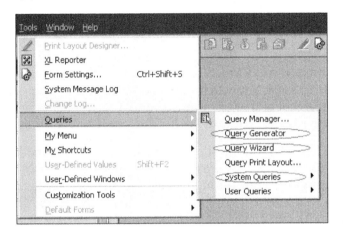

The previous screenshot shows you how to access these different tools from the SAP Business One menu. You can find all tools for this chapter from it. They are all under the **Tools | Queries** menu. **Query Generator** is the second item; **Query Wizard** is the third item; and **System Queries** is number five.

Query Generator

Query Generator is the first tool to be discussed. It is located above the Query Wizard in the menu item list.

Query Generator overview

Query Generator enables you to create queries using the SQL query engine. Like all other tools, it is designed for data retrieval/selection only. You are not able to do any DML queries such as updates, insert, or delete. This menu item can be accessed from **Tools | Queries | Query Generator**.

With this tool, you are able to:

- Create many queries yourself from a fixed set of tables in SAP Business One
- Access all the data in those tables and evaluate it according to your needs
- Create individual reports without writing any single query statements

Left part of Query Generator form

After you click on the Query Generator menu item, you can bring up the main form of Query Generator. On the top left of the form, you may find a yellow cell. Click the **Tab** key from the empty cell to bring up **Choose from List**, as in the following screenshot:

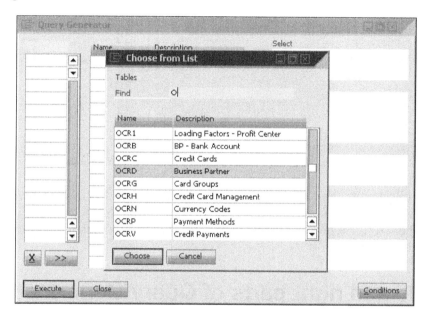

The set of table names will then show up. You could type any letters in the **Find** textbox to bring up the table names starting with that letter. In the example, you could find that the letter **O** is typed in. All tables starting with O would be on the top list. You could either use the scroll bar or page up/down key to find the tables you are looking for.

You'll remember we discussed the importance of the Data Dictionary in the previous chapter. Without the dictionary, it might be too hard to find which tables you need. If **Table References** is available, you could easily find the table quickly. For the sake of time, if you already know the names then you could just type in the full table names.

However, here is still one of the best places to find all commonly used tables for SAP Business One in case the help file is not available to you. In this less than ideal case, you probably need to go through the table name list quite a few times to become familiar with them.

In the example screenshot, the highlighted table **OCRD** (Business Partner table) will be selected when you click **Choose**:

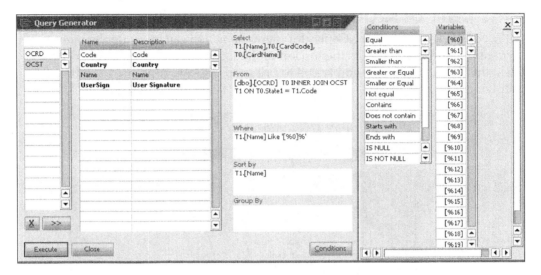

You may select more than one table in the same way as the first table was selected. In the screenshot you just saw, the **OCST** (State table) has also been selected. If you selected the wrong table or changed your mind, the **X** button here could be used to remove it from the list.

Middle and right parts of Query Generator form

After the table selection, you would see that the middle part of the form shows you the fields from the highlighted table in alphabetical order. The right part shows the query component when you double-click the field name or table names on a proper box.

Under **Select**, three fields are selected from two tables. Under **From**, the table names are automatically shown with the default alias **T0** and **T1**. The default link by system is also shown. If the link is not correct, you can manually fix it.

Under **Where**, you can choose any fields to restrict the query result. Here, **T1.[Name]** has been selected for the purpose of bringing the Business Partner according to the State/Province names.

You may notice that there is an additional form shown. This appears after clicking on the **Conditions** button. You may find 12 conditional formulas from the form that can be selected. The **Variables** part allows you to select variable as [%0], [%1], and so on. The percent sign plus a number represents a variable for SQL query in SAP Business One. It can allow the user to select or input values during query execution.

In the last example, **Start With** formula plus [%0] variable gives the result as **T1.[Name] like '[%0]'**. The additional % on the right of [%0] is a manual input wildcard character that can be used as a suffix to match any string of zero or more characters.

Under **Sort, T1.[Name]** is also selected to allow query results to be sorted by State/Province names.

Executing a query from Query Generator form

When all the required information has been selected, click on **Execute**. Then the following form **Query – Selection Criteria** will pop up for you to input any letters:

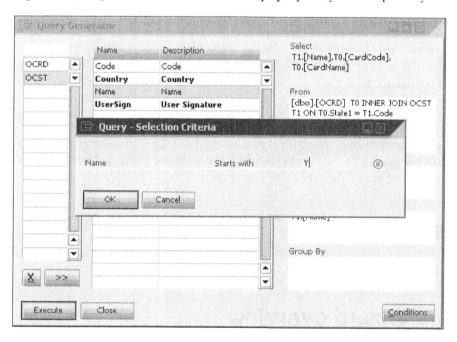

In the previous example, a letter **Y** has been entered. That means you will get the query result with all business partner code and names from the state/province with the name starting with Y.

The result looks like the next screenshot:

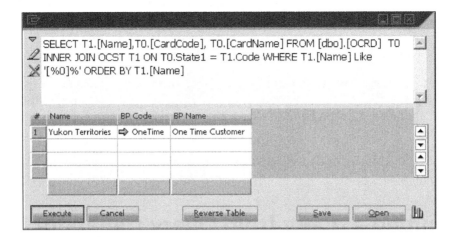

If this query could be used later, click on Save near the bottom to save your query. It might be saved under any query categories with the name you entered. The topic regarding query saving will be discussed in detail later.

The **Reverse Table** button at the bottom of the form is used to help you choose to display the table either from right-to-left or from left-to-right. This is because unlike English, some of the other languages may not start from left-to-right, but in reverse order.

You may notice that all query script from different sections of the generator has been linked together for you. Remember, you do not need to write any single statement. This is such a good gift for you to reduce your learning curve in terms of query learning. Do not waste this valuable resource!

Query Wizard

Query Wizard is the second tool to be discussed in this chapter. It is similar to Query Generator. We are going to compare both tools later in the book.

Query Wizard overview

Query Wizard enables easy access to the database and an easy way of building user-defined reports. It is designed for data retrieval/selection only. You are not able to do any DML queries such as updates, insert, or delete. This menu item can be accessed from **Tools | Queries | Query Wizard**.

With this tool, you can do the following:

- Create queries through five steps from a fixed set of tables from SAP Business One

- Access all data in those tables and get help from tips on each step

- Create individual reports without writing any single query statements

Step 1—Splash screen

The first step is very simple. After you click on **Query Wizard** menu item, you get the first screen that simply tells you: **This wizard will guide you step-by-step through the definition of parameters required for a query. The screenshot is omitted here since it is nothing but a splash screen for you to know you are starting this wizard.**

Step 2—Select tables for the report

The second step is similar to the left part in Query Generator. You can select as many tables as you need. However, you must try to minimize the number of tables for system performance and query efficiency.

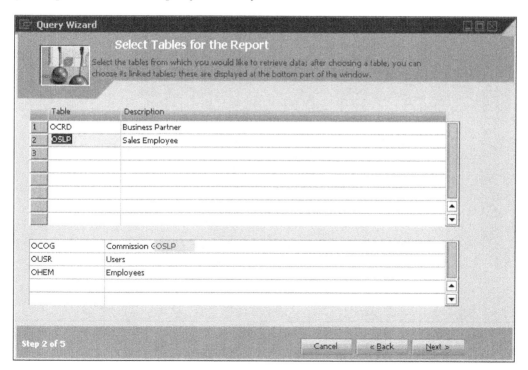

In the example screenshot you just saw, you may find that the first table selected is **OCRD** (Business Partner table). The second table selected is **OSLP** (Sales Employee table). Each table selected is placed in a separate row in the window. The second column displays the full description of the tables.

One thing here is, it is noticeably better than Query Generator. When you select any table, it automatically shows all linked tables under the lower part of the form. You will then find it very convenient to just choose the necessary tables by double-clicking.

This process applies to all tables selected in the upper part of the form.

A linked table list in the lower part of the form changes when you highlight different tables from the upper part of the form.

Step 3—Select fields and sort orders

Step 3 in Query Wizard has the same function as the middle part of Query Generator. In addition, you have more options to select fields.

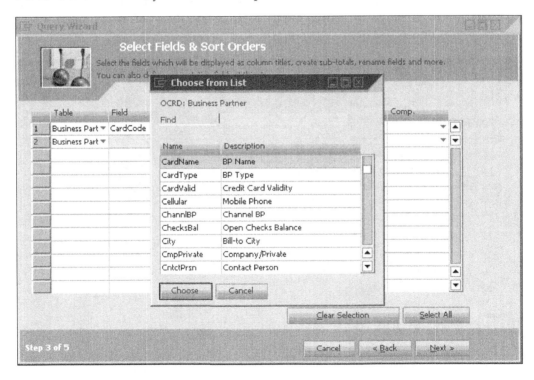

You may tab out the **Field** column to bring up **Choose from list** from the selected table. It is just like when you selected tables from both tools. You may type in any letters on the Find textbox to search your requested fields. There are two columns on the list:

- Name: Field names
- Description: Field description

As you know from the previous chapter, you can get all field information from the Table References for SAP Business One in advance. If that is not available to you, this might be the second best place to find all commonly used field information. You will probably need to go through them many times before you can reach frequently used fields at ease.

You can type the letter **C** to bring the field names starting with C on top of the list, so that you can get to the fields quicker. Or, you may not need to type any letters. Just use the mouse or page down to browse through the list in order to become familiar with those fields.

From the previous screenshot, you can see that two fields in OCRD have been selected. Another field from OSLP has also been selected. They are:

- CardCode: Business Partner Code from OCRD
- CardName: Business Partner Name from OCRD
- SlpName: Sales Employee Name from OSLP

The third column, **Heading**, displays the field description by default. You can change them to anything you want such as Customer Name instead of BP Name. It will show on the top of the query result screen as a column heading.

The fourth column, **Sort Order**, uses an integer (1, 2, 3) to set the sort priority; you can assign any orders to the field you have selected.

The fifth column defines the sort type as **Ascending** or **Descending**.

The sixth column allows you to set the group on any fields you would like to add. You just need to select **Y** for the field you would like it to be grouped to. If you have not selected this, the default value would be **N**.

The last column in the previous screenshot, **Comp.**, offers six computation options:

- **Total Records**: Displays the number of records retrieved
- **Total Distinct Records**: Displays the number of distinct records retrieved
- **Amount**: Displays the sum of the values for numeric field in the retrieved records
- **Average**: Calculates and displays the average of the values of that field in the retrieved records
- **Minimum**: Displays the smallest value of this field from within the retrieved records
- **Maximum:** Displays the largest value of this field from within the retrieved records

Step 4—Conditions and relations

Step 4 is for defining the conditions and relations for retrieving data. Both conditions and relations are based on the database structure and logic.

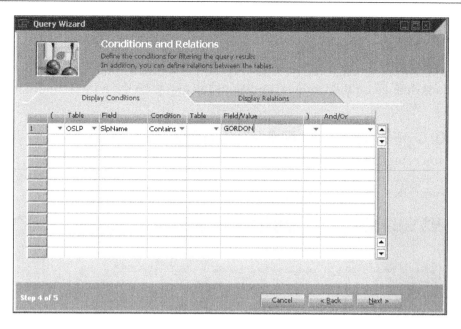

For the previous example, it is the **Display Conditions** tab. You can see the condition entered is **Sales Employee's name**, which contains **Gordon**.

You may select **(** or **)** on these two tabs to define the priority sequence of the conditions. You may also select **And/Or** to define complex conditions.

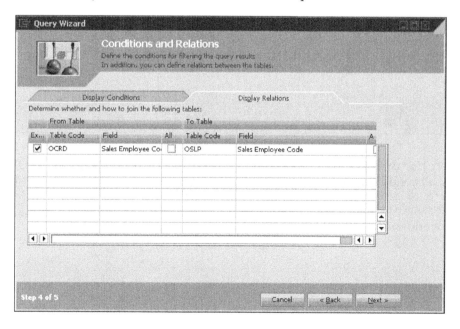

The other tab is for **Display Relations**. Under this tab, you will find the first column's checkbox, **Execute**. It applies the defined relationship between the tables that appear in the row. When this checkbox is selected, SAP Business One adds another condition. This means that the records you want to retrieve must comply with the conditions defined on the **Define Conditions** tab and with the added condition.

Step 5—Query Wizard completion

When you complete all Conditions and Relations, clicking on **Next** will bring you to the final step, which shows you the Query script created by the system that applies all of your selections.

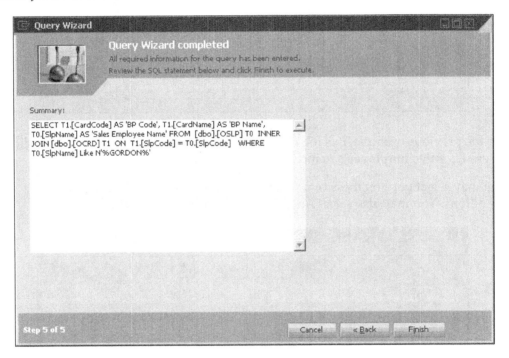

You may review the query to check if it is all you need. If you find that it did not include all conditions, you can go back to edit some of them in the previous steps.

In the example case, there are no problems. Click **Finish** to bring up the query result window.

You can find all Business Partner Codes and Names under the selected State/ Province from the query results.

Like Query Generator, if the query is useful, you can click Save to save your query. The topic regarding query saving will be discussed in the *Creating and saving user queries* section of the next chapter.

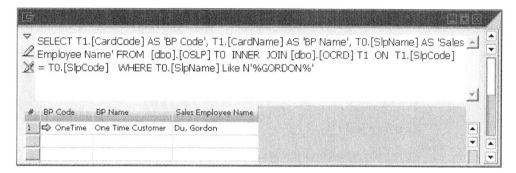

 There is a video tutorial available for Query Wizard by SAP. You can find it here: http://www.youtube.com/watch?v=xaLO_4JnG-E. From this video, you will have additional information in a classroom-like instruction for the topic here.

What is the difference between Query Generator and Query Wizard?

When you go through the first part of the chapter, you have probably already noticed the differences between the Query Generator and Query Wizard tools.

You will find the summarized differences here to clarify any doubts you may have.

The first tool, Query Generator, is one of the simplest tools for building SQL Queries. It just uses one simple **User Interface (UI)** for you to create queries. You can start to use it whenever you wish to find the tables, fields, and their relationship.

The second tool, Query Wizard, has added five steps with different forms, so that you can find the table relationship more easily. Also, finding fields becomes much easier because you have the option to bring up **Choose from list**.

Here is the list showing the similarities between these two tools:

- There is no need to write full query statements
- Allows selection of tables and fields
- Prohibits updating data
- Uses the mouse alone to add conditions

Differences	Query Generator	Query Wizard
	Single step User Interface	Multiple steps User Interface
	Requires more tables and fields knowledge	Requires less tables and fields knowledge
	Less help and tips	More help and tips
	Field level selection is basic	Field level selection is sophisticated

In summary, the Query Generator is designed to get quick results in a single step, while Query Wizard is more concentrated on step-by-step instructions to help you build queries with clear selection in different phases.

I prefer the Query Generator over the Query Wizard because I am familiar with all tables and fields. To me, the simpler the steps, the better. To a beginner, I would suggest you try Query Wizard because it gives you more power to select different tables and fields. You will also be provided with more helpful tips.

Benefitting from built-in system queries

Besides Query Generator and Query Wizard, there is another powerful tool for you to learn SQL Query in SAP Business One. That is: **System Queries.**

System queries enable you to generate additional reports and retrieve data that is not available by running the other reports. You may access system queries either from the different modules—in each module the relevant system queries appear as entries under report menu, identified with the icon **?** or by choosing them from **Tools | Queries | System Queries**.

The following screenshot shows you the names of all the available system queries. You may find as many as 18 queries here. Most queries are related to finance and banking.

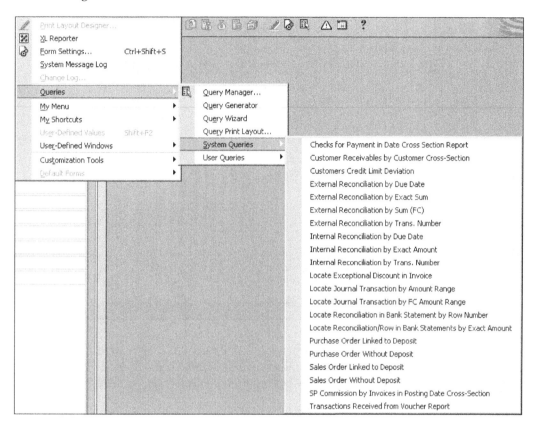

You can see the query results from one of the system queries: **Purchase Order Linked to Deposit**.

The result is actually empty because there is no deposit linked to the purchase order in the database. You would like this result, wouldn't you?

What you need to know is the top part of the query result. You will see there is a Left Arrow (*Show* icon) there. When you click on the arrow, you will get the full body of the query statements.

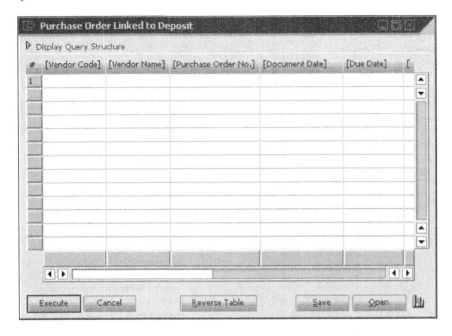

As soon as you click on the Left Arrow icon, it will become Down Arrow (*Hide* icon). You will notice there are two additional icons displayed. One is Pencil Only. The other is a Pencil with Cross. All query statements are shown as well.

This is only available if you run those system queries under the tools menu instead of each module under report.

When you click on the Pencil Only icon, the background of the query statement area will become yellow instead of grey. You are now able to modify the query for your own use.

 Be careful about changing this. You need a good understanding of the SAP Business One data structure in advance. Don't panic here either. You can try anything to amend the query. There is no harm to the system unless you try to overwrite the system query.

When you finish editing, you may click the other icon (Pencil with Cross). That will change back to the read only mode of the query body.

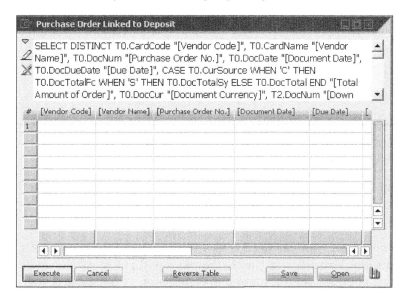

If you are interested, here is the complete statement of this query:

```
DECLARE @Factor as numeric(1,0)

SELECT @Factor =
CASE (SELECT TOP 1 DispPosDeb FROM OADM)
 WHEN 'N' THEN 1 ELSE -1
END

SELECT T0.CardCode,
T0.CardName,
T0.Balance,
T0.CreditLine,
(T0.CreditLine + @Factor*T0.Balance) "Deviation"

FROM OCRD T0
WHERE (select T0.CreditLine + @Factor*T0.Balance) < 0 AND T0.CardType
= 'C'
```

If you come across any difficulties in creating your query later, you can always come back to system queries to find some useful tips.

Summary

In this chapter, you have learned about the following tools for creating or using SQL queries in SAP Business One:

- Query Generator
- Query Wizard
- System Queries

You have also learned the differences between Query generator and Query wizard. This is a good start for your progress in mastering SQL Queries for SAP Business One.

By practicing these tools, you could have better understanding of the tables and table relationship within SAP Business One. Some of the system queries will give you more hints than others regarding how to create the correct query.

If you are a beginner, you may need to try those tools quite a few times. Only when you feel comfortable in creating simple queries – without problems – with these tools, will you build a solid foundation to create more sophisticated queries. In order to benefit from Business Intelligence, it would be better to try to master these tools to as high a level as possible. To learn the details of each statement and the complicated syntax, continue to read the following chapters.

In the next chapter, you will learn about the Query Manager and all the commonly used statements and functions, one by one, and in detail.

3

Query Manager and Query Statements

In the previous chapter, you learned about two basic tools, **Query Generator** and **Query Wizard**. Meanwhile, you also learned about system queries so that you can create or use queries with these tools. However, those tools have certain limitations.

The most inconvenient limitation is that only a fixed set of tables is available to you with these tools. For example, the table list does not show all tables in the database. When the queries become complicated, these tools may not work for you.

You must be eager to know how to create queries freely without those restrictions. Do you have other ways of creating queries when you need to create them in complex logic? The answer is definitely: "Yes". This is the topic of this chapter.

This chapter illustrates the most important business intelligence tool for SAP Business One: **Query Manager**. You will learn how to manage your queries by creating, saving, and deleting them directly from the Query Manager. At the same time, you will learn how to organize your queries into categories. The detailed query statements, keywords, and functions will be presented to you as well.

In the first section, you will learn everything related to the Query Manager such as User Interface, including each button. The query categories for saved query will also be discussed. The next section will show you the most commonly used basic statements for queries one by one. All statements are fully explained. They cover the most frequently used statements. The last section covers the query functions, including the most commonly used functions or expressions.

Query Manager user interface

The following screenshot shows you how to access this tool from the SAP Business One menu:

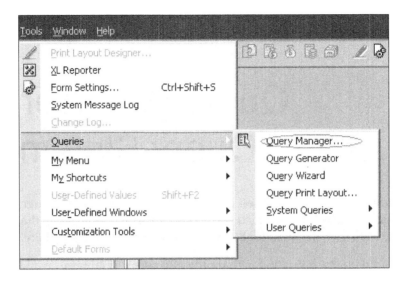

Just like the other query tools, Query Manager can be accessed through the first menu item under **Tools | Queries**.

You can also access it directly from the toolbar. The Query Manager icon can be found on the toolbar between the **Form Settings** and **Message/Alert** icons. This icon is shown in the previous screenshot on the left side of **Query Manager**.

In the Query Manager window, you can:

- Display all existing queries
- Create and save user queries
- Delete user queries
- Manage query categories

Query Manager is used for query management. All queries can be saved, edited, or deleted by using the Query Manager tool. It does not matter if the query is created by tools like Query Generator/Query Wizard, or by users directly from the query result windows.

Display all existing queries

This is the simplest function for the Query Manager. You can find all your saved queries or system queries through the Query Manager User interface.

The first text block on the top of the Query Manager can display the query name you have selected or allow you to type a query name for a new query before you save it.

The next text block below the query name can display the query category you have selected or allow you to type a query category name for a new query category before you save it through the **Manage Category** function.

The big window under these two boxes is the place to display all query categories and the query names for the expanded categories you have selected.

The first screenshot shows the system query names:

The second example shows the query categories plus the query names under expanded query categories:

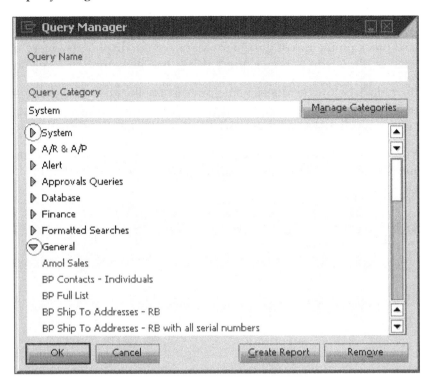

You may notice that there are two different icons in front of each query category: the **Down Arrow** icon next to the **General** category and the **Right Arrow** icon next to **System** as well as other categories. The Down Arrow icons stand for the query categories that are expanded to display the query names under the categories. The Right Arrow icons refer to the query categories that are not expanded. When you click on the icon, the status will change from **expanded** to **non-expanded** or vice versa. To find a query under a specific category, you just need to click on the icon in front of the query category to expand it.

You can display any queries in two ways:

1. The first way is from the Query Manager window directly. You can find the required query name and double-click on the name or you can click **OK** when you select a specific query name. The selected query will be displayed on the query result window with either method.

2. The second way is bypassing the Query Manager window. You can also find the query name directly from **Tools | Queries | User Queries**. One click is good enough to bring up the query result window with this method.

The second method presents a limitation. If the query name is too long, it might be cut off when you display their names directly from the **Tools** menu. Or if you have special characters, it may not display them fully either. It is advisable to use shorter names for queries whenever possible. Avoid using special characters whenever possible.

> When you name a query, it is better not to name them similar to each other. You may have the misfortune wherein, all names are not easily distinguishable if the first 40 characters are the same.

Creating and saving user queries

Creating user queries can be done directly after you run any queries in order to bring up the query result window. The query you want to run can either be from query tools directly or selected from the Query Manager.

When you open the query result window by either of the methods mentioned earlier, you might be able to edit or create a query from scratch, if you have the right authorization. In case you don't have the user privilege, check with the **Superuser** in your company.

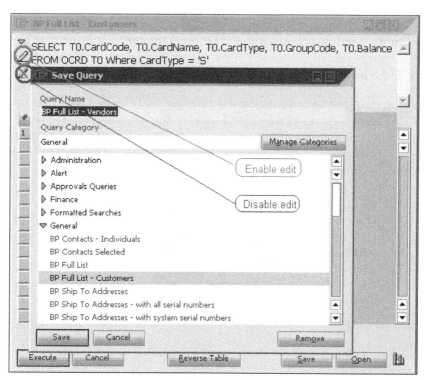

Once you have got proper user rights, you will be able to find two icons on the left screen beside the query script. They look like a pencil or a pencil with a red line cross. From the previous screenshot, you can find that the first icon is used for enabling edit queries and the second icon is the opposite, that is, to disable the editing ability. When you click on the pencil icon, you will have the power to write any queries to retrieve data from any tables in the database.

Unlike the other query tools, you have to write every single statement, keyword, column name, table name, function, and parameter on your own. The freedom to write query as you wish requires that you have both high level SQL query knowledge and SAP Business One database structure knowledge. If you find it is difficult, you need to go back to the previous chapter. Spend your time with the tools until you are ready.

To save your query, you just need to follow these steps:

1. Click on **Save**. The **Save Query** window will show up.

2. Select any categories from the list.

3. Type in a proper query name.

4. Click on **Save** under the bottom of the window.

Your query will be saved immediately with the previously mentioned steps.

The **Save Query** window is similar to the **Query Manager** window. Any query categories or query names displayed in the **Query Manager** window, will be displayed in the **Save Query** window too.

The following example shows that the existing query, **BP Full List — Customer**, has been edited. The new query can be saved by selecting the category **General** and selecting a query name to modify it to. The new name **BP Full List — Vendors** has been entered. After clicking on **Save**, this new query is saved under the **General** category. You can just type in the name if the name is not very long.

 Warning: Although you can write some DML queries such as **UPDATE**, **DELETE**, or **INSERT** in the query result windows, those DML queries have to be restricted to only your **User Defined Tables (UDT)**. Even **User Defined Field (UDF)** in the system tables is not allowed to be updated by the SQL Query directly. You face great risk of losing your SAP support in case of any corruptions in your database, if you have directly updated system tables.

If you need to create a query from scratch without bringing up other queries, you can create an empty query such as SELECT '' and save it by a name **Blank** or **Empty**. If you run this query, you will see nothing in the query result but empty space that allows you to create a brand new query.

Deleting user queries

It is simple to delete a user query. You don't need to open the query to run it, but delete it from the Query Manager window directly. After you have selected the Query Manager from the menu or through the icon, you can select the query you want to delete. Click on the **Remove** button, and a warning message will popup to confirm that you want to delete the query. If you have not reached this point through a wrong mouse click, you can click on **Yes** to proceed. The query will be deleted from the database.

There is an alternative way to delete queries. That is to bring up the **Save Query** window by clicking **Save** under the query result window. Instead of saving queries, you may select any user queries to delete. Clicking on the **Remove** button is all you need to do.

After deleting queries, you can click on **Cancel** to return to the query result window.

Be careful when you delete your query. There is no Undo function like some other applications. Once the query is deleted, there is no way to retrieve it unless you restore your entire database! A practical remedy is to copy and save all queries to a text document after you have created them. It will save you time whenever you find the queries have to be revised or deleted.

Managing query categories

Categories are the folders for queries. They include categories for system queries and categories for user queries. You always get a default category called **General** when you have a new database. There is nothing else beside these **system** and **general** categories in the beginning. It is dependent on an administration user to create and maintain your queries with any categories you like.

If you only have few queries, categories may not be that important to you. However, this will change as soon as you have more saved queries. Good category management can save you tremendous time. You can maintain the categories with the same structure as the SAP Business One menu system. Any queries can be found quickly in this way.

Categories are similar to directories or folders in an operating system, with one exception. This is not a trivial exception. There is only one level for categories under the Query Manager. You don't have the option to create multi-level categories.

Due to the limitations of having only one level category, your plan to create categories should avoid any overlap structure. If your categories have not clearly divided the scope of your queries, you may face a dilemma in saving your new query to a proper category. When you try to find the saved queries in the future, it may actually increase your troubles in getting the right queries, instead of saving you time.

To manage categories, you can click **Manage Category** beside the second text box. After you click the button, a window with a title **Create/Edit Categories** will pop up like in the following screenshot:

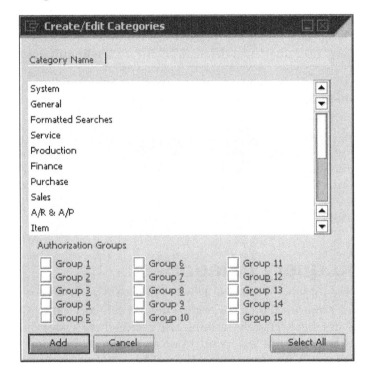

When this window pops up, it is always in **Add** mode. You can add a new category by typing any letters in the text box close to the top of window. Then click **ADD**. The new category will be added right away.

If you are not satisfied with the category name, it is very easy to edit it. Just select a category name when you are in the **Add** mode. The **Add** button will change to an **Update** button instantly, like the example in the following screenshot. **A/R & A/P** category is selected to be a candidate for update.

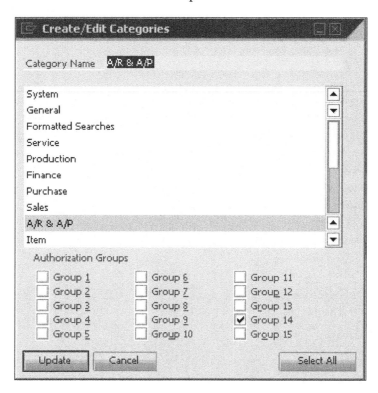

 User rights for category maintenance should be left to the person who has full administration right. Only Superusers must handle this function. Detailed discussion can be found in Chapter 5 for query security.

You can type in your preferred category name at this time. In the example, **Gordon** is typed in. When you click **Update**, the category name changes to **Gordon** instead of **A/R & A/P**.

The query names under the same category will not be affected when you are editing category names. Actually, this is the category ID to be used by the system. This category ID is not changed during your category name update.

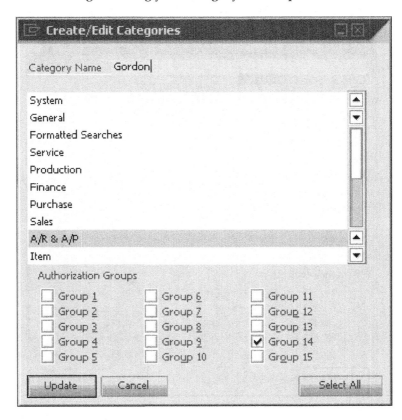

After you click **Update**, the window is changed to find mode. The button is changed again from **Update** to **OK**. You can still select any categories just like in the Add mode. However, the button will not change to **Update** this time. It still shows **OK**.

To add another new category, you have to change the window mode to Add mode. This can be done through the menu item **Data | Add**, keyboard shortcut *Ctrl+A* or the icon on the toolbar.

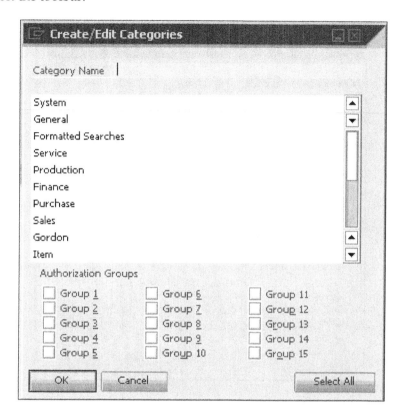

The last button to be discussed is the **Select All** button. This button allows you to select all **Authorization Groups**. If you want to assign your query category to more than half of the authorization groups, it will be easier to click on this button first. Then you can deselect any groups. If you just assign to less than half of the groups, you can check them one by one. It will save you time compared with unchecking many boxes after **Select All**.

Whenever you have not selected all groups, the **Select All** button will be available. As soon as all groups are selected, the button will change to **Clear All**. The authorization groups are used for query report user authorizations. The details for query report user authorizations will be discussed in Chapter 5.

Commonly used statements

SQL queries comprise a statement, keyword, function, expression, and parameters. To see how commonly used query statements work, you can have a look at the following query example that includes most of the statements and some of the functions. The query contents and meaning of these query results will be discussed in the next chapter:

```
SELECT TOP 5 T0.ShortName 'Customer',
Max(T2.CardName) 'Customer Name',
SUM(ISNULL(T0.Debit,0) - ISNULL(T0.Credit,0)) as "Amount(LC)"
FROM dbo.JDT1 T0
INNER JOIN dbo.OJDT T1 ON T1.TransID = T0.TransID and T0.TransType IN
(13,14)
INNER JOIN dbo.OCRD T2 ON T2.CardCode = T0.ShortName
WHERE t1.RefDate >= [%0] and t1.RefDate <= [%1]
```

```
GROUP BY T0.ShortName
HAVING SUM(ISNULL(T0.Debit,0) - ISNULL(T0.Credit,0)) > 0
ORDER BY SUM(ISNULL(T0.Debit,0) - ISNULL(T0.Credit,0)) DESC
```

This query can be used to return the top five customers for sales in any period based on the date range you selected. It includes most of the statements that are going to be discussed in this chapter.

Let us go through those statements or functions in **Bold** from the sample query one by one:

SELECT—first statement to retrieve data

It is quite obvious from the meaning of the word that **SELECT** is used to display or retrieve data from certain data sources.

The SELECT statement is used to return data from a set of values or database tables.

The result is stored in a result table, called the **result-set.**

SELECT is one of the most commonly used **Data Manipulation Language (DML)** commands. It seems very simple. However, something important needs to be explained for this statement:

- The scope of the value that can be retrieved
- The numbers of columns to be included
- Column name descriptions
- Keywords followed to this statement

The scope of the value that can be retrieved

Here is a return value list that SELECT can be used for:

- A single value
- A group of values
- Return a single database table column
- Return a group of database table columns
- Return complete database table columns
- Used in a subquery

A single value

The simplest SELECT query would be just to get a constant or text without any additional statements. An example would be:

```
SELECT 'YES' AS 'Yes/No' or
SELECT 10 AS 'No.'
```

These queries will display **Yes** or **10** in one column when executed.

A group of values

You may also use this statement to get a group of values. For example:

```
SELECT 'YES' AS 'Yes/No', 10 AS 'No.', 'This is an example' AS
'Content'
```

This query will display **Yes**, **10**, **This is an example** in three columns named **Yes/No**, **No.**, and **Content** when you execute it.

Some special uses of this statement to display a single value or group of values will be discussed in other chapters when we introduce more specific topics.

Please note the comma used above. Following the SELECT statement, each comma will define a new column to be displayed.

Do not forget to delete the last comma in a SELECT statement. This simple mistake is one of the most frequent problems for a query. It is mainly due to the fact that we are often used to copying columns in our queries, which include the comma, and forget to remove the last one before testing the query.

Return a single database table column

Similar to the single value SELECT, we can use it for a database table column. Here is an example:

```
SELECT CompnyName
FROM OADM
```

This simple example will retrieve your company name from table **OADM**.

The formal query should be this:

```
SELECT T0.CompnyName
FROM dbo.OADM T0
```

It is an important step to include **Alias** (T0) and **Database Owner** (dbo) for the table in the query. It will ensure the query's consistency and efficiency. This topic will be discussed in the FROM clause in more detail.

Return a group of database table columns

There is no big difference with the previous example. We can use the same principle to select multiple database table columns. For instance:

```
SELECT CompnyName, CompnyAddr, Country, Phone1
FROM OADM
```

This example will retrieve not only your company name, but also your company's address, country, and phone number from table **OADM**.

The formal query should be as follows:

```
SELECT T0.CompnyName, T0.CompnyAddr, T0.Country, T0.Phone1 FROM dbo.
OADM T0
```

Return complete database table columns

This is the simplest query to return all column values from table. That is:

```
SELECT *
FROM OADM
```

This example will retrieve every single column from table **OADM**. There is no need to assign alias to the query because this kind of query is usually a one-time only query. Here, * is a wildcard that represents everything in the table.

Be careful when running SELECT * from a huge table such as JDT1. It may affect your system's performance! If you are not sure about the table size, it is safer for you to always include the WHERE clause with reasonable restrictions. Or you can run SELECT COUNT(*) FROM the table you want to query first. If the number is high, do not run it without a condition clause.

Used in a subquery

SELECT can be used in a subquery within SELECT column(s). The topic of using SELECT for subqueries will be discussed in the last chapter of the book, since it needs above average experience level to use it sufficiently.

The numbers of columns to be included

How many columns are suitable for a query? I don't think there are any standard answers. In my experience, I can only suggest to you: the shorter, the better.

Some people have the tendency to include all information in one report. This kind of request may even come from certain executives of the company's management.

One simple test would be a fair criterion. Can you fit the query result within the query result window? If you can, great; that would be a proper number of columns. If not, then I would strongly suggest you double check every column to see if you can cut one or more of them out.

If it is a query for alert, it needs even more special care. The column numbers in any alert queries have to be trimmed to the minimum. Otherwise, you may only get part of the result due to the query result size limitation. You will get more explanation for this issue in the chapter for alert queries.

If you are requested to create super long and wide queries, explain the consequences to the person in charge. Sometimes, they can change their mind depending on the way you communicate with them. In my experience, if a print out report cannot be handled within the width of a page, it might make the report difficult to read. Show the result to a non-technical person. It is easily understandable when you can bring the first hand output to the report readers.

Column name descriptions

Column names usually come directly from column descriptions, if you have not reassigned them in the query. You can, however, change them to make the query result more useful for special cases. Some people use this method to translate the description into their local language. Some people use it to make the column description more clear.

For some of the value-only columns or formula columns it is mandatory to assign descriptions, otherwise the column headings would be empty. This not only looks unprofessional, but you will also have no way to export the query results to Excel for those columns without the description.

You can use single or double quotation marks for the description. If the description has only one word, you can even omit the quotation mark. The syntax is shown next:

```
[ColumnName] AS 'Column Description Here'
```

You can omit AS, so that you just keep `[ColumnName] 'Description Here'`. However, whenever possible, you should keep the AS to make the query script more consistent.

Clauses can follow this statement

Not many clauses can directly follow a SELECT statement. The short list we discuss here is this:

- Distinct
- Top

These two clauses will be discussed one by one as follows.

DISTINCT—duplicated records can be removed

A **DISTINCT** clause is used for getting rid of duplicated records to return only distinct (different) values.

The syntax of this clause is:

```
SELECT DISTINCT column_name(s)
FROM table_name(s)
```

column_name and *table_name* are self explanatory. They represent column name and table name respectively. There will be no additional denotation for these two clauses in this book. A DISTINCT clause is always the first one after the SELECT statement. It is optional. When you specify Distinct in the query, it will not allow any identical rows in the query result. All lines are unique from each other.

Some users claim this clause may still allow duplicate rows. This can never be true. The fact is: although most of the values are the same between two lines, the query results always include at least one column, which contains the different values. Those columns have to be taken out in order to benefit from this clause. You cannot get both the DISTINCT working and some columns which have different values within the scope you selected.

There are criticisms of this clause because it adds burden to the SQL Server. Be careful while using it if the result-set is huge. You can reduce the amount of the data returned by restricting the query scope within a specific date range.

TOP—number of lines returned by ranking

A TOP clause is used to specify the maximum number of records to return in a query result-set. It is usually used together with the Order By clause at the end of the query.

The syntax of the clause is as follows:

```
SELECT TOP (number)|percent[with ties] column_name(s)
FROM table_name(s)
```

The query result can be the top 10 sales orders, for example. In this case, descending order must be used for the document amounts. Or you may get the top 20 percent purchase invoices, if you specify the TOP by percentage. When you use percentage, you need to write 20 percent instead of 20% after SELECT TOP.

The WITH TIES option specifies the additional rows that need to be returned from the base result set with the same value in the ORDER BY columns appearing at the end of the TOP n (PERCENT) rows. TOP...WITH TIES can be specified only if an ORDER BY clause is specified.

 TOP can be very useful on large tables with thousands of records. Returning a large number of records may have an impact on database performance. If you just need part of the result, give the top clause a try.

Microsoft suggests SELECT TOP (n) with parentheses. It is better to follow the suggestion to be safe for the query results.

FROM—data resource can be assigned

It is very clear that FROM means where to find the data. A FROM clause is actually not a standalone statement since it must be used with SELECT. Most queries need this clause because to only assign a fixed value or a group of values would not be very useful. However, this is one of the most often misused parts of SQL queries. More discussion is needed on this clause.

A FROM clause can be followed by the data sources mentioned next:

- A single table
- A group of linked tables
- Multiple tables separated by commas

If you have read through Chapter 1, *SAP Business One Query Users and Query Basic*, you should understand the concept of Table and Table Relationships. If you directly jumped here bypassing that previous chapter, you may need to go back to check.

A single table

This is the simplest query including a FROM statement. A simple example:

```
SELECT Code, Name, Remarks FROM OUDP
```

This will only touch one table—OUDP. This table is for a department. You can get the Department Code, Department Name, and the Description from the query result.

The better format would be:

```
SELECT T0.Code, T0.Name, T0.Remarks FROM dbo.OUDP T0
```

Now, it is time to explain why those additional T0 and dbo are necessary here.

Actually, it may not make any difference if we only deal with this particular query and this query is only run by one user. However, that is not generally true. In most cases, we often have more than one table and more than one user to run the same query.

T0 here stands for an **Alias** of OUDP table. It is the standard convention and most frequently used alias. **T** means table. **0** is a sequence number. You can have T0, T1, T2, …until Tn. If you have 10 tables in the query, n would be equal to 9 for alias. This naming convention is convenient to use. You just need to name them in sequential numbers.

The syntax for table alias looks like this:

```
SELECT alias_table_name.column_name
FROM table_name [AS] alias_table_name
```

An alias table name can be anything, but usually it is the shortest possible one.

If a query is not created by query tools, it is not mandatory for alias to take the Tn sequence. You may just use A, B, C, …… to have one letter shorter than the standard way, or make them easier to remember. However, it is advisable that you follow the norm. It can save you time for maintaining your query in the long run.

When you have more than 10 tables in the query, an A, B, C, ... sequence would be better than the normal T0, T1, T2, ... convention because T10 and above need more spaces.

The function for alias is mainly for saving resources. If no alias is defined, you have to enter the full table names for every single column in the query. Be careful when you are using alias; you should use alias exclusively throughout your query. You are not allowed to mix them with the actual table name. In other words, you may only use alias or the actual table name, but you are not allowed to use them both in the same query.

The other added word **dbo** means **Database Owner**. This is a special database user. This user has implied permissions to perform all activities in the database. All tables of SAP Business One have the owner of dbo. It is useful to add dbo in front of a table name when you have more than one user running the query, but this is beyond the scope of the book. I will try to use the simplest method to give you a rough idea.

Query running needs an execution plan. A **query execution plan (or query plan)** outlines how the SQL Server query optimizer (query optimizer is too complicated to explain here, you just need to know it is a tool built into SQL server) actually ran (or will run) a specific query. There are typically a large number of alternate ways to execute a given query, with widely varying performance. When a query is submitted to the database, the query optimizer evaluates some of the different, correct possible plans for executing the query and returns what it considers the best alternative. This information is very valuable when it comes to finding out why a specific query is running slowly.

The hard fact is: no one can control this plan manually at runtime. Once a plan is created, it is reusable for the same user to run the query. If you are not entering **dbo** in front of the table name, the query will check every user who runs the query. A new plan may be added for every new user because the owner is not included in the query body. That might cause too much unnecessary burden to the database.

To save time and increase your system performance, **dbo** is highly recommended in front of table names for every query unless they are only for temporary use. These three letters mean database performance gain. Do not ignore, but add them to your query!

A group of linked tables

This is the category that most queries will be included in. One example may not be enough to show this clearly. You have two query examples to show. The first one is as follows:

```
SELECT Distinct T0.[DocNum], T1.DocNum, T0.[DocType], T0.[CardCode],
T0.[CardName], T0.[UserSign], T0.[UserSign2], T1.[UserSign],
T1.[UserSign2]
FROM dbo.ADOC T0
INNER JOIN dbo.ORIN T1 ON T0.DocNum = T1.DocNum
WHERE T0.[ObjType] = '14' AND T0.[UserSign2] != T1.[UserSign2]
```

This query links ADOC (Document History) and ORIN (Credit Memo Headers) tables to show the credit memo document number, document type, user information, and the change log user code for the credit memo. A detailed explanation can be found in the next chapter.

The second query example is as follows:

```
SELECT T1.CardCode as "CustCode", T1.CardName as "CustName",
T2.SlpName, T1.DocNum "Incoming#", T1.DocDate, T1.DocTotal as "Payment
Total", T4.DocNum as "Invoice#", T3.SumApplied as "Applied Total"
FROM dbo.OCRD T0
INNER JOIN dbo.ORCT T1 ON T0.CardCode = T1.CardCode
LEFT JOIN dbo.OSLP T2 ON T0.SlpCode = T2.SlpCode
INNER JOIN dbo.RCT2 T3 ON T3.DocNum = T1.DocNum
INNER JOIN dbo.OINV T4 ON T4.DocEntry = T3.DocENtry AND T3.InvType =
'13'
WHERE T1.DocDate >= [%0] AND T1.DocDate <= [%1]
ORDER by T1.DocDate
```

This query links five tables OCRD (Business Partners), ORCT (Incoming Payment Headers), RCT2 (Incoming Payments – Invoices), OSLP (Sales Employees), and OINV (Invoice Headers) together. It shows customers' payment with invoice details. Again, the business case explanation is available in the next chapter.

Among the five links in the query, there are two different kinds of links. One is INNER JOIN. The other is LEFT JOIN; more explanation of these joins can be found later in the chapter.

 Again, one special case needs to be pointed out here. If your table is a User Defined Table (UDT), do not forget that @ is the first letter of your table name.

Multiple tables separated by commas

When you link tables together, SQL Server just treats them as a view, or it acts as one big table. However, there is another way to add your tables into the query without linking them first. The syntax is similar to comma delimited columns. You simply need to enter a comma in between tables. In this case, table linking has to be done under the WHERE conditions.

Technically, the way of linking tables without joining is the most ideal method because you can get the minimum records out with the least database operations, if you are very good at database structure. However, like the difference between manual and automatic cameras, most people prefer automatic cameras because it is very convenient, especially if you do not have extensive training or extraordinary experience, and the ideal manual control may not help you get a better picture!

I always refuse to create queries without joining the tables first. Comma-separated table query is too dangerous. If you have the wrong conditions defined in the WHERE clause, you may end up with countless loops. In the worst case scenario, it may lock your system up. On the contrary, if you link all tables together, the worst case scenario would be no results because of a bad link or bad conditions.

In other words, if you want to add all tables' linking conditions under the WHERE clause, you are giving yourself an unnecessary burden in making sure they are correct. Those verifications have to be done manually.

Whenever possible, you are better to avoid using comma separated table queries. In most cases, it may use more resources and put you at a higher risk of system instability.

JOIN—addition table or tables can be linked

You have learned the FROM statement. With this statement, you know that more than one table can be put into one query.

In most cases, those additional tables should be **linked** together. The reason we need to link tables before the WHERE clause has been discussed in the previous paragraph. To link those extra tables, **JOIN** is used to combine rows from multiple tables.

A join is performed whenever two or more tables are listed in the FROM clause of a SQL statement without using a comma to separate them. Joined tables must include at least one common column in both tables that contain comparable data. Column names across tables don't have to be the same. But if we have the same name columns to join with correct relation, use them first.

There are different types of JOIN statements to be discussed, listed as follows:

- Inner join
- Outer joins
- Self-join

One of the special join types is omitted from the list. This is called the **Cross Join**. This type of join can list all possible combinations of your linked tables. You may end up with 90,000 lines of huge output even if you have only 300 records in each table. I have no idea who can benefit from this Cross Join. They must be very special.

First, let's look at the most commonly used one.

Inner Join

An **INNER JOIN** is also called a Simple Join. It is the simplest table join. INNER JOIN is the default link type to join tables. You may even omit INNER to leave only JOIN. When you see JOIN without any words in front, it means INNER JOIN. In order to distinguish other types of JOIN, omission is not encouraged unless your query length is an issue that requires you to reduce your query to the minimum size.

An INNER JOIN syntax looks like the following:

```
SELECT T[0]|[1].column_name(s)
FROM table_name0 T0
INNER JOIN table_name1 T1
ON T0.column_name=T1.column_name
```

In an INNER JOIN statement, the link is defined by the keyword ON with common columns from each table to retrieve the matching records from those tables. To link two or more tables correctly, the linking columns are very important. INNER JOIN will select all rows from linked tables as long as there is a match between the columns you are matching on. If you forget the keyword ON in the joined table list, you will get an error message right away when you try to run the query.

The best way to link tables is by using the **Key Columns** such as the primary key or the foreign key. That is because Key Columns are usually indexed. That makes links easier and faster. In case there is no such columns' pair to link, care must be taken to select the best efficient common columns between tables. When you have more than one way to link, you can consider the shorter columns first.

A/R Invoice Headers (OINV)

BP Code	Doc Entry	Doc No.	Posting Date
C100001	1	10000001	9-Sep-10
C100002	2	10000002	10-Sep-10

A/R Invoice Rows (INV1)

Doc Entry	Item Code	Price	Quantity	Row Total
1	A1000001	100	1	100
1	A1000002	200	2	400
2	A1000003	300	3	900
2	A1000004	400	4	1600

Query Result by INNER JOIN OINV with INV1 ON DocEntry

BP Code	Doc Entry	Doc No.	Posting Date	Item Code	Price	Quantity	Row Total
C100001	1	10000001	9-Sep-10	A1000001	100	1	100
C100001	1	10000001	9-Sep-10	A1000002	200	2	400
C100002	2	10000002	10-Sep-10	A1000003	300	3	900
C100002	2	10000002	10-Sep-10	A1000004	400	4	1600

The previous example shows a real query about how an inner join works.

The query script is:

```
SELECT T0.CardCode as 'BP Code', T0.DocNum as 'Doc No.', T0.DocDate,
T1.ItemCode, T1.Price as 'Price', T1.Quantity, T1.LineTotal
FROM dbo.OINV T0
INNER JOIN dbo.INV1 T1 ON T1.DocEntry = T0.DocEntry
```

Two tables, OINV (A/R invoice headers) and INV1 (A/R invoice rows), are joined by DocEntry columns. This DocEntry column is actually not included in the query result. It is only for illustration purposes for easier understanding. From the previous example, you can see how INNER JOIN works. For DocEntry 1 and 2, two rows each are formed by the query. The query result shows four lines in total.

You should avoid linking by lengthy text only columns. To match those columns, not only system performance becomes an issue, but also no ideal query results might be shown. In general, if the column length is over 30 characters, the link efficiency will be reduced dramatically.

Keep in mind, an inner join will effectively filter your query result by linking columns. If there are no common values between linked columns, those records are going to be dropped out. If you find that the query result does not meet your requirements, some other types of joins can be used instead.

Outer Join

Some may call **OUTER JOIN** a complex join. Actually, it may not be that complicated at all and is only a little bit more complicated than INNER JOIN. You do not need to worry about the complexity. When you find the true meaning of OUTER JOIN, it is similar and comparable with INNER JOIN.

There are three types of Outer Joins:

- Left Outer Join
- Right Outer Join
- Full Outer Join

We will examine each type as follows.

Left Outer Join

A **LEFT OUTER JOIN** is one of the most used outer joins in queries. Outer here is optional. It can be omitted so that you just need **LEFT JOIN**. There is no added benefit to using the full name of LEFT OUTER JOIN. Unless a query is automatically created, you should keep using only LEFT JOIN.

A LEFT JOIN clause syntax looks like the following:

```
SELECT T[0]|[1].column_name(s)
FROM table_name0 T0
LEFT JOIN table_name1 T1
ON T0.column_name=T1.column_name
```

In the previous syntax, the first table `table_name0 T0` is the **LEFT** table, while `table_name1 T1` is the right table. **LEFT JOIN** means all records in the left table will be returned, regardless of the right table linking condition. If the match cannot be found in T1 table, it simply returns `Null` value for any columns coming from T1 table.

A LEFT JOIN is very useful when you need to display all data records from one table but also want to know some secondary table data without restricting the query results. You will find more examples in the next chapter. If you are still not very clear about this LEFT JOIN clause, I hope the following example can help you:

Business Partners (OCRD)

BP Code	BP Name	Account Balance
C100001	Test 1	$0.00
C100002	Test 2	$1,000.00
C100003	Test 3	$0.00
C100004	Test 4	$0.00

A/R Invoice Headers (OINV)

BP Code	Posting Date	Document Number	Document Total
C100002	9/1/2010	10000003	$1,000.00

Query Result by LEFT JOIN OCRD with OINV ON CardCode

BP Code	BP Name	Account Balance	Document Number	Posting Date	Document Total
C100001	Test 1	$0.00			
C100002	Test 2	$1,000.00	10000003	9/1/2010	$1,000.00
C100003	Test 3	$0.00			
C100004	Test 4	$0.00			

The previous example shows a real query about how LEFT JOIN works.

The query script is as follows:

```
SELECT T0.[CardCode], T0.[CardName], T0.[Balance], T1.[DocNum],
T1.[DocDate], T1.[DocTotal]
FROM dbo.OCRD T0
LEFT JOIN dbo.OINV T1 ON T0.CardCode = T1.CardCode
WHERE T0.CardCode < 'C100005'
```

From the example, you can get a clear view. If you can only find one BP Code C100002 in the right table (OINV), you will get only one line with full information. All other lines will still show left table columns though.

One thing is important for a LEFT JOIN: do not use secondary Left Join if possible. Suppose you put more than one level of LEFT JOIN; the query result may become less clear.

Right Outer Join

A **Right Outer Join** is not used as often as a LEFT JOIN in a query. OUTER here is also optional. It can be omitted so that you just need RIGHT JOIN.

A RIGHT JOIN clause syntax looks like the following:

```
SELECT T[0]|[1].column_name(s)
FROM table_name0 T0
RIGHT JOIN table_name1 T1
ON T0.column_name=T1.column_name
```

In the previous syntax, the second table `table_name1 T1` is the right table while `table_name0 T0` is the left table. A **RIGHT JOIN** means all records in the right table will be returned, regardless of the left table linking condition. If the match cannot be found in T0 table, it simply returns `Null` value for any columns coming from the T0 table.

Most people would be more interested in the first table than the second table. That is why not so many people use this RIGHT JOIN. Here is an example for you:

A/R Invoice Headers (OINV)			
Posting Date	**Document Number**	**Document Total**	**BP Code**
9/1/2010	10000003	$1,000.00	C100002

Business Partners (OCRD)		
BP Name	**Account Balance**	**BP Code**
Test 1	$0.00	C100001
Test 2	$1,000.00	C100002
Test 3	$0.00	C100003
Test 4	$0.00	C100004

Query Result by RIGHT JOIN OINV with OCRD ON CardCode

Document Number	Posting Date	Document Total	BP Name	Account Balance	BP Code
			Test 1	$0.00	C100001
10000003	9/1/2010	$1,000.00	Test 2	$1,000.00	C100002
			Test 3	$0.00	C100003
			Test 4	$0.00	C100004

The query script is as follows:

```
SELECT T1.[DocNum], T1.[DocDate], T1.[DocTotal],T0.[CardName],
T0.[Balance], T0.[CardCode]
FROM dbo.OINV T1
RIGHT JOIN dbo.OCRD T0 ON T0.CardCode = T1.CardCode
WHERE T0.CardCode < 'C100005'
```

Unless you are used to reading from right to left, I bet no user prefers this result instead of the LEFT JOIN.

Full Outer Join

A **Full Outer Join** syntax looks like the following:

```
SELECT T[0]|[1].column_name(s)
FROM table_name0 T0
FULL OUTER JOIN table_name1 T1
ON T0.column_name=T1.column_name
```

A Full Outer Join will return all rows from both tables, regardless of matching conditions. It is one of the most dangerous clauses for SELECT queries too. Try to avoid this kind of join wherever you have other options.

There is no example query for this kind of join because it may only be useful in very special cases.

For people who like to use a Full Outer Join, you should always check what alternatives you have. If only Full Outer Join can solve your issue, some big problems might be hidden. Check them out!

Self-Join

A **Self-Join** is a special join in which a table is joined to itself. Self-Joins are used to compare values in a column with other values in the same column in the same table. It can be used for certain special needs such as obtaining running counts or running totals in a SQL query. It is often used in subqueries.

To write a query that includes a Self-Join, select from the same table listed twice with different aliases, set up the comparison, or eliminate cases where a particular value would be equal to itself.

A Self-Join is mostly an INNER JOIN. However, it can also be an OUTER JOIN. It is all dependent on your needs.

To my knowledge, this join is only a particular type of INNER JOIN or OUTER JOIN. The classification makes it outstanding only because it is too special.

You will get some example queries of Self-Join in later chapters.

WHERE—query conditions to be defined

It is very clear that the **WHERE** clause is to define query conditions. By using the WHERE clause, you may extract only those records that fulfill a specified criterion.

The WHERE clause is optional. However, it is a good idea to make it mandatory for your own sake to keep your query results safer. When you create your query without a WHERE clause, all records will be retrieved no matter how big the table is. It is highly recommended that you put the WHERE clause for all of your query scripts before you test to run them. This can save you much more time if you just enter these few letters.

If the WHERE clause exists in a query, it always follows the FROM clause. Its syntax is as follows:

```
SELECT column_name(s)
FROM table_name(s)
WHERE [(]expression operator expression [and/or] [expression operator
expression ][)]
```

In the previous syntax, *expression* stands for a column name, a constant, a function, a variable, or a subquery. An operator can be set from the following list:

Operator	Description
=	Equal
<>/!=	Not equal
>	Greater than
<	Less than
!>	Not Greater than
!<	Not Less than
>=	Greater than or equal
<=	Less than or equal
BETWEEN	Between an inclusive range
LIKE	Search for a pattern, used only for string
IN/EXISTS	Test if a specified value matches any value in a subquery (or a list for IN operator only)

If a column used in the WHERE clause is one of the character data types, the value must be enclosed in single quotes. In contrast, if the column used in the WHERE clause is of a numeric data type, the value should not be enclosed. The numeric values enclosed in quotes will always return 0.

To make the WHERE clause more efficient, it is better to avoid using Not Equal (<> /!=) wherever possible. Some of the other conditions with NOT also need to be used with care.

Five operators include >, <, =, >=, and <= symbols are very common for comparisons. They are not needed for the purpose of this book. Therefore they are omitted from the examples. Only three special comparisons will be discussed next.

BETWEEN—ranges to be defined from lower to higher end

A BETWEEN operator is to specify a range to test.

The syntax for a BETWEEN operator is:

```
Value1 [ NOT ] BETWEEN Value2 AND Value3
```

All arguments are discussed as follows:

- Value1 is the value to be tested in the range defined by Value2 and Value3.
- NOT specifies that the result of the predicate be negated. It is optional.
- Value1 is any valid value with the same data type as Values.
- Value3 is any valid value that is greater than Value2 with the same data type.
- AND is mandatory and acts as a placeholder that indicates Value1 should be within the range indicated by Value2 and Value3.
- This clause is equivalent to Value1 >= Value2 and Value1 <= Value3.
- When you use BETWEEN, it means that the start value and end value are included. If you need to specify an exclusive range, you have to use the greater than (>) and less than (<) operators instead.

There is a condition in the first query example in this chapter before discussing the statement:

```
WHERE t1.RefDate >= [%0] and t1.RefDate <= [%1]
```

Actually, it is equivalent to the following:

```
WHERE t1.RefDate BETWEEN [%0] and [%1]
```

The query result is exactly the same. I have chosen to use the longer expression only because the system prompt for the first one is better and clear.

Be careful; if any input to the BETWEEN or NOT BETWEEN predicate is null, the result is UNKNOWN. When you do not get the desired result, check if there is Null involved. If you are not sure about the data having NULL or not, you better not use BETWEEN at all.

IN/EXISTS—the value list that may satisfy the condition

IN or NOT IN is an operator to compare a value with an existing value list that has more than one value. You are allowed to have only one value in the list. However, that should be by equal operator. It is not logical to define only one value in the list. An IN operator can be used to determine whether a specified value matches or does not match any values in a list. The list can be a result of a subquery. This subquery must have only one column to return. In order for two sides to be comparable, both sides must have matched data types.

This operator is similar to the OR condition but is much shorter. With the OR condition, you not only have to repeat the similar conditions one by one, but you also need parentheses if there are other co-existing conditions.

In the list to be compared, duplicate values are allowed. You do not need to specify the DISTINCT keyword if the same values are the same. After all, you are comparing the left side value to the right side value list. The result will be the same no matter how many times the same values present in the list are compared with.

Any null values returned by a subquery or a list that are to be compared using IN or NOT IN will return UNKNOWN. It can produce unexpected results. Get rid of the Null value for the list wherever possible.

EXISTS or NOT EXISTS is also an operator to compare a value with a list. The list is only a result of a subquery. This subquery can have more than one column to return. In order for two sides to be comparable, both sides must have matched data types.

IN and EXISTS are almost the same, only that IN allows both fixed list and subquery. The only other exception is the way they treat Null values. If the subquery contains Null value, EXISTS will perform better than IN. This is because EXISTS only cares if the value exists in the query result. It doesn't care if there is Null value or not.

The bottom line is: whenever using these operators, predict if you may get Null values. Choose a proper one based on the prediction.

LIKE—similar records can be found

A LIKE operator allows you to do a search based on a pattern rather than specifying exactly what is desired (as in IN) or spell out a range (as in BETWEEN). LIKE determines whether a value to be tested matches a specified pattern. A pattern can include wildcard characters. During this matching, wildcard characters play flexible roles to allow partly unmatched values to go through.

Using wildcard characters makes the LIKE operator more flexible than using the = or != string comparison operators. In case any one of the values is not of the character string data type, the SQL Server Database Engine converts them to character string data type if possible.

A LIKE operator syntax is as follows:

```
Value [ NOT ] LIKE Pattern
```

Two arguments are as follows:

- Value is any valid value of character string data type.
- Pattern is the specific string of characters to search for in the Value, and can include the following valid wildcard characters. Pattern can be a maximum of 8,000 bytes.

Wildcard character	Description
%	Any string with zero or more characters
_(underscore)	Any single character
[ ]	Any single character within the specified range ([a-d]) or set ([abcd])
[^]	Any single character not within the specified range ([^x-z]) or set ([^xyz])

Most of the LIKE operators include % and/or _ wildcard characters. % can be put in the front, in the middle, or at the end. If you can find a certain condition such as **A LIKE 'xy%'** instead of **A LIKE '%xy'**, the query result would be faster.

Although NOT is an optional keyword for LIKE, you should try to avoid it in any way possible. It is not an effective way to compare a value with any patterns.

GROUP BY—summarizing the data according to the list

A GROUP BY clause is very useful if you need to aggregate your data based on certain columns. It is optional and must follow the FROM and WHERE clauses.

If you remember the first query before discussing statements, you have:

```
GROUP BY T0.ShortName
```

GROUP BY specifies T0.ShortName i.e. Business Partner column would be the base for summarizing debit and credit amounts for each Business Partner.

Whenever you use the GROUP BY clause, it is mandatory to include all your columns under this clause unless they are aggregated columns.

The following example shows a simple query:

A/R Invoice Headers (OINV)

BP Code	BP Name	Doc No.	Posting Date	DocTotal
C100001	Test 1	10000001	9-Sep-10	$1,000.00
C100002	Test 2	10000002	10-Sep-10	$2,000.00
C100001	Test 1	10000003	11-Sep-10	$3,000.00
C100002	Test 2	10000004	12-Sep-10	$4,000.00
C100002	Test 2	10000004	13-Sep-10	$5,000.00

Query Result by GROUP BY

BP Code	BP Name	Total
C100001	Test 1	$4,000.00
C100002	Test 2	$11,000.00

The query script is simple:

```
SELECT T0.CardCode AS 'BP Code', T0.CardName AS 'BP Named', SUM(T0.
DocTotal) AS 'Total'
FROM dbo.OINV T0
WHERE T0.CardCode < 'C100003'
GROUP BY T0.CardCode, T0.CardName
```

In the previous example, neither the DocNum nor the DocTotal columns can be included in the query. Otherwise, the group will not work for each customer.

HAVING—conditions to be defined in summary report

A HAVING clause is normally used with a GROUP BY clause. This clause is optional. It is equivalent to a WHERE clause under the main query body. It specifies that a SELECT statement should only return rows where aggregate values meet the specified conditions. This clause was added to the SQL language after the main clause had already been defined because the WHERE keyword could not be used with aggregate functions.

If you remember the first query before discussing, you have:

```
HAVING SUM(ISNULL(T0.Debit,0) - ISNULL(T0.Credit,0)) > 0
```

It can be found under the GROUP BY clause in the query. This means the query result will only include those records if the aggregate summary function's result of T0.Debit minus T0.Credit is greater than zero. In case there are Null values, they will be replaced with zero from all occurrences before summary operation.

ORDER BY—report result can be by your preferred order

An ORDER BY clause is very simple when you need to sort your query result based on certain columns. This clause is always the last clause to be used in the query. If you have UNION or UNION ALL to combine more than one query, this clause may only be added to the end of the entire query.

There are two types of orders: One is ascending and the other is descending. Descending can be abbreviated to DESC in the end. Ascending can be abbreviated to ASC. If DESC is not included, the default ORDER BY will be ascending. Since ascending is the default order, it is usually omitted from the query.

An ORDER BY clause can have more than one column. The rule for query result is: the order first applies to the first column in the left. Then will be the second column, the third column, and so on.

Remember, not all types of columns are orderable. Some image columns, memo columns, etc. cannot be ordered.

If you remember the first query before the discussion statement, the last statement is as follows:

```
ORDER BY SUM(ISNULL(T0.Debit,0) - ISNULL(T0.Credit,0)) DESC
```

It means the query result will be ordered by descending order according to the summary of T0.Debit minus T0.Credit. If there are Null values, they will be replaced with zero for all occurrences.

UNION/UNION ALL—to put two or more queries together

The UNION clause combines the results of two or more SQL queries into one query result set. To use this clause, the number and order of columns from those queries must be the same with compatible data types. Any duplicate records are automatically removed by the UNION clause. It works like DISTINCT.

One thing you need to be aware of: UNION results do not care about the order of the rows. Rows from the first query may appear before, after, or mixed with rows from the following one. If you need a specific order, the ORDER BY clause must be used.

The UNION ALL clause is almost the same as the UNION clause, except it allows duplicated records.

UNION ALL may be much faster than plain UNION due to fewer checks in the query process. Whenever duplication is not a concern, or duplication is needed, UNION ALL should be used first.

A UNION or UNION ALL query is usually longer than a normal query because it is at least double the lines of query scripts. The example query that includes this clause will be shown in later chapters.

Some important functions to return values

Some important functions to return values are discussed as follows:

ISNULL() predicate

An ISNULL() function is used for replacing Null with the specified replacement value.

The syntax for the function is as follows:

```
ISNULL (Value1,Value2)
```

Value1 is normally a column value or a variable to be checked. Value2 is a fixed value to be replaced to.

In the first example query you read before the discussion of statement, there is an instance of ISNULL(T0.Debit,0) or ISNULL(T0.Credit,0). Here, a column T0.Debit or T0.Credit is checked. If it is Null, then it will be replaced with 0. Otherwise, the query will not be able to return the correct results. That is because: only 0 can be added but not Null. Even if you have one Null in the formula, the final result will be Unknown or an error.

Misunderstanding of how Null works is not a rare case. These mistakes are usually the result of confusion between Null and either 0 (zero) or an empty string (''). Null is actually different from both values. Null indicates the absence of any value. Null means nothing. ISNULL() function is very effective for getting rid of Null. Use it whenever you need it.

SUM() function

A SUM() function is used for returning the summed total of all the values, or only the DISTINCT values, from the numeric columns.

The syntax for the function is as follows:

```
SUM ([ ALL | DISTINCT ] value)
```

Both ALL and DISTINCT keywords are optional. If you add DISTINCT keyword to the function, it will only return the sum of distinct values. ALL is the default selection. There is usually no need to add to the function at all.

The value here can be a constant, column, or a function, and any combination of arithmetic operators.

MAX() function

A MAX() function is used for returning the maximum value from all checked values.

The syntax for the function is as follows:

```
MAX ([ ALL | DISTINCT ] value)
```

Both ALL and DISTINCT keywords are optional. If you add a DISTINCT keyword to the function, it will only return the maximum of the distinct values. The result will be exactly the same as the one without this keyword. ALL is default selection. There is usually no need to add to the function at all.

The value here can be a constant, column, or function, and any combination of arithmetic, bitwise, and string operators. MAX function can be used with numeric, character, and datetime columns.

An example query would be as follows:

```
SELECT T0.CardCode, MAX(T0.DocTotal) 'Total'
FROM dbo.OINV T0
WHERE T0.CardCode LIKE '[%0]%'
GROUP BY T0.CardCode
ORDER BY MAX(T0.DocTotal) DESC
```

With this query, the maximum A/R invoice total will be returned in a range of customers or all customers if you input nothing when you run the query.

MIN() function

A `MIN()` function is used for returning minimum value from all checked values.

The syntax for the function is as follows:

```
MIN ([ ALL | DISTINCT ] Value)
```

Both ALL and DISTINCT keywords are optional. If you add DISTINCT keyword to the function, it will only return the minimum of the distinct values. The result will be exactly the same as the one without this keyword. ALL is the default selection. There is usually no need to add to the function at all.

The value here can be a constant, column, or function, and any combination of arithmetic, bitwise, and string operators. MIN can be used with numeric, character, and datetime columns.

An example query would be as follows:

```
SELECT T0.CardCode, MIN(T0.DocTotal) 'Total'
FROM dbo.OPCH T0
WHERE T0.CardCode LIKE '[%0]%'
GROUP BY T0.CardCode
ORDER BY MIN (T0.DocTotal)
```

With this query, the minimum A/P invoice total will be returned in a range of vendors or all vendors, if you input nothing when you run the query.

COUNT() function

A `COUNT()` function returns the number of items in a group.

The syntax for the function is as follows:

```
COUNT { [ [ ALL | DISTINCT ] Value ] | * })
```

Both ALL and DISTINCT keywords are optional. If you add DISTINCT keyword to the function, it will only return the count of the distinct values. ALL is the default selection. There is usually no need to add to the function at all.

The value here can be of any type except text or image. Aggregate functions and subqueries are not permitted.

COUNT(*) cannot be used with DISTINCT. * specifies that all rows should be counted to return the total number of rows in a table. COUNT(*) does not require any values because it does not use information about any particular columns. COUNT(*) returns the number of physical rows in a specified table including duplicate rows and the rows that contain null values. On the contrary, if it is not COUNT(*), only non-null rows will be counted.

An example query is as follows:

```
SELECT Count(*) FROM OUSR
```

You will immediately know how many users you have set up in your system from day one of your system. Remember all users, including deleted users, will be counted. If you have a long history, this number could be well above your current number of users.

Another useful query example is as follows:

```
SELECT Count(*) FROM JDT1
```

You will get the number of records for one of your largest tables.

DATEDIFF() function

A DATEDIFF() function returns an integer number of intervals of a specified type between two dates.

The syntax is simple:

```
DATEDIFF ( Datepart , Date1 , Date2 )
```

Three arguments are:

- **Datepart** is the parameter that specifies on which type of the date or time to calculate the difference. The Datepart and abbreviations can be found from the following table. These Datepart and abbreviations are an exclusive list that cannot be supplied as a user-declared variable.

Datepart	Abbreviations
Year	yy, yyyy
Quarter	qq, q
Month	mm, m
Dayofyear	dy, y
Day	dd, d

Datepart	Abbreviations
Week	wk, ww
Weekday	dw
Hour	hh
Minute	mi, n
Second	ss, s
Millisecond	ms

- **Date1** is the starting date for the interval. It is an expression that returns a datetime value, or a character string in a date format.

- **Date2** is the ending date for the interval. It is also an expression that returns a datetime value, or a character string in a date format.

Date and time values included in the function must be within a valid range. Years must be less than or equal to 9999. Months must be between 1 and 12. Days must be between 1 and 31. Hours: 0 through 23. Minutes: 0 through 59. Seconds: 0 through 59.

For year format, it is recommended to always use four-digit years. If you specify only the last two digits of the year, it may cause uncertainty. It will be affected by the two-digit year cutoff configuration option in your system. For example, if the two-digit year cutoff is 2049 (default), 49 is interpreted as 2049 and 50 is interpreted as 1950. The difference calculated across the boundary will be surprising.

DATEDIFF() function is one of the most useful date functions for getting proper results. This is always the first function to be used if you need a date compare operation. For using abbreviations, two-letter abbreviations are recommended because this is one of the most easily remembered options with the consistent format.

Here is an example:

```
SELECT DATEDIFF(DD, '10-10-2010', '01-01-2011')
```

It will return 83 since the difference between these two dates is 83 days. You could change the date order to the following:

```
SELECT DATEDIFF(DD, '01-01-2011', '10-10-2010')
```

This will return -83 because the first date is greater than the second one.

DATEADD() function

A `DATEADD()` function returns a new datetime value based on adding or subtracting an interval to a specified date.

The syntax is as follows:

```
DATEADD (Datepart , Number, Date )
```

Three arguments are as follows:

- Datepart is the parameter that specifies the part of the date or time to return. The lists of the Dateparts and abbreviations can be found above, under the `DATEDIFF()` function.

- Number is the value used to increment Datepart. If you specify a value that is not an integer, the decimal part of the value is truncated. For example, if you specify day for Datepart and 3.68 for number, date is incremented only by 3.

- Date is an expression that returns a datetime value, or a character string in a date format. When you enter datetime values, always enclose them in quotation marks.

An example query is as follows:

```
SELECT DateAdd(mm, 5, '05-05-2011')
```

It will return 10-05-2011, if your date format is mm-dd-yyyy, or it returns 05-10-2011, if your date format is dd-mm-yyyy.

DATEPART() function

A `DATEPART()` function returns an integer that represents the specified Datepart of the specified date or time.

The syntax is very simple:

```
DATEPART ( Datepart , Date )
```

Two arguments are as follows:

- **Datepart** is the parameter that specifies the part of the date or time to return. The lists of the Dateparts and abbreviations can be found above, under the `DATEDIFF()` function.

- **Date** is an expression that returns a datetime value, or a character string in a date format. When you enter datetime values, always enclose them in quotation marks.

An example query would be as follows:

```
SELECT DatePart(WW, '05-05-2011')
```

This would return 19 since the date May 5th, 2011, belongs to the nineteenth week of 2011.

CAST()/CONVERT() function

To convert an expression of one data type to another explicitly, CAST and CONVERT can be used. They provide similar functionality with different syntaxes.

Syntax for CAST:

```
CAST ( Value AS Data_type [ (Length ) ])
```

Syntax for CONVERT:

```
CONVERT ( Data_type [ ( Length ) ] , Value [ , Style ] )
```

Here, **Value** is any valid expression.

Data_type is the target system-supplied data type such as integer data, character data, monetary data, date and time data, binary strings, and so on. Alias data types cannot be used with this function.

Length is an optional parameter of string data types. For CONVERT, if length is not specified, the default length is 30 characters.

Style is the style of the value to be returned. When style is Null, the result returned is also Null. In other words, you have to define style in the CONVERT function, otherwise, you may get nothing.

 Do not use any unsupported styles or an unsupported combination of style and target data type. Otherwise, it might return an error or unreliable results. To find the supported style by SQL Server, check SQL Server references.

CASE expressions

A CASE expression is a unique conditional statement providing if/then/else logic for any ordinary SQL statement. It returns a single value from one of the multiple possible result expressions by evaluating a list of conditions.

The CASE expression has two formats:

- The simple CASE expression
- The searched CASE expression

Both formats support an optional ELSE expression that gives an alternative action, if no THEN expression is executed.

The simple CASE expression compares an expression to a set of simple expressions to determine the result. The searched CASE expression, on the other hand, evaluates a set of Boolean expressions to determine the result.

CASE can be used in any statement or clause that allows a valid expression. You can use CASE in statements such as SELECT, SET, or in clauses, such as WHERE, IN, ORDER BY, and HAVING.

CASE expressions can be extremely useful when you have very complex requirements. Through CASE expression, some complex queries can be changed into simpler, more efficient SQL statements.

CASE is a very powerful tool to get query results that cannot be done through other functions or expressions. It is mainly the topic of a later chapter.

The syntax for CASE expression is better shown by a query example:

```
SELECT CASE WHEN (DATEDIFF(dd,T0.refdate,getdate())) >= 90
THEN CASE
WHEN T0.SYSCRED= 0 THEN T0.SYSDEB
WHEN T0.SYSDEB= 0 THEN -T0.SYSCRED
END
END "90 + DAYS"
FROM DBO.JDT1 T0
WHERE T0.SHORTNAME LIKE '[%0]%'
```

This simple query can be used to show a selected business partner's aging balance that is greater than or equal to 90 days. In the query, the ELSE is not used. Only when the conditions meet the requirement the results can be returned. With the condition `(DATEDIFF(dd,T0.refdate,getdate())) >= 90`, only those records in the JDT1 table will be returned.

There are two levels of CASE clauses that have been applied. After the first CASE check, the second level CASE will check whether T0.SYSCRED equals zero or T0.SYSDEB equals zero. When one of them is zero, the opposite column will be returned.

Notice there is only END without BEGIN. END is to be used to end the CASE expression. A CASE expression will always imply BEGIN of the SQL block. END is needed for every CASE expression. WHEN and THEN is the branch to make the CASE expression work. If you need to cover all conditions, ELSE is required to get all other records without meeting any of the WHEN conditions.

IF expressions

An IF expression introduces a condition that determines whether the next statement is executed. The optional ELSE expression can give an alternate action to be executed when the IF condition is not satisfied.

The IF statement is logically equivalent to a searched CASE expression. In other words, an IF expression will cover less than a CASE expression.

In SAP Business One, IF can be used in many places such as **Formatted Search**.

Similar to CASE expression, the syntax for IF expression is better shown with a query example:

```
If Exists
(SELECT T1.DocEntry
FROM OIGE T0 INNER JOIN IGE1 T1
ON T0.DocEntry=T1.DocEntry
WHERE T0.DocEntry = @list_of_cols_val_tab_del
Group By T1.DocEntry
Having Sum(T1.Quantity) <=T0.U_nQty)
Begin
SELECT @error = 111,
@error_message = 'error quantity entered'
End
```

In the query example, the IF expression is used to check whether the query after EXISTS returns anything. If it is positive, this query could be used for effectively blocking the Goods Receipt being created. Notice that the parentheses are needed when there is a SELECT statement included in the query body.

Summary

In this chapter, you learned about the most important tool for creating or using SQL queries in SAP Business One, Query Manager. This included Query Manager user interface and query display, creation, and save. We also discussed query categories.

You learned the most commonly used query statements such as SELECT, DISTINCT, TOP, and more. You also learned some functions or expressions such as ISNULL(), SUM(), and CASE.

From those statements, functions, and expressions, you have built a good foundation to build your own SQL queries. When you are in doubt about your query building knowledge, it is always advisable to come back here to have a good overview of the statement you need.

In the next chapter, you will have more real world query examples to deal with.

Section 2

SQL Query in Action

Query Examples

Securities and Approval

SQL Query for Formatted Search (FMS)

SQL Query for Other Reporting Tools

SQL Query for Stored Procedure (SP)

More Complicated SQL Query Topics

Appendix

4
Query Examples

In the previous chapter, you learned about Query Manager and the most commonly-used statements and functions. That gave you a necessary tool to create any SQL queries within SAP Business One system freely. However, it may not be that easy to create a query to meet your specific needs.

This chapter will show you the following:

- The most widely used query examples to give you more powers to build your own queries. These include:
    - Query variables
    - Date selection
    - Drill-down arrows
    - Subtotals

- Detailed solution examples give all readers an idea about how business intelligence works within SAP Business One and breaks it down into three primary categories:
    - Marketing documents
    - Inventory transactions
    - Financial transactions

- Alert query examples and miscellaneous query examples for better use of on demand information.

You will find the questions or some queries that do not fully satisfy what is required first. Then, the right queries to solve these problems. Finally, there will be an explanation of the solution queries.

Within this chapter, any table or column in the queries can be found through the table references mentioned in the previous chapters. If you do not know the meaning of the tables or columns, you can refer to *Chapter 1* to find where to get those references.

The column names in this book are often in two different formats. You can find some of them within brackets, that is, [Column]. However, more than half of them are without brackets. Usually the differences between them can be ignored. Column within brackets is only the result of query tools by SAP Business One. For the sake of time, if the original queries have brackets, the solution queries may have brackets too. If it is created from scratch, the query will have no brackets.

Please refer back to the the preface for more information on the specific naming conventions of the query examples in this chapter.

Why three categories have been chosen

In this chapter, besides some examples for special areas, most of the query examples are categorized based on Marketing Documents, Inventory Transactions, and Financial Transactions.

You may wonder why these three categories have been picked for the book. These are not randomly selected but are the result of investigation based on the query examples, which I have written from the many requests received. You may get a clearer picture of the query usage area from the following pie chart based upon a sample of 100 queries:

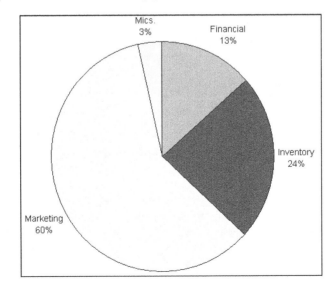

From this chart, you can have a good idea which one is the most frequently used category. Actually, the term Inventory here is not limited to stock only. It also includes Production. Purchasing and sales are the main areas for query reports. It is also one of the most important areas where business intelligence is definitely a must.

Defining variables for queries

The first type of query example to discuss is regarding query variables or parameters. Query variables or parameters are important because the correct parameters in the query will greatly increase the query flexibility and the query intelligence. One query with variables may mean hundreds of hard-coded queries. If you input different data for the variables, you can have pertinent information just related to what you are interested in.

If you have read the previous chapters, you will remember [%0], [%1], etc. That is the way SAP Business One defines variables.

 Remember, you must define an alias for the table in order to use these variables. If you omit the table alias, you will get an error message when you include the variables in your query.

Look at the cases below for variables usage.

Case 4-R1: Four variables in one query

One request is to create a simple query that needs four parameters. The information required includes order no., date, customer data, amount, and status from the sales order table. When a user selects **OPEN**, it should display open sales order; if the user enters **CLOSED** it should display closed sales order during a specific period. An additional requirement is to add selectable customer groups besides initial request.

The solution can be found as follows:

```
SELECT T0.DocNum,
T0.DocDate,
T0.CardCode,
T0.CardName,
T0.DocTotal,
T0.DocStatus

FROM dbo.ORDR T0
INNER JOIN dbo.OCRD T1 ON T1.CardCode = T0.CardCode
```

```
INNER JOIN dbo.OCRG T2 ON T2.GroupCode = T1.GroupCode

WHERE T0.DocStatus = [%0] and
T0.DocDate BETWEEN [%1] and [%2] AND
T2.GroupName LIKE '[%3]%'
```

With this query, users can select a sales order with a different document status within a certain period for selected customer groups. You probably noticed there are two more tables in addition to the sales order table ORDR. One is OCRD that holds all Business Partner data. Another is OCRG that holds Business Partner Group data. In order to have a variable to select a customer group, these two tables are absolutely necessary. Without these two tables, you will not be able to put in the customer group selection variable, because in the sales order table, you can only find the CardCode and CardName columns. You need to link to the OCRD table first. Then you can link to the OCRG table in order to access business partner group information.

`T0.DocDate BETWEEN [%1] and [%2]` is equal to `T0.docdate >= [%1] and T0.docdate <= [%2]`, which gives users the power to select a specific period.

Case 4-R2: Variables first or last

A user created a questionable query that could not run. The problematic query is as follows:

```
IF [%2] IS NULL
SELECT T0.[CardCode], T0.[CardName], T0.[DocNum], T0.[DocTotal],
T0.[GrosProfit], T0.[DocDate] FROM ADOC T0 WHERE T0.[CardCode] like
'C%' and T0.[DocDate] between [%0] and [%1]
ELSE
SELECT T0.[CardCode], T0.[CardName], T0.[DocNum], T0.[DocTotal],
T0.[GrosProfit], T0.[DocDate] FROM ADOC T0 WHERE T0.[CardCode] like
'C%' and T0.[DocDate] between [%0] and [%1] and T0.[CardCode] = [%2]
```

The previous query is not runnable. It pops up an error message when it is executed.

The solution query script is listed here:

```
SELECT DISTINCT
T0.CardCode,
T0.CardName,
T0.DocNum,
T0.DocTotal,
T0.GrosProfit,
T0.DocDate
```

```
FROM dbo.ADOC T0

WHERE T0.CardCode like 'C%' and
T0.DocDate between [%0] and [%1]
AND T0.CardCode like '%[%2]%'
```

With this query, there is no need to check the condition of the variable. The variable for T0.CardCode will only appear once. It effectively replaces the conditional check. The way to put parameter like '%[%2]%' is very useful. This is because:

- [%2] can be Null. When it is Null, this query will return all CardCodes starting with 'C'.

- [%2] can be very short, with one or two characters. This gives you great flexibility instead of inputting the complete CardCode.

This query can still be improved by changing the following condition:

T0.[CardCode] like 'C%' to be replaced by T0.CardType = 'C'.

Obviously this condition is to restrict the query result to the customers only. The second condition will be stronger to get everything you need without binding to your customers' coding convention. Due to possible end-user error during creation of the customer, the "C" could have been accidently left off the customer code. By checking the CardType (BP Type) you will be certain to pick up all customers, no matter what the naming convention used in your company.

The problem for the first query is: no parameter is allowed for the IF clause. IF EXISTS is the most common way to use the IF clause. Unless you declare them first, all variables should be located inside the WHERE clause.

> Be careful when you define variables; all variables like [%0], [%1], [%2], and so on must be unique. If you use them in more than one place, all values for one specific variable will be identical no matter where they are. The column to compare with identical variables must have exactly the same data type.

Date function—where the most problems emerge

The date function is one of the most problematic areas for SQL query. It is often used to return date-related results from a database. Some date functions were explained in the previous chapter. Get familiar with them first, if you are still not clear.

Case 4-D1: Balance of production for a month

A question which I received dealt with a query that needs to display the balance of production for the current month or for the past month.

```
SELECT SUM(T0.SYSDeb - T0.SYSCred) AS 'Production'
FROM JDT1 T0
WHERE T0.Account in ('_SYS00000000238','_SYS00000000239','_
SYS00000000244')
UNION
SELECT SUM(T0.SYSDeb - T0.SYSCred) AS 'Production'
FROM JDT1 T0
WHERE T0.Account = '_SYS00000000053'
```

As this query will work in the Add-on it cannot specify `T0.RefDate >= [%0]` AND `T0.RefDate <= [%1]`.

The solution is very simple:

```
SELECT SUM(T0.SYSDeb - T0.SYSCred) AS 'Production'

FROM dbo.JDT1 T0

WHERE T0.Account in ('_SYS00000000238','_SYS00000000239', '_
SYS00000000244', '_SYS00000000053') AND
MONTH(T0.RefDate)=Month(Getdate()) AND YEAR(T0.
RefDate)=YEAR(Getdate())
```

If the results need to be for the last month, it can simply be done by replacing `MONTH(T0.RefDate)=Month(Getdate())` with `MONTH(T0.RefDate)=Month(Getdate())-1`.

This example shows that when dealing with a date range, flexibility is important. You don't need to compare the date range with specific dates all the time. If the date function is available, use function instead. Here, the YEAR and MONTH functions are quite handy to solve the problem.

Another difference is, the UNION clause has been taken away completely. Because two parts joined by UNION have identical columns and tables, here, the UNION clause is not necessary at all. The second query can be included to the first query condition without any problems.

If you want to try this query, you need to replace the G/L account numbers with some valid numbers from your system first. This specific example is using a segmented account. These accounts in the query are probably not the same as yours. All accounts beginning with _SYS are system generated account codes for segmented accounts. They differ from system to system.

Case 4-D2: How to input a fixed date range

Another example has a different requirement from the first one. The query's main structure has been created but not the date part. The query is as follows:

```
SELECT T0.DocNum as 'SO No.', T0.DocDate as 'Date', T0.CardCode as
'CustCode', T0.CardName as 'Customer Name', T0.NumAtCard as 'Ref/PO
No.', T0.DocCur as 'Currency', (T0.DocTotal - T0.VatSum) as 'SO Amt'
FROM ORDR T0
WHERE T0.DocDate >= Date1 and T0.DocDate <= Date2
```

Date1 = current date - 7 days

Date2 = current date - 1 day

The requester wants this query's date range to be between the current date minus seven days and the current date minus one day. However, the user could not find a proper way to complete it.

The solution for this query is:

```
SELECT T0.DocNum as 'SO No.',
T0.DocDate as 'Date',
T0.CardCode as 'Customer Code',
T0.CardName as 'Customer Name',
T0.NumAtCard as 'Ref/PO No.',
T0.DocCur as 'Currency',
(T0.DocTotal - T0.VatSum) as 'SO Amount'

FROM dbo.ORDR T0

WHERE DateDiff(DD, T0.DocDate, GetDate()) > 0 and
DateDiff(DD, T0.DocDate, GetDate()) < 8
```

This is a perfect example to show the power of the DateDiff function. As you can find from the previous chapter, the DateDiff function is the first and the foremost date function available to you. It would be a great tool to compare dates. It usually works in many cases to solve date-related problems.

This query could be used to display all sales orders created within the past week. No matter what their status is, all documents can be browsed with the query result viewer. If it is associated with an alert, the alert can be sent automatically based on the alert setting.

You may notice the > and < signs used instead of >= and <=. They are equivalent when you adjust the date boundaries by one day, that is: 1-1 = 0 and 7+1 = 8.

To show the power of the `DateDiff()` function, even the first example can be changed using it. The following can be replaced:

```
MONTH(T0.RefDate)=Month(Getdate()) AND YEAR(T0.
RefDate)=YEAR(Getdate())
```

With the following:

```
DateDiff(mm,T0.RefDate,Getdate())=0 AND
DateDiff(yy,T0.RefDate,Getdate())=0
```

Orange arrow—an excellent tool for drill down

"Orange arrow" or "Golden arrow" is a linked button in SAP Business One. I prefer calling it "Orange arrow" because the color of the arrow is orange. It is not golden.

However, it will be called "**Link Arrow**" in the book to prevent any confusion.

Link arrow is an excellent tool to get detailed information directly from the query result. This is one of the best functions within SAP Business One that makes SQL query a much more powerful tool than some other printable only reporting tools. When you click on the link arrow, you will immediately open the linked document. It is very convenient.

Some queries will hide link arrows by default. Here is a partial list:

- Queries with a Union clause
- Queries for Formatted Search
- Queries with parameters declared
- Queries with certain restricted names in comment section
- Queries with only historical "A" tables

In the last case, you may still find certain link arrows. However, they are only from foreign keys.

If your query is not subjected to the previous list, it is always better to place "For Browse" at the end of each and every SQL query to ensure that link arrows appear.

Case 4-O1: Make it simple

A good example is a working query that returns all AR Invoices posted before the current day, excluding weekends. However, when this query executes, there are no drill-down arrows in the result for DocNum. So the question is: "Is there a way that the drill-down arrows can appear in this query?" The original query is as follows:

```
declare @dt_today datetime,
@dt_yesterday datetime
select @dt_today = DATEADD(dd, DATEDIFF(dd,0,GETDATE()), 0)
select @dt_yesterday = case DATEPART(DW,@dt_today)
when 2 then DATEADD(dd, -3, @dt_today)
when 1 then DATEADD(dd, -2, @dt_today)
else DATEADD(dd, -1, @dt_today) end
SELECT T0.DocNum As 'Invoice number', T0.DocDate As 'Posting Date',
T0.DocTotal As 'Invoice Total', T0.GrosProfit As 'Gross Profit',
((T0.GrosProfit / (T0.DocTotal - T0.GrosProfit))*100) As 'Profit %',
T1.CardCode, T1.CardName, T0.NumAtCard As 'Customer PO#',
T2.GroupName,
T1.Phone1, T1.CntctPrsn
FROM OINV T0 INNER JOIN OCRD T1 ON T0.CardCode = T1.CardCode INNER
JOIN OCRG
T2 ON T1.GroupCode = T2.GroupCode WHERE T0.DocDate = @dt_yesterday
```

The solution query is listed as follows:

```
SELECT T0.DocNum As 'Invoice number',
T0.DocDate As 'Posting Date',
T0.DocTotal As 'Invoice Total',
T0.GrosProfit As 'Gross Profit',
(T0.GrosProfit/(T0.DocTotal-T0.GrosProfit))*100 As 'Profit %',
T1.CardCode,
T1.CardName,
T0.NumAtCard As 'Customer PO#',
T2.GroupName,
T1.Phone1,
T1.CntctPrsn

FROM dbo.OINV T0
INNER JOIN dbo.OCRD T1 ON T0.CardCode = T1.CardCode
INNER JOIN dbo.OCRG T2 ON T1.GroupCode = T2.GroupCode

WHERE DATEDIFF(DD, T0.DocDate, GetDate()) = 1 OR
(DATEDIFF(DD, T0.DocDate, GetDate()) = 3 AND DATEPART(dw,GetDate()) in
(1,2))
```

As you know, there will be no link arrow if there are parameters used in the query. The solution is to get rid of those parameters. The condition under the WHERE clause handles the various weekdays, so that parameters can be omitted. Here, `DATEDIFF(DD, T0.DocDate, GetDate()) = 1` covers current weekdays, while `DATEDIFF(DD, T0.DocDate, GetDate()) = 3 AND DATEPART(dw,GetDate()) in (1,2)` handles days for weekends.

This solution just assumes that the original logic works. If you find out that it may not cover all possibilities, it is necessary to fine tune it to fit your condition.

The most important hint from this example is: whenever possible, do not use parameters if the link arrow is very important to you.

Case 4-O2: Sales order updating alert with drill down

A requested query is needed to list a sales order's amendments. Then, an alert can be created based on this query, so that it runs once a day and shows the sales orders that have been amended during that particular day. The sales order has to allow you to drill down.

The solution is:

```
SELECT DISTINCT T1.DocNum,
T0.DocStatus,
T0.DocDate,
T0.DocDueDate,
T0.CardCode,
T0.CardName

FROM dbo.ADOC T0
INNER JOIN dbo.ORDR T1 ON T1.DocNum = T0.DocNum AND T0.ObjType = '17'

WHERE DateDiff(d,T0.UpdateDate,GETDATE()) <= 0

FOR BROWSE
```

In the query, joining table ORDR is the key to overcome the difficulty due to all history log tables' inability to show link arrow. By linking the current table to the ADOC table, the sales order can be opened through query result without any problem.

The T0.ObjType = '17' in the query is the way to extract only the sales order from the ADOC table. Sales order's object type is '17'.

If you have multiple series for document number, a third condition is needed for INNER JOIN clause: AND T1.Series = T0.Series.

There is an interesting difference for this particular query. It can get the link arrow in 2007A version without the last FOR BROWSE clause. However, it is mandatory for version 8.8. This book is tested in both versions. I believe, even 2005 version users could run most (if not all) of the queries within this book.

> The ADOC table is a very useful table. It holds all historical records for all marketing documents and certain inventory documents such as Goods Receipt and Goods Issue. As I mentioned in the previous chapter, this table is wrongly called Invoice History. In fact, it should be called Documents History. You can find individual type documents by their object type. This object type list can be found at the end of the book.

Getting a subtotal from the query

Quite frequently someone will want to display either a subtotal or total within the query. It is possible in the following ways. This is not the complete list, but they are the most often used methods:

- By Union ALL
- By running total
- By system

The last method is very simple. It is a SAP Business One internal function. You can get the column total under the query result window using *Ctrl+Click* on the column header if the column is a numeric value. The following screenshot shows you an example:

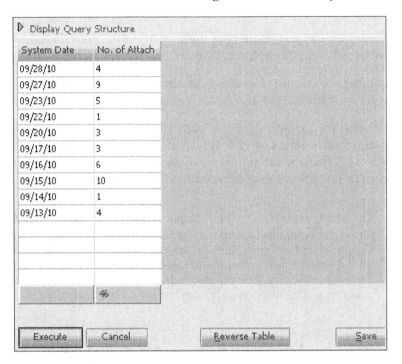

Case 4-T1: By Union ALL

A request to add a summary to the following query script:

```
SELECT T0.[DocNum] as 'SO No.',
T0.[DocDate] as 'Date',
T0.[CardCode] as 'CustCode',
T0.[CardName] as 'Customer Name',
T0.[NumAtCard] as 'Ref/PO No.',
(T0.[DocTotalSy] - T0.[VatSumSy]) as 'SO Amt',
T2.[FrozenComm], T0.Comments

FROM ORDR T0
INNER JOIN OCRN T1 ON T0.DocCur = T1.CurrCode
INNER JOIN OCRD T2 ON T0.CardCode = T2.CardCode

WHERE DateDiff(DD, T0.DocDate, GetDate()) > 0 AND
DateDiff(DD, T0.DocDate, GetDate()) < 8 and
T0.[Canceled]='N'

ORDER BY T0.[DocDate], T0.[DocNum]
```

Here is the solution:

```
SELECT T0.[DocNum] as 'SO No.',
T0.[DocDate] as 'Date',
T0.[CardCode] as 'CustCode',
T0.[CardName] as 'Custome Name',
T0.[NumAtCard] as 'Ref/PO No.',
(T0.[DocTotalSy] - T0.[VatSumSy]) as 'SO Amt',
T2.[FrozenComm], T0.Comments

FROM dbo.ORDR T0
INNER JOIN dbo.OCRN T1 ON T0.DocCur = T1.CurrCode
INNER JOIN dbo.OCRD T2 ON T0.CardCode = T2.CardCode

WHERE DateDiff(DD, T0.DocDate, GetDate()) > 0 and
DateDiff(DD, T0.DocDate, GetDate()) < 8 AND
T0.[Canceled]='N'

UNION ALL
SELECT '', NULL,'Total','','', SUM(T0.[DocTotalSy] - T0.[VatSumSy]) ,
'', ''

FROM dbo.ORDR T0
INNER JOIN dbo.OCRN T1 ON T0.DocCur = T1.CurrCode
INNER JOIN dbo.OCRD T2 ON T0.CardCode = T2.CardCode

WHERE DateDiff(DD, T0.DocDate, GetDate()) > 0 and
DateDiff(DD, T0.DocDate, GetDate()) < 8 AND
T0.[Canceled]='N'
```

In the previous solution, the Union All clause is used. It can effectively add the same data from the first part of the query. Other than the SUM(T0.[DocTotalSy] - T0.[VatSumSy]) column, all other columns are set to a null value or replaced by text. The number of columns as well as the data types must be the same for the first part of the query above UNION ALL and for the second part of the query below the UNION ALL as well.

Case 2: By running total

A very common requirement is to add a running total to each line within the query with the last line giving you a total of the entire query result. There is a way to do this but it is extremely difficult and would take a long time. I would suggest you don't attempt to provide a running total, but instead use the Export to Excel feature available and then produce the running total column within Excel.

Query for marketing documents

Marketing Documents is the term used in SAP Business One to represent both purchasing and sales documents. They also include A/P and A/R documents such as A/P Invoice or A/R Credit Memo. This category is one of the most targeted areas for query. Based on the chart shown in the first part of the chapter, it represents more than 60 percent of the query questions, which I have dealt with in the past.

Case 4-M1: Overview of BP with selection of realized balance

Here is an example request to get an overview of all customers which realized sales greater than 1,000 for the current year. The columns in need are the business partner's name, address, zip code, city, and email address.

The following is the solution query:

```
SELECT T0.cardname, T0.address, T0.zipcode, T0.city, T0.e_mail

FROM dbo.OCRD T0

WHERE T0.CardCode IN
(SELECT T1.CardCode
FROM dbo.OINV T1 WHERE Year(T1.DocDate) = Year(Getdate())

GROUP BY T1.CardCode
Having SUM(T1.DocTotal) > [%0])
```

This solution will check much more than a fixed 1,000 amount. It can be any amount the users are interested in. The subquery under IN clause is the real solution. This query summarizes all customers' current year invoice totals. Then it compares with the user entered value. The last statement in the subquery is the key to the solution.

```
GROUP BY T1.CardCode
Having SUM(T1.DocTotal) > [%0]
```

This means that only the customers with sales amounts greater than a user-defined amount will be shown. The discussion of the subquery will be pushed to the end of the book.

Case 4-M2: Top five items sold

Sales ranking is one of the hot topics everywhere. There is no difference for SAP Business One users. There are quite a few questions with similar requests. They need certain top items sold during a certain period of time.

The solution query is as follows; it has top five items along with sales values between the user's definable date ranges:

```
SELECT TOP 5 T1.ItemCode,
MAX(T1.Dscription) as 'Item Description',
SUM(T1.LineTotal) as 'Amount(LC)'

FROM dbo.OINV T0
INNER JOIN dbo.INV1 T1 ON T1.DocENtry = T0.DocENtry

WHERE T0.docdate >= [%0] and T0.docdate <= [%1]
AND T0.doctype = 'I'

GROUP BY T1.ItemCode

ORDER BY SUM(T1.LineTotal) DESC
```

This query has just looked up Invoice tables OINV and INV1. The first table is the header. The other table is line detail of A/R invoices.

- `TOP 5 T1.ItemCode` here will list five item codes that have the highest sale values during a specific period. You can change it to any number you like, or go by the percentage.

- `Max(T1.Dscription)` here has two advantages:
  - It is convenient to omit the column from grouping.
  - It is very useful when your query includes multiple values in the document. It can just return one item name instead of many different names in the document for the same item. In other words, the query only cares about item code.

- `SUM(T1.LineTotal)` means the summary amount – in local currency – of the items sold in all invoice lines.

- `T0.docdate >= [%0] and T0.docdate <= [%1]` define the user input date range. Although this code is longer than using **between**, an advantage of this is clearly showing the description of the date range **greater than or equal to** and **smaller than or equal to** on the screen. If using **between**, the description displayed before variables will not be very clear.

- `T0.doctype = 'I'` is to limit the document to item type only.

- `GROUP BY T1.ItemCode` is used to make sure summary will be based on Item code.

- The last line `ORDER BY SUM(T1.LineTotal) DESC` means the query result will be based on the descending order of the summary of the line total.

This query is only a rough estimate of the items sold. It has not taken credit memo into consideration. In order to make sure the credit memos are taken into consideration, it is best to include the UNION function and then the complete query should be as follows:

```
SELECT TOP 5 S.ItemCode,
MAX(S.Description) as 'Item Description',
SUM(S.LineTotal) as 'Amount(LC)'

FROM

(SELECT T1.ItemCode AS 'ItemCode',
T1.Dscription AS 'Description',
T1.LineTotal AS 'LineTotal'

FROM dbo.OINV T0
INNER JOIN dbo.INV1 T1 ON T1.DocENtry = T0.DocENtry

WHERE T0.docdate >= [%0] and T0.docdate <= [%1]
AND T0.doctype = 'I'

UNION
SELECT T1.ItemCode AS 'ItemCode',
T1.Dscription AS 'Description',
-T1.LineTotal AS 'LineTotal'

FROM dbo.ORIN T0
INNER JOIN dbo.RIN1 T1 ON T1.DocENtry = T0.DocENtry

WHERE T0.docdate >= [%0] and T0.docdate <= [%1]
AND T0.doctype = 'I') S

GROUP BY S.ItemCode

ORDER BY SUM(S.LineTotal) DESC
```

This solution requires a subquery. The topic of the subquery will be discussed in the last chapter of the book. There are two queries inside the subquery. They are linked together by the Union clause. The second query only changes the tables from INV related to RIN related, or invoice related to credit memo. Another change is adding a minus sign for the T1.LineTotal column for credit memo.

GROUP BY S.ItemCode will ensure only one line for each item code with summary data.

Case 4-M3: A filter by notes from OCRD

The following query is an example for displaying pending sales orders, which have not been shipped completely to the customer. The requirement is to add a filter by notes column from the OCRD table.

```
SELECT T1.DocNum as 'Sales Order No', T1.DocDate as 'Sales Order
Date',
 T1.CardName, T0.Dscription, T0.Quantity as 'Sales Order Qty',
T0.Quantity-T0.OpenQty as 'Delivered Qty', T0.OpenQty as 'Balance
Qty',T0.Price as 'Selling Price', T0.OpenQty*T0.Price as 'Open Amount'
FROM dbo.RDR1 T0
INNER JOIN dbo.ORDR T1 ON T0.DocEntry = T1.DocEntry
INNER JOIN dbo.ITM1 T2 ON T0.ItemCode = T2.ItemCode AND T2.PriceList =
1
where T1.DocDate between [%0] and [%1] AND T1.U_Department =[%2] AND
T0.LineStatus = 'O'
```

The solution is:

```
SELECT T1.DocNum as 'Sales Order No',
T1.DocDate as 'Sales Order Date',
T1.CardName, T0.Dscription,
T0.Quantity as 'Sales Order Qty',
T0.Quantity-T0.OpenQty as 'Delivered Qty',
T0.OpenQty as 'Balance Qty',
T0.Price as 'Selling Price',
T0.OpenQty*T0.Price as 'Open Amount', T3.Notes

FROM dbo.RDR1 T0
INNER JOIN dbo.ORDR T1 ON T0.DocEntry = T1.DocEntry
INNER JOIN dbo.ITM1 T2 ON T0.ItemCode = T2.ItemCode AND T2.PriceList =
1
INNER JOIN dbo.OCRD T3 ON T3.CardCode = T1.CardCode

WHERE T1.DocDate between [%0] and [%1] AND
T0.LineStatus = 'O' AND T3.Notes LIKE '%[%2]%'
```

This is a very simple question with an easy solution. I put it here to help you understand the table relationship and how to add another table.

The OCRD table holds all business partners' data. It is used very often in marketing documents. No matter whether it is for sales analysis or purchase analysis queries, this table is often needed to get more business partner related information.

Case 4-M4: Adding sales employees' names to a query

A user would like to add the name of the Sales Employee that created the Sales Order to an existing query. However, the user is not sure which JOINS need to be added to which table. Here is what the query looks like:

```
SELECT T0.DocNum as 'SO No.', T0.DocDate as 'Date', DateDiff(DD,
T0.DocDate,
GetDate()) AS 'DayDiff', T0.CardCode as 'Customer Code', T0.CardName
as 'Customer Name',
T0.NumAtCard as 'Ref/PO No.', (T0.DocTotal - T0.VatSum) as 'SO Amt'
FROM OINV T0
WHERE
DateDiff(DD, T0.DocDate, GetDate()) >= '1' AND DateDiff(DD,
T0.DocDate, GetDate()) <= '7'
```

The solution is:

```
SELECT T0.DocNum as 'SO No.',
T0.DocDate as 'Date',
DateDiff(DD, T0.DocDate,GetDate()) AS 'DayDiff',
T0.CardCode as 'Customer Code',
T0.CardName as 'Customer Name',
T0.NumAtCard as 'Ref/PO No.',
(T0.DocTotal - T0.VatSum) as 'SO Amt',
T1.SLPName

FROM dbo.ORDR T0
INNER JOIN dbo.OSLP T1 ON T1.SLPCODE=T0.SLPCODE

WHERE DateDiff(DD, T0.DocDate, GetDate()) BETWEEN 1 AND 7
```

Although the solution mentioned earlier is the right solution, the person found out they actually required the Sales Employee in the context of it being the "Owner", as seen in the field under the Sales Employee box on a Sales Order instead. So, the final solution is:

```
SELECT T0.DocNum as 'SO No.',
T0.DocDate as 'Date',
DateDiff(DD, T0.DocDate,GetDate()) AS 'DayDiff',
T0.CardCode as 'Customer Code',
T0.CardName as 'Customer Name',
T0.NumAtCard as 'Ref/PO No.',
(T0.DocTotal - T0.VatSum) as 'SO Amt',
```

```
T1.LastName+', '+T1.firstName as 'Owner'

FROM dbo.ORDR T0
INNER JOIN dbo.OHEM T1 ON T1.empID=T0.OwnerCode

WHERE DateDiff(DD, T0.DocDate, GetDate()) BETWEEN 1 AND 7
```

To join tables, the first thing to do is to find the relationship between tables. This task cannot be done without a good data dictionary. Again, the table reference from SDK help should be used to find this information. `T1.empID=T0.OwnerCode` gave the right link between the ORDR and OHEM tables.

The first solution gave the right link between the ORDR and OSLP tables. That link is simpler because the primary key name SlpCode in the OSLP table is the same as the foreign key name SlpCode in the ORDR table. The actual name of the Sales Person in the OSLP table can be retrieved through these table joins.

Case 4-M5: A case for solution just from deduction

Depending on your localization, sometimes you might need to know which A/R Credit Memos still have not been converted into Incoming Excise Invoices.

The following query was initially created to display the Incoming Excise Invoices, and has the AR Credit Memo as a base document. However, the initial attempt was not successful.

```
SELECT distinct T0.[DocNum], T0.[DocDate], T0.[CardName], T1.[BaseRef]
as 'Credit Memo No', T1.[BaseType]
FROM OIEI T0 INNER JOIN IEI1 T1 ON T0.DocEntry = T1.DocEntry
WHERE T0.[DocDate] between '[%0]' and '[%1]' and T1.BaseType ='14'
```

Here is the solution:

```
SELECT distinct T0.[DocNum],
T0.[DocDate],
T0.[CardName]

FROM dbo.ORIN T0
INNER JOIN dbo.RIN1 T1 ON T0.DocEntry = T1.DocEntry

WHERE T0.[DocDate] between '[%0]' and '[%1]' and T1.TargetType != XXX
```

This is a typical case of getting the query solution to test without the actual tables. To find out if something is not being done, you always need to check the source table. There is no way to get such information from the target table. This is because, before copying the source table to a target table, nothing can be found in the target table yet.

With the solution, the source Credit Memo tables ORIN and RIN1 are checked. The ORIN table is the header table to get the date range. The RIN1 table is the row table to check if the target Incoming Excise Invoices have been converted or not. Since the TargetType for Incoming Excise Invoices is unknown to me, I have left it as XXX. It can be found easily if you have this object.

The symbol != instead of <> is used within the book. They are equivalent; the latter symbol (Greater Than or Smaller Than) may not be able to display well on the web. Also, the symbol != is more straightforward to stand for Not (!) Equal (=).

Case 4-M6: Goods Receipt PO within 10 days

A good way to manage warehouse receipts is to create a list of Goods Receipt POs and review it periodically. However, there is a special requirement of all distinct vendors who have supplied material in user defined 10 days and whose total quantity – transaction wise – is less than 10. For example, suppose the date range is five days, then if the total number of Goods Receipt PO on any given day is in the range less than or equal to five, the document's total summary for the vendor should be listed.

The solution:

```
SELECT T0.CardCode,
Max(T0.Cardname) 'Vendor Name',
SUM(T0.DocTotal) 'Total'

FROM dbo.OPDN T0

WHERE T0.DocDate >= '[%0]'
AND T0.DocDate <= '[%0]' + 10
AND T0.CardCode NOT in (SELECT T1.CardCode FROM OPDN T1 WHERE
T1.DocDate >= '[%0]' AND T1.DocDate <= '[%0]' + 10
GROUP BY T1.CardCode, T1.DocDate Having COUNT(T1.DocDate) > 10)

GROUP BY T0.CardCode

ORDER BY T0.CardCode
```

This request is somewhat special compared to all other query requirements. The tricky part is how to get the count of the documents correctly.

The key part of the solution is again by a subquery:

```
SELECT T1.CardCode FROM OPDN T1 WHERE T1.DocDate >= '[%0] ' AND
T1.DocDate <= '[%0] ' + 10
GROUP BY T1.CardCode, T1.DocDate Having COUNT(T1.DocDate) > 10
```

This subquery will return the list of vendors that have more than 10 transactions during any specific day in the selected date range. Those vendors who are not in this list will be displayed. The 10 days can be changed to a variable. However, the display of the variable will be misleading because it is the same as the first one. If you change this 10 to [%1], you will soon find out that the variable description changes to "posting date smaller or equal".

Case 4-M7: Quantity purchased, received, and returned

A very common requirement in the purchasing function inside companies is to have a query to capture the quantity purchased, quantity received, and quantity returned.

The solution is to link the required tables by left join:

```
SELECT T0.ItemCode,
SUM(T0.Quantity) 'PO Qty',
SUM(T1.Quantity) 'GRPO Qty',
SUM(T2.Quantity) 'Return Qty'

FROM dbo.POR1 T0
LEFT JOIN dbo.PDN1 T1
ON T0.DocEntry = T1.BaseEntry AND T0.LineNum = T1.BaseLine
LEFT JOIN dbo.RPD1 T2
ON T1.DocEntry = T2.BaseEntry AND T1.LineNum = T2.BaseLine

WHERE T0.ItemCode is not NULL AND T0.DocDate >= [%0] AND T0.DocDate <=
[%1]

GROUP BY T0.ItemCode

ORDER BY T0.ItemCode
```

There are three tables used within the query:

- POR1: Purchase Order Rows
- PDN1: Goods Receipt PO Rows
- RPD1: Goods Return Rows

LEFT JOIN is essential here. We need to list all Purchase Orders during the user selected periods. However, not all Purchase Orders have been received yet. There are even fewer Goods Returns. (No business can survive if all goods purchased have been returned!) By LEFT JOIN clause, it will not bind any Goods Receipt PO or Goods Returns to the Purchase Order. Only when there are target documents, will they be included. Therefore, all Purchase Orders will be in the report regardless of whether the target documents exist or not. This unbinding feature is a useful tool to get a complete list with or without data binding to the main entry.

In this way, quantity purchased, quantity received, and quantity returned will be listed in three columns for each item number. The first column is item code. The second column must be full, because all item codes are taken from POR1. The third and the last column should have empty lines if the Purchase Orders have not been received in full during the selected period.

Case 4-M8: Customized sales analysis report

Sometimes users are looking for a customized Sales Analysis query report so that they can export the query result to Excel.

This query should include Invoices and Credit Memos, or the debit and the credit columns in the journal entries details.

Here is the half done query that needs to be completed:

```
SELECT Distinct T0.[CardCode],
T0.[CardName],
(SELECT (SUM(T2.Debit) - sum(T2.Credit))
FROM OCRD T0 INNER JOIN JDT1 T1 ON T1.ShortName = T0.CardCode
WHERE T0.CardType = 'C' AND DateDiff(DD,T2.Duedate,GetDate()) between
0 and 30) AS 'Present Month',
FROM OCRD T0
INNER JOIN JDT1 T1 ON T1.ShortName = T0.CardCode
WHERE T0.CardType = 'C'
```

The query should pick up all sales amounts for those months such as July and August. It also needs to remove payment transactions from the query results to show only the invoices/credit memo amounts.

The solution is:

```
SELECT T0.[CardCode],
T0.[CardName],
(SUM(T1.Debit) - sum(T1.Credit)) AS 'July',
(SUM(T2.Debit) - sum(T2.Credit)) AS 'August'
```

```
FROM dbo.OCRD T0
LEFT JOIN dbo.JDT1 T1 ON T1.ShortName = T0.CardCode AND Month(T1.
Duedate) = 7 AND Year(T1.Duedate) = Year(GetDate()) AND T1.TransType
in ('13','14')
LEFT JOIN dbo.JDT1 T2 ON T2.ShortName = T0.CardCode AND Month(T2.
Duedate) = 8 AND Year(T2.Duedate) = Year(GetDate()) AND T2.TransType
in ('13','14')


WHERE T0.CardType = 'C'


Group By T0.[CardCode], T0.[CardName]
```

Since this solution query only deals with journal entry tables, it should be under the financial query section. However, in common sense, sales analysis should be covered within sales. That is why it is under this category. All query records are extracted from the journal lines with `TransType in ('13','14')`. All those lines are the result of automatic posting of A/R Invoices or A/R Credit Memos. So it makes sense to be under this category.

The first thing you should notice is that `TransType in ('13','14')` is equivalent to `ObjType in ('13','14')` in the ADOC table. The difference is only the column name. Under the journal entry, they are different transactions. Before the journal entry, they are only different objects.

In this query, you can see the JDT1 table joined twice to the OCRD table. By using two aliases from two joins, the query result can show the same table with different selections for the same Shortname (equivalent to CardCode in the OCRD table).

Case 4-M9: Average sales per month

A user worked out a query to get the average sales for 2009:

```
SELECT T0.CardCode, T0.CardName, (SUM(T1.Debit) - sum(T1.Credit)) AS
'2009', ((SUM(T1.Debit) - sum(T1.Credit))/12)
FROM OCRD T0
LEFT JOIN JDT1 T1 ON T1.ShortName = T0.CardCode LEFT JOIN JDT1 T2
ON T2.ShortName = T0.CardCode WHERE T0.CardType = 'C' AND Year(T1.
Duedate) = 2009 Group By T0.CardCode, T0.CardName
```

The question is how to include the average sales for 2010 in the same query too.

The solution is:

```
SELECT T0.CardCode, T0.CardName,
(SUM(T1.Debit) - sum(T1.Credit)) AS '2009',
((SUM(T1.Debit) - sum(T1.Credit))/12) AS '2009 Avg',
(SUM(T2.Debit) - sum(T2.Credit)) AS '2010',
((SUM(T2.Debit) - sum(T2.Credit))/Month(GetDate()))AS '2010 Avg'

FROM dbo.OCRD T0
LEFT JOIN dbo.JDT1 T1 ON T1.ShortName = T0.CardCode AND Year(T1.
Duedate) = 2009 AND T1.TransType in ('13','14')
LEFT JOIN dbo.JDT1 T2 ON T2.ShortName = T0.CardCode AND Year(T2.
Duedate) = 2010 AND T2.TransType in ('13','14')

WHERE T0.CardType = 'C'

Group By T0.CardCode, T0.CardName
```

This query structure is similar to the previous example. The concept is the same. You can always use two separate joins to the same table by different aliases and selections to get the different scopes of data under the same line of query result. Maybe your company also has a requirement to see the average sales per month. This average is a good tool for the sales personnel to forecast and project their upcoming year.

Case 4-M10: Credit Memo user check

This example is to show the credit memo, document number, and the change log user name for the credit memo.

A user had tried to use the ADOC table but could not find the link between this and the credit memo.

```
SELECT T0.[DocNum], T0.[DocType], T0.[ObjType], T0.[CardCode],
T0.[CardName], T0.[UserSign], T0.[UserSign2]
FROM ADOC T0 WHERE T0.[ObjType] = '14'
```

This query does not show the same data as the change log screen. With the query, updated user is always the same user as the original user.

The solution is:

```
SELECT Distinct T0.[DocNum], T1.DocNum, T0.[DocType], T0.[CardCode],
T0.[CardName], T0.[UserSign], T0.[UserSign2], T1.[UserSign],
T1.[UserSign2]

FROM dbo.ADOC T0
```

```
INNER JOIN dbo.ORIN T1 ON T0.DocNum = T1.DocNum

WHERE T0.[ObjType] = '14' AND T0.[UserSign2] != T1.[UserSign2]
```

The first query just looks at the historical log of credit memos from ADOC. It therefore could not get the required information.

In the solution query, by joining the ORIN table, that is, the current credit memo table and adding the column from this table, the query result should satisfy the needs. The condition T0.[UserSign2] != T1.[UserSign2] will list all records in the query results if the user who updates the document is not the same as the current one.

This is a good example of what many users are looking for in the instance of who has changed a document. It is an extension to "Change Log" for showing all changes.

Case 4-M11: Delivery date on sales order

A user requests an SQL query that identifies when the delivery date on a Sales Order is modified from the original date. This query needs to list who made the change and the date of the change. It will be a base query for an alert in case any changes are made on a sales order.

It has been doubly confirmed that the query results do not need to include the delivery dates from the initial set up of a Sales Order.

The solution is:

```
SELECT T0.DocNum,
MAX(T1.UpdateDate) 'Last Update'

From dbo.ADOC T0
JOIN dbo.ADOC T1 on T1.DocNum = T0.DocNum AND T1.ObjType = '17'

WHERE T0.ObjType = '17' and T0.DocDuedate != T1.DocDueDate

Group BY T0.DocNum
```

In this solution query, a self join is used for the ADOC table. T0 and T1 are all referred to in the same table. The query checks the same document number with the object type of '17', that is, sales order records. If the query finds that the DocDueDates are not the same, the results of the document number and the latest update will be returned.

Be careful to run this query if you have a long history and a large size database. ADOC table has too many records. Self join of this table is not recommended. Unless you know exactly what you are looking for, do not try any other self join of ADOC. This applies to AJDT and AJD1 tables too.

Case 4-M12: Reducing from two to one line for the sales summary

A user wants to show quantity, sales dollar amount, and tax amount for each warehouse and customer group.

The following is the query by the user, but the query results have two lines for each warehouse and customer group combination.

```
SELECT
T1.WhsCode AS 'WH',
T3.GroupName AS 'Cust Grp',
Sum(T1.Quantity) AS 'Quantity',
Sum(T1.LineTotal) AS 'Sls Dlr Amt',
Sum(T1.LineVat) AS 'Tax Amt'

FROM OINV T0
INNER JOIN INV1 T1
ON T0.DocEntry = T1.DocEntry
INNER JOIN OCRD T2
ON T0.CardCode = T2.CardCode
INNER JOIN OCRG T3
ON T2.GroupCode = T3.GroupCode

WHERE
T1.DocDate >= '[%0]' AND T1.DocDate <= '[%1]'
AND T0.DocType = 'I'
GROUP BY
T1.WhsCode,
T3.GroupName

UNION

SELECT
T1.WhsCode AS 'WH',
T3.GroupName AS 'Cust Grp',
Sum(T1.Quantity) * -1 AS 'Quantity',
```

```
Sum(T1.LineTotal) * -1 AS 'Sls Dlr Amt',
Sum(T1.LineVat) * -1 AS 'Tax Amt'

FROM ORIN T0
INNER JOIN RIN1 T1
ON T0.DocEntry = T1.DocEntry
INNER JOIN OCRD T2
ON T0.CardCode = T2.CardCode
INNER JOIN OCRG T3
ON T2.GroupCode = T3.GroupCode

WHERE
T1.DocDate >= '[%0]' AND T1.DocDate <= '[%1]'
AND T0.DocType = 'I'
GROUP BY
T1.WhsCode,
T3.GroupName
ORDER BY
T1.WhsCode,
T3.GroupName
```

The solution is:

```
SELECT
T3.WhsCode AS 'WH',
T1.GroupName AS 'Cust Grp',
(Sum(ISNULL(T3.Quantity,0)) - Sum(ISNULL(T5.Quantity,0))) AS
'Quantity',
(Sum(ISNULL(T3.LineTotal,0)) - Sum(ISNULL(T5.LineTotal,0))) AS 'Sls
Dlr Amt',
(Sum(ISNULL(T3.LineVat,0)) - Sum(ISNULL(T5.LineVat,0))) AS 'Tax Amt'

FROM dbo.OCRD T0
INNER JOIN dbo.OCRG T1 ON T0.GroupCode = T1.GroupCode
INNER JOIN dbo.OINV T2 ON T0.CardCode = T2.CardCode AND T2.DocType =
'I'
INNER JOIN dbo.INV1 T3 ON T2.DocEntry = T3.DocEntry
LEFT JOIN dbo.ORIN T4 ON T0.CardCode = T4.CardCode AND T4.DocType =
'I'
LEFT JOIN dbo.RIN1 T5 ON T4.DocEntry = T5.DocEntry AND T3.WhsCode =
T5.WhsCode

Group By
T3.WhsCode, T1.GroupName
```

This solution returns one line per warehouse and customer group combination. This is again taken out by the Union clause. If the Union clause is in use, the query will always have two lines for each individual combination.

Left Joins are used in the query for ORIN and RIN1 tables to ensure no invoice will be missing from the query results. Otherwise, if by inner join, only invoice with credit memo will be shown. All other invoices will be filtered out.

ISNULL(T3.Quantity,0) and other similar formula are here to ensure no NULL value will affect the query result.

Case 4-M13: Tax code summary

Taxation is always an important topic in companies due to the complexity of taxes and possible errors with the entry of tax codes. An excellent report to have is to show if there are two types of tax codes in one document.

```
SELECT M.CardCode,M.CardName as 'Vendor Name',
(SELECT Sum(TaxSum) FROM PCH4 where (statype=1 or statype=7) and
relatetype = 1 and DocEntry=M.DocEntry) as 'AmountOfTax'FROM OPCH M
Inner JOIN PCH1 L on L.DocEntry=M.DocEntry
Inner JOIN PCH4 T on T.DocEntry=L.DocEntry
Inner JOIN PCH12 T0 on T.DocEntry=L.DocEntry
INNER JOIN OLCT T2 ON L.LocCode = T2.Code
WHERE M.DocDate >= %1 and M.DocDate <= %2 and t.statype = 1 GROUP BY
M.CardCode,M.CardName,M.DocEntry, T.stccode ORDER BY
M.CardName,M.DocEntry
```

The solution is:

```
SELECT M.CardCode,M.CardName as 'Vendor Name',
(SELECT Sum(TaxSum) FROM PCH4 where statype=1 and relatetype = 1 and
DocEntry=M.DocEntry) as 'AmountOfTax1',
(SELECT Sum(TaxSum) FROM PCH4 where statype=7 and relatetype = 1 and
DocEntry=M.DocEntry) as 'AmountOfTax2'

FROM dbo.OPCH M Inner JOIN PCH1 L on L.DocEntry=M.DocEntry
Inner JOIN dbo.PCH4 T on T.DocEntry=L.DocEntry
Inner JOIN dbo.PCH12 T0 on T.DocEntry=L.DocEntry
INNER JOIN dbo.OLCT T2 ON L.LocCode = T2.Code

WHERE M.DocDate >= [%1] and M.DocDate <= [%2] AND
(t.statype = 1 or t.statype = 7)

GROUP BY
M.CardCode,M.CardName,M.DocEntry, T.stccode

ORDER BY
M.CardName,M.DocEntry
```

This is another example query that is solved just by logical checking. LocCode is only available in the purchase order detail in certain localizations, so it is not available to test. However, the right query solution only needs the right logic. If the original query is working, the new query will work one hundred percent because it follows the same logic. The only difference is to change the OR condition under one or two columns.

PCH related tables are for A/P Invoices. OPCH is the header. PCH4 is for the Tax Amount per Document. PCH12 is the Tax Extension.

Using mixed aliases in the query such as M, L, T, T0, etc is not good practice. I left the original unchanged just as an example to show you that this is awkward.

Case 4-M14: Sales by states

Depending upon the size and organizational sales department structure of your company, you might need to show monthly sales by each state.

The solution is:

```
SELECT T0.State1 AS 'Bill-to State',
(SELECT SUM(T1.DocTotal) FROM OINV T1 with (NOLOCK)
INNER JOIN OCRD T2 ON T2.CardCode=T1.CardCode
WHERE MONTH(T1.DOCDATE) = 1 AND T2.State1 = T0.State1
AND YEAR(T1.DOCDATE) = YEAR(GETDATE())) AS 'JAN Amt',
(SELECT SUM(T1.DocTotal) FROM OINV T1 with (NOLOCK)
INNER JOIN OCRD T2 ON T2.CardCode=T1.CardCode
WHERE MONTH(T1.DOCDATE) = 2 AND T2.State1 = T0.State1
AND YEAR(T1.DOCDATE) = YEAR(GETDATE())) AS 'FEB Amt',
(SELECT SUM(T1.DocTotal) FROM OINV T1 with (NOLOCK)
INNER JOIN OCRD T2 ON T2.CardCode=T1.CardCode
WHERE MONTH(T1.DOCDATE) = 3 AND T2.State1 = T0.State1
AND YEAR(T1.DOCDATE) = YEAR(GETDATE())) AS 'MAR Amt',
(SELECT SUM(T1.DocTotal) FROM OINV T1 with (NOLOCK)
INNER JOIN OCRD T2 ON T2.CardCode=T1.CardCode
WHERE MONTH(T1.DOCDATE) = 4 AND T2.State1 = T0.State1
AND YEAR(T1.DOCDATE) = YEAR(GETDATE())) AS 'APR Amt',
(SELECT SUM(T1.DocTotal) FROM OINV T1 with (NOLOCK)
INNER JOIN OCRD T2 ON T2.CardCode=T1.CardCode
WHERE MONTH(T1.DOCDATE) = 5 AND T2.State1 = T0.State1
AND YEAR(T1.DOCDATE) = YEAR(GETDATE())) AS 'MAY Amt',
(SELECT SUM(T1.DocTotal) FROM OINV T1 with (NOLOCK)
INNER JOIN OCRD T2 ON T2.CardCode=T1.CardCode
WHERE MONTH(T1.DOCDATE) = 6 AND T2.State1 = T0.State1
AND YEAR(T1.DOCDATE) = YEAR(GETDATE())) AS 'JUN Amt',
```

```
(SELECT SUM(T1.DocTotal) FROM OINV T1 with (NOLOCK)
INNER JOIN OCRD T2 ON T2.CardCode=T1.CardCode
WHERE MONTH(T1.DOCDATE) = 7 AND T2.State1 = T0.State1
AND YEAR(T1.DOCDATE) = YEAR(GETDATE())) AS 'JUL Amt',
(SELECT SUM(T1.DocTotal) FROM OINV T1 with (NOLOCK)
INNER JOIN OCRD T2 ON T2.CardCode=T1.CardCode
WHERE MONTH(T1.DOCDATE) = 8 AND T2.State1 = T0.State1
AND YEAR(T1.DOCDATE) = YEAR(GETDATE())) AS 'AUG Amt',
(SELECT SUM(T1.DocTotal) FROM OINV T1 with (NOLOCK)
INNER JOIN OCRD T2 ON T2.CardCode=T1.CardCode
WHERE MONTH(T1.DOCDATE) = 9 AND T2.State1 = T0.State1
AND YEAR(T1.DOCDATE) = YEAR(GETDATE())) AS 'SEP Amt',
(SELECT SUM(T1.DocTotal) FROM OINV T1 with (NOLOCK)
INNER JOIN OCRD T2 ON T2.CardCode=T1.CardCode
WHERE MONTH(T1.DOCDATE) = 10 AND T2.State1 = T0.State1
AND YEAR(T1.DOCDATE) = YEAR(GETDATE())) AS 'OCT Amt',
(SELECT SUM(T1.DocTotal) FROM OINV T1 with (NOLOCK)
INNER JOIN OCRD T2 ON T2.CardCode=T1.CardCode
WHERE MONTH(T1.DOCDATE) = 11 AND T2.State1 = T0.State1
AND YEAR(T1.DOCDATE) = YEAR(GETDATE())) AS 'NOV Amt',
(SELECT SUM(T1.DocTotal) FROM OINV T1 with (NOLOCK)
INNER JOIN OCRD T2 ON T2.CardCode=T1.CardCode
WHERE MONTH(T1.DOCDATE) = 12 AND T2.State1 = T0.State1
AND YEAR(T1.DOCDATE) = YEAR(GETDATE())) AS 'DEC Amt'

FROM dbo.OCRD T0
LEFT JOIN dbo.OINV T1 ON T1.CardCode = T0.CardCode

GROUP BY T0.State1

ORDER BY T0.State1
```

This is an example of the traditional way of building a query based on months. You might have noticed, all columns beside `T0.State1` have the same logic. The only difference between them is the months selected. This query is for the current year and includes only invoices. The year can be changed easily such as: `(T1.DOCDATE) = YEAR(GETDATE()) -1` for last year.

There is a shorter way to complete the same task. This will be the topic in the last chapter for complicated queries. It is much easier with the other query to include the credit memo, so that the result will be more accurate.

Case 4-M15: Many linked tables in one query

An initial request is to link seven tables including OJDT, JDT1, OCRD, OCRG, OINV, OITM, and OITB.

Query input would be posting date range (from OJDT OR OINV) and item group name (OITB).

Then an initial query was tried based on some other users' recommendation:

```
SELECT distinct T2.CardCode, T2.[CardName],T1.[RefDate],T0.[BaseRef],
T0.[Debit],T0.[Credit],T0.[BalDueDeb], T0.[BalDueCred]
FROM JDT1 T0
INNER JOIN OJDT T1 ON T0.TransId = T1.TransId
INNER JOIN OCRD T2 on T2.CardCode = T0.ShortName
INNER JOIN OCRG T3 ON T2.GroupCode = T3.GroupCode
INNER JOIN OINV T4 ON T2.CardCode = T4.CardCode
left JOIN OITM T5 ON T2.CardCode = T5.CardCode
left outer JOIN OITB T6 ON T5.ItmsGrpCod = T6.ItmsGrpCod
WHERE T0.[RefDate] BETWEEN '[%0]' AND '[%1]' AND T0.[BalDueDeb]'0' AND
T3.GroupName != 'Vendors' and T6.[ItmsGrpNam] = '[%2]'
```

However, there is no result from this query.

The solution is as follows:

```
SELECT distinct T2.CardCode,
T2.[CardName],
T1.[RefDate],
T0.[BaseRef],
T0.[Debit],
T0.[Credit],
T0.[BalDueDeb],
T0.[BalDueCred]

FROM dbo.JDT1 T0
INNER JOIN dbo.OJDT T1 ON T0.TransId = T1.TransId
INNER JOIN dbo.OCRD T2 on T2.CardCode = T0.ShortName
INNER JOIN dbo.OCRG T3 ON T2.GroupCode = T3.GroupCode
INNER JOIN dbo.OINV T4 ON T2.CardCode = T4.CardCode
INNER JOIN dbo.INV1 T5 ON T5.DocEntry = T4.DocEntry
LEFT JOIN dbo.OITM T6 ON T6.ItemCode = T5.ItemCode
LEFT JOIN dbo.OITB T7 ON T7.ItmsGrpCod = T6.ItmsGrpCod

WHERE T0.[RefDate] BETWEEN '[%0]' AND '[%1]'
AND T0.[BalDueDeb] != 0 AND T3.GroupName != 'Vendors'
AND T7.[ItmsGrpNam] = '[%2]'
```

The difference is one more table added. That is INV1—the A/R invoice row table. The idea is to display item sales by item group. All sales item details could only be found under the INV1 table. In the original query, linking CardCode in OITM with OCRD cannot reach the goal.

Within this query, eight tables are used. Their functions are listed as follows:

- OJDT: Journal Entry Header
- JDT1: Journal Entry Row
- OCRD: Business Partners Master
- OCRG: Business Partners Groups
- OINV: A/R Invoice Header
- INV1: A/R Invoice Row
- OITM: Items Master
- OITB: Items Groups

The first two tables are for the financial section. We will discuss them in detail under the financial query section. OITB is not mentioned before. It holds item group information.

Using this query, you can select the item group to display detailed sales transactions for the specified item group only.

Case 4-M16: Sales Order with PO

If you do any kind of drop-ship or consignment processing, it usually requires that Purchase Orders are created directly from an individual Sales Order. For those companies who rely mainly on drop-ship or consignment, a query showing the connections between the documents is required. A user created the following query:

```
SELECT DISTINCT T0.DocNum as "Sale Order NO.",T0.CardName,
T1.Project,T1.ItemCode, T1.Quantity,T1.LineTotal, T0.DocTotal,
T2.CardName as BP Name,
T2.DocNum as PO Number, T2.DocDate as PO Date, T3.ItemCode as Stock
Item,
T3.Quantity, T3.OpenQty, T5.DocNum as Goods Receipt No, T5.DocDateas
GR Date,
T4.ItemCode as Stock Item, T4.Quantity, T4.OpenQty as Left to Deliver
FROM ORDR T0 INNER JOIN RDR1 T1 ON T0.DocEntry = T1.DocEntry,
dbo.OPOR T2
INNER JOIN dbo.POR1 T3 ON T2.DocEntry = T3.DocEntry
LEFT JOIN dbo.PDN1 T4 ON T4.BaseEntry = T2.DocEntry AND T4.BaseLine =
T3.Linenum
```

```
LEFT JOIN dbo.OPDN T5 ON T5.DocEntry = T4.DocEntry
WHERE T3.ItemCode = T1.ItemCode and T3.BaseRef = T0.DocNum and
T1.Project Like '%%%0%%'
```

The problem for the query is: it only shows the sale order with the purchase order posted. However, all sale orders should be shown no matter if there is any purchase order posted or not based on the user's request.

The solution is:

```
SELECT DISTINCT T0.DocNum as 'Sale Order NO.',
T0.CardName,
T1.Project,
T1.ItemCode,
T1.Quantity,
T1.LineTotal,
T0.DocTotal,
T2.CardName as 'BP Name',
T2.DocNum as 'PO Number',
T2.DocDate as 'PO Date',
T3.ItemCode as 'Stock Item',
T3.Quantity, T3.OpenQty,
T5.DocNum as 'Goods Receipt No',
T5.DocDate as 'GR Date',
T4.ItemCode as 'Stock Item',
T4.Quantity,
T4.OpenQty as 'Left to Deliver'

FROM dbo.ORDR T0
INNER JOIN dbo.RDR1 T1 ON T0.DocEntry = T1.DocEntry
LEFT JOIN dbo.POR1 T3 ON T1.Docentry = T3.Baseentry and T1.LineNum=T3.
Baseline
LEFT JOIN dbo.OPOR T2 ON T3.Docentry = T2.Docentry
LEFT JOIN dbo.PDN1 T4 ON T4.BaseEntry = T2.DocEntry AND T4.BaseLine =
T3.Linenum
LEFT JOIN dbo.OPDN T5 ON T5.DocEntry = T4.DocEntry

WHERE T1.Project Like '%[%0]%'
```

Comparing the solution with the original query, you can find a big difference. The solution query has all tables joined. The original query has a comma inside the FROM clause. If you have read the previous chapters of this book, you will know this could lead to some problems.

In this case, the problem is not having too many records returned, but the opposite. Due to the improper links between POR1, ORDR, and RDR1 by `T3.ItemCode = T1.ItemCode and T3.BaseRef = T0.DocNum`, it filtered out all RDR1 lines if there is no purchase order linked.

In the solution, sales order rows will be shown just by one condition of `T1.Project Like '%[%0]%'`. In other words, only user inputted project code will affect query results. It will not be affected by four Left Join tables.

Query for inventory transactions

Inventory transactions and inventory status are the second hot topics for SAP Business One users. Here within the book, inventory will cover production too because they are closely related.

Case 4-I1: Adding stock total to the query

The first example is a simple one: to have an overview of total stock in all warehouses sorted on items group with the total amount per item group and total amount of units.

The user tried a report by **XL Reporter** for the goal. However, the result from that report is different from the standard stock report in SAP Business One. So it is not useful.

System report, however, is not sorted on item group; that could not meet their needs either. The user only needs the total on hand for item groups. The other totals are not of any interest.

The solution is:

```
SELECT T1.ItmsGrpNam, SUM(T0.OnHand) 'Total On Hand', SUM(T0.
OnHand*Case WHEN T0.AVGPRICE = 0 THEN T0.LastPurPrc ELSE T0.AVGPRICE
END) 'Total Amount'

FROM dbo.OITM T0
INNER JOIN dbo.OITB T1 ON T1.ItmsGrpCod = T0.ItmsGrpCod

WHERE T0.OnHand > 0

GROUP BY T1.ItmsGrpNam
```

Using this query, the summary of the item on hand will be grouped by item groups. This query can be used to get a rough idea of your total value of inventory. If you need the accurate results, AvgPrice for item must not be zero. That is the item cost value used by the system.

Case clause is included in the query. To understand this usage, wait until the last chapter where you will find a detailed explanation.

Case 4-I2: Adding a total to the query bottom

It is quite often required by the user to add a line to the query that also gives the total of quantity and amount at the bottom. We use the previous case as an example. The prices used in the query will be from price list number 10 instead of Avgprice or Lastpurprc from the OITM table.

A solution is to add an UNION ALL clause under the query:

```
SELECT T1.ItmsGrpNam,
SUM(T0.OnHand) 'Total On Hand',
SUM(T0.OnHand*T2.Price) 'Total Amount'

FROM dbo.OITM T0
INNER JOIN dbo.OITB T1 On T1.ItmsGrpCod = T0.ItmsGrpCod
INNER JOIN dbo.ITM1 T2 On T2.ItemCode = T0.ItemCode AND T2.PriceList =
9

WHERE T0.OnHand > 0
GROUP BY T1.ItmsGrpNam

UNION ALL

SELECT 'Grand Total',
SUM(T0.OnHand) 'Total On Hand',
SUM(T0.OnHand*T2.Price) 'Total Amount'

FROM dbo.OITM T0
INNER JOIN dbo.ITM1 T2 ON T2.ItemCode = T0.ItemCode AND T2.PriceList =
9

WHERE T0.OnHand > 0
```

Comparing this query with the one in the first part of the chapter, you will notice the similarity. Union All is the universal way in getting this job done.

The second query under Union All is almost the same as the first one. A small difference is no Group By clause. The other difference is the T1.ItmsGrpNam column is replaced by the text '**Grand Total**'. This means the total for all records in the OITM table, as long as items' on hands are greater than zero, will only return one line at the end of the query result.

Case 4-I3: Items not delivered within 15 days

Good customer service requires almost any company to review the status of the customer's orders. Sometimes you want to have a list of all items which are not delivered from the last month.

The query to meet the requirement is:

```
SELECT Distinct T0.ItemCode,
T0.ItemName

FROM dbo.OITM T0

WHERE T0.SellItem = 'Y' AND
T0.ItemCode NOT IN
(SELECT Distinct T1.ItemCode FROM dbo.DLN1 T1
INNER JOIN dbo.ODLN T2 ON T2.DocEntry = T1.DocENtry
WHERE DateDiff(DD,T2.DocDate,GetDate()) <31)
```

This is a simple case.

The solution is in the subquery. The query lists all item codes from the delivery document DLN1 table if those deliveries have been done within 30 days. T0.ItemCode NOT IN will meet the requirement. T0.SellItem = 'Y' will make sure only sellable items are displayed by the query result.

To know more about subquery, check the last chapter.

Case 4-I4: Active item list

An active item list is to list all items for which the item code cannot be changed anymore, in other words, which have been used at least in a document or a transaction.

The solution is:

```
SELECT T0.ItemCode
FROM dbo.OITM T0
```

```
WHERE T0.ITEMCODE IN (SELECT DISTINCT CODE FROM dbo.ITT1) OR
T0.ITEMCODE IN (SELECT DISTINCT CODE FROM dbo.OITT) OR T0.ITEMCODE
IN (SELECT DISTINCT ITEMCODE FROM dbo.OINM) OR T0.ITEMCODE IN (SELECT
DISTINCT ITEMCODE FROM dbo.ADO1)
```

This solution is similar to the previous case. It also depends on subquery. This time there is more than one of them.

The first two subqueries check if the item is in the **Bill of Material (BOM)** or so called **Production Tree** in SAP Business One. The third query checks if it has been posted for inventory transaction before. The last one checks if it has been included in the marketing documents in the history.

Filtered by these subqueries, the listed items will be active items. However, a more accurate term should be: nonremovable item list.

Case 4-I5: How to find stock taking details

A common occurrence of stock taking (inventory count) is to receive an error message "quantity falls below minimum quantity" appearing during the process.

The problem is how to check which items are giving that error if 100 items have been posted.

The solution query is as follows:

```
SELECT T1.WhsName,
T0.ItemCode,
SUM(T0.InQty - T0.OutQty) as 'On Hand Changed'

FROM dbo.OINM T0
INNER JOIN dbo.OWHS T1 ON T0.Warehouse = T1.WhsCode

WHERE T0.DocDate >= '[%0]' and
T1.WhsName like '[%1]%' and
T0.ItemCode like '[%2]%'

GROUP BY T1.WhsName, T0.ItemCode
Having SUM(T0.InQty - T0.OutQty) != 0
```

This query links OINM with OWHS. The second table is the warehouse table. You can get warehouse names from this table. If warehouse code is good enough for you, it can be omitted from the query altogether.

The last clause is as follows:

```
GROUP BY T1.WhsName, T0.ItemCode
Having SUM(T0.InQty - T0.OutQty) != 0
```

It is to ensure the query only returns those items that have on hand changed for certain warehouses.

)The `T0.DocDate >= '[%0]'` condition by user input is used to enter the date for stock take. All transactions after this date will be checked. This will greatly help you to reduce the list from hundreds to just a couple. `T1.WhsName like '[%1]%'` and `T0.ItemCode like '[%2]%'` give you further options to limit the output range in case you have too many posted items in the same time.

Case 4-I6: Query on price updates

Price updates are extremely important for companies to maintain proper profits and margins. A frequent request deals with receiving a report on a daily basis showing information on updated price lists. Preferred columns would be Item Code, Item Description, Price list Number, Old price, New Price, and User code (who updated the prices). Parameters would be beginning date and ending date.

The solution is:

```
SELECT DISTINCT T0.ItemCode,
T1.ItemName,
T0.PriceList,
T2.Price 'OLD',
T0.Price 'New',
MAX(T2.LogInstanc) 'Last Changed'

FROM dbo.ITM1 t0
INNER JOIN dbo.OITM T1 ON T1.ItemCode = T0.ItemCode
INNER JOIN dbo.AIT1 T2 ON T2.ItemCode = T0.ItemCode AND T2.PriceList =
T0.PriceList

WHERE ISNULL(T0.Price,0) != ISNULL(T2.Price,0) AND
T0.ItemCode Like '[%0]%' AND T0.PriceList = '[%1]'

GROUP BY T0.ItemCode,T1.ItemName,T0.PriceList,T2.Price, T0.Price
```

This query links item price table ITM1 with its history table AIT1 through OITM, and then compares the prices to get the difference. All different records will be found by the query. But only the latest changes will be returned. That is due to the Group By clause.

The requirements cannot be satisfied in full because there is no column saving the date and user information for when and who updated the prices.

Case 4-I7: Planned quantity versus in stock

A user looks for a report that would show the planned quantity (based on production order) and in stock of the raw material, so that the user in charge of planning can decide whether to purchase the raw material or not.

There is added difficulty to the request. Some items in the production order are also BOM item. The material needs for those components also need to be checked. It is confirmed that they do not use multiple levels BOM very much. 99 percent of the BOMs are one level or two levels.

The following query had been tried by the user but the result is unsatisfactory. It can only show the components from the top level BOM:

```
SELECT T0.[DocNum], T0.[Status], T0.[DueDate], T0.[ItemCode],
T2.[ItemName], T1.[ItemCode],T2.[OnHand],
 T1.[BaseQty], T1.[PlannedQty]
FROM [dbo].[OWOR] T0 INNER JOIN [dbo].[WOR1] T1
ON T0.DocEntry = T1.DocEntry INNER JOIN [dbo].[OITM] T2 ON T1.ItemCode
= T2.ItemCode
WHERE T0.[ItemCode] = [%0] AND T0.[DocNum] = [%1]
```

The solution is:

```
SELECT T0.[DocNum],
T0.[Status],
T0.[DueDate],
T0.[ItemCode],
T3.[ItemName],
T3.[ItemCode],
T3.[OnHand],
T1.[BaseQty]*T2.Quantity 'Base Qty', T1.[PlannedQty]*T2.Quantity
'Planned Qty'

FROM [dbo].[OWOR] T0
INNER JOIN [dbo].[WOR1] T1 ON T0.DocEntry = T1.DocEntry
INNER JOIN [dbo].[ITT1] T2 ON T1.ItemCode = T2.Father
INNER JOIN [dbo].[OITM] T3 ON T2.Code = T3.ItemCode
WHERE T0.[ItemCode] = [%0] AND T0.[DocNum] = [%1]
```

This solution may only apply to two-level BOM to get those component's quantity under the second level. This query needs to be used together with the original query to get a complete picture of planned quantity and in stock.

Case 4-I8: Adding to the production orders list from a sales order

Another example falls between inventory and marketing documents. Because the main table used is the production order table, it is reasonable to include here:

```
SELECT distinct T0.DocNum As ProdOrder, T0.ItemCode, (select itemname
from OITM where T0.ItemCode = OITM.itemcode) As ProdName, T0.PostDate,
T0.PlannedQty As Planned FROM OWOR T0, OITM T1 where T0.Status 'C'
```

The user wants to add the NumAtCard column from ORDR to this query. This column is for BP reference. What change should be made to the existing query?

Here is the solution:

```
SELECT distinct T0.DocNum As ProdOrder,
T0.ItemCode,
T1.itemname As ProdName,
T0.PostDate,
T0.PlannedQty As Planned,
T2.NumAtCard

FROM dbo.OWOR T0
INNER JOIN dbo.OITM T1 ON T0.ItemCode = T1.itemcode
LEFT JOIN dbo.ORDR T2 ON T2.DocEntry = T0.OriginAbs AND T0.OriginType
= 'S'

WHERE T0.Status != 'C'
```

The challenge for the query is to find the relationship between the production order and sales order. The link is T2.DocEntry = T0.OriginAbs AND T0.OriginType = 'S'. Instead of BaseEntry column in marketing document rows, OriginAbs column in production header is used. OriginType = 'S' will ensure it is from a sales order.

Two tables under FROM without link in the original query is not recommended. It will check the complete table many times to return the result. This will affect database performances especially for a large database.

Case 4-I9: Complete item list with or without transactions

If you are maintaining different item groups and need to display all the items by grouping that particular warehouse or location (even though there are no transactions in that given date range).

The initial request is to change a query that only displays the items which have transactions on that particular given date range.

Declare @FromDate Datetime:

```
Declare @ToDate Datetime
Declare @Group nvarchar(10)
Declare @Whse nvarchar(10)
Set @FromDate = (Select min(S0.Docdate) from dbo.OINM S0 where
S0.Docdate >='[%0]')
Set @ToDate = (Select max(S1.Docdate) from dbo.OINM s1 where
S1.Docdate <='[%1]')
Set @Group = (Select Max(s2.ItmsGrpCod) from dbo.OITB S2 Where
S2.ItmsGrpNam = '[%2]')
Set @Whse = (Select Max(s3.Warehouse) from dbo.OINM S3 Where
S3.Warehouse = '[%3]')
SELECT
@Whse as 'Warehouse',
a.Itemcode,
max(a.Dscription),
sum(a.Opening Balance) as Opening Balance,
sum(a.IN) as IN,
sum(a.OUT) as OUT,max(a.Price) as 'Price',
((sum(a.Opening Balance) + sum(a.IN)) - Sum(a.OUT)) as Closing
from(
Select
N1.Warehouse,
N1.Itemcode,
N1.Dscription,N1.Price,
(sum(N1.inqty)-sum(n1.outqty)) as Opening Balance,
0 as IN,
0 as OUT
From dbo.OINM N1
Where
N1.DocDate < @FromDate and N1.Warehouse = @Whse
Group By
N1.Warehouse,N1.ItemCode,N1.Dscription,N1.Price
Union All
select
N1.Warehouse,
N1.Itemcode,
N1.Dscription,N1.price,
0 as Opening Balance,
sum(N1.inqty) as IN,
0 as OUT
```

```
From dbo.OINM N1
Where
N1.DocDate >= @FromDate and N1.DocDate <= @ToDate and
N1.Inqty >0
and N1.Warehouse = @Whse
Group By
N1.Warehouse,N1.ItemCode,N1.Dscription,N1.price
Union All
select
N1.Warehouse,
N1.Itemcode,
N1.Dscription,N1.price,
0 as Opening Balance,
0 as IN,
sum(N1.outqty) as OUT
From dbo.OINM N1
Where
N1.DocDate >= @FromDate and N1.DocDate <=@ToDate and
N1.OutQty > 0
and N1.Warehouse = @Whse
Group By
N1.Warehouse,N1.ItemCode,N1.Dscription,N1.price) a, dbo.OITM I1
where
a.ItemCode=I1.ItemCode and
I1.ItmsGrpCod = @Group
Group By
a.Itemcode
Having sum(a.Opening Balance) + sum(a.IN) + sum(a.OUT) > 0
Order By a.Itemcode
```

The solution is:

```
Declare @FromDate Datetime
Declare @ToDate Datetime
Declare @Group nvarchar(10)
Declare @Whse nvarchar(10)

Set @FromDate = (Select min(S0.Docdate) from dbo.OINM S0 where
S0.Docdate >='[%0]')
Set @ToDate = (Select max(S1.Docdate) from dbo.OINM s1 where
S1.Docdate <='[%1]')
Set @Group = (Select Max(s2.ItmsGrpCod) from dbo.OITB S2 Where
S2.ItmsGrpNam = '[%2]')
Set @Whse = (Select Max(s3.Warehouse) from dbo.OINM S3 Where
S3.Warehouse = '[%3]')
```

```
SELECT @Whse as 'Warehouse',
a.Itemcode,
a.max(a.Dscription) as 'Item Description',
sum(a.[Opening Balance]) as [Opening Balance],
sum(a.[IN]) as [IN],
sum(a.OUT) as OUT,
max(a.Price) as 'Price',
((sum(a.[Opening Balance]) + sum(a.[IN])) - Sum(a.OUT)) as Closing

FROM dbo.OITM I1
Left JOIN (Select N1.Warehouse, N1.Itemcode, N1.Dscription,N1.Price,
(sum(N1.inqty)-sum(n1.outqty)) as [Opening Balance],
0 as [IN],
0 as OUT

From dbo.OINM N1

WHERE N1.DocDate < @FromDate and N1.Warehouse = @Whse

Group By N1.Warehouse,N1.ItemCode,N1.Dscription,N1.Price

Union All
SELECT N1.Warehouse,
N1.Itemcode,
N1.Dscription,
N1.price,
0 as [Opening Balance],
sum(N1.inqty) as [IN],
0 as OUT

From dbo.OINM N1

Where N1.DocDate >= @FromDate and N1.DocDate <= @ToDate and N1.Inqty
>0 and N1.Warehouse = @Whse

Group By N1.Warehouse,N1.ItemCode,N1.Dscription,N1.price

Union All
SELECT N1.Warehouse,
N1.Itemcode,
N1.Dscription,
N1.price,
0 as [Opening Balance],
0 as [IN],
```

```
sum(N1.outqty) as OUT

From dbo.OINM N1

Where N1.DocDate >= @FromDate and N1.DocDate <=@ToDate and N1.OutQty >
0 and N1.Warehouse = @Whse
Group By N1.Warehouse,N1.ItemCode,N1.Dscription,N1.price) a ON
a.ItemCode=I1.ItemCode

WHERE I1.ItmsGrpCod = @Group

Group By a.Itemcode

Order By a.Itemcode
```

This is one of the longest queries in this book. In general, I am reluctant to create any long queries like this one. That is because the longer the query, the more system resources might be used. It also creates maintenance difficulty for other users.

If you compare the solution query to the original one, you will find the difference is only a little. This proves that such a long query is indeed problematic.

If you find this query works for you, good. If not, that is no problem either. This query may only work under 2007 version or below. OINM is changed from a table to a view so the parameter may not work for version 8.8 or higher.

To put this query here is to show what kind of queries should be avoided.

Query for financial transactions

Under this category, all banking related issues are included. There are fewer financial transactions related query requests than other queries. This is probably because:

- System provides more financial reports than other reports
- The need for such reports is less
- It is too difficult to produce a proper report

No matter how many queries can be built, we should still go through some of the queries so that we can find more information related to business operations.

Case 4-F1: Top five customers

Sales ranking is discussed in the previous section. However, there are many questions with some different requests. One example is top N customers during any period.

Since this query only deals with the Journal Entry table, I have put it under the financial transactions section. Here is the query list:

```
SELECT TOP 5 T0.ShortName 'Customer',
Max(T2.CardName) 'Customer Name',
SUM(ISNULL(T0.Debit,0) - ISNULL(T0.Credit,0)) as "Amount(LC)"

FROM dbo.JDT1 T0
INNER JOIN dbo.OJDT T1 ON T1.TransID = T0.TransID and T0.TransType IN
('13','14')
INNER JOIN dbo.OCRD T2 ON T2.CardCode = T0.ShortName

WHERE T1.RefDate >= [%0] and T1.RefDate <= [%1]

GROUP BY T0.ShortName

ORDER BY SUM(ISNULL(T0.Debit,0) - ISNULL(T0.Credit,0)) DESC
```

This query has just looked up Journal Entry table OJDT and JDT1. It is only for displaying customer names to link with the Business Partner table OCRD.

`Max(T2.CardName)` is used for convenience to omit the column from grouping. It will be very useful when your query includes some multiple value documents such as OINV or ORIN. It can just return one customer name in case you have any different names in the documents for the same customer.

`T0.TransType IN ('13','14')` limits query results to A/R Invoice and A/R Credit Memo transactions only.

This is similar to the top five items query in the beginning. Something discussed there will probably also apply here.

Case 4-F2: Incoming payment

An auditor would like to see a report that shows all the incoming payments between two given dates along with the following columns:

- BPCode
- BPName

- Payment No
- Amount Paid
- Payment Date
- Invoice No (that was reconciled against the payment)
- Invoice Date

The user has no idea which tables to query to get the payment and reconciliation information.

Here is the solution:

```
SELECT T0.[CardCode] AS 'Customer Code',
T0.[CardName] AS 'Customer Name',
T0.[DocNum] AS 'Payment Number',
T1.[SumApplied] AS 'Paid to Invoice',
T0.[DocDate] AS 'Payment Date',
T2.[DocNum] AS 'Invoice Number',
T2.[DocDate] AS 'Invoice Date'

FROM [dbo].[ORCT] T0
INNER JOIN [dbo].[RCT2] T1 ON T0.[DocNum] = T1.[DocNum]
INNER JOIN [dbo].[OINV] T2 ON T1.[DocEntry] = T2.[DocEntry]

WHERE T0.[DocDate] >= [%0] AND T0.[DocDate] <= [%1]
```

This query is the first one in which I have used query generator for the solution, so that you can see all brackets.

Incoming payment table links are different with marketing document links. They use DocNum column for the link. I believe this is for the convenience of the table structure. DocEntry columns are used by marketing documents. So you can find that the link between RCT2 and OINV is by the DocEntry column.

Case 4-F3: Linking an incoming payment with an invoice

There is another one shown in the previous chapter too.

The original query is:

```
SELECT T1.CardCode as "CustCode", T1.CardName as "CustName",
T2.SlpName, T1.DocNum, T1.DocDate, T1.DocTotal as "Amount Total"
FROM [dbo].[OCRD] T0 INNER JOIN [dbo].[ORCT] T1 ON T0.CardCode =
T1.CardCode INNER JOIN [dbo].[OSLP] T2 ON T0.SlpCode = T2.SlpCode
WHERE T1.DocDate >=[%0] AND T1.DocDate <=[%1] order by T1.DocDate
```

The initial attempt was to link the query result with A/R invoice data to have the invoice details but it failed.

The solution is:

```
SELECT T1.CardCode as "CustCode",
T1.CardName as "CustName",
T2.SlpName,
T1.DocNum as "Incoming#",
T1.DocDate,
T1.DocTotal as "Payment Total",
T4.DocNum as "Invoice#",
T3.SumApplied as "Applied Total"

FROM dbo.OCRD T0
INNER JOIN dbo.ORCT T1 ON T0.CardCode = T1.CardCode
LEFT JOIN dbo.OSLP T2 ON T0.SlpCode = T2.SlpCode
INNER JOIN dbo.RCT2 T3 ON T3.DocNum = T1.DocNum
INNER JOIN dbo.OINV T4 ON T4.DocEntry = T3.DocENtry AND T3.InvType =
'13'

WHERE T1.DocDate >= [%0] AND T1.DocDate <= [%1]

ORDER by T1.DocDate
```

The link between Incoming Payment and A/R Invoice is through the RCT2 table. You have seen that in the previous case. The linking column is DocEntry. The SumApplied column in RCT2 holds each applied total for individual invoice. This example is almost the same as the Case 2. However, due to the additional column SlpName, OCRD, and OSLP are added.

Case 4-F4: Listing both types of payment transactions

Some companies receive incoming payments in two ways. If it is by check, by cash, or by bank transfer from a single party then they are posting Incoming Payment transactions.

But in certain instances like the field persons, they collect the money from dozens of customers and the total amount of cash is deposited directly into the bank. At that time, they are posting the payments just by passing a Journal Entry to the customer.

In order to get the total payments collected (either by Incoming Payment or by Journal Entry) from all the customers for a particular dates frame, their client tried to use the General Ledger report for BP but it is taking too much time to execute and display.

The solution given is:

```
SELECT T1.TransID,
T0.ShortName,
T0.Debit,
T0.Credit

FROM dbo.JDT1 T0
INNER JOIN dbo.OJDT T1 ON T0.TransID = T1.TransID
INNER JOIN dbo.OCRD T2 ON T2.CardCode = T0.ShortName AND T2.CardType =
'C'

WHERE T0.ShortName LIKE '[%2]%' AND T0.TransType IN ('24', '30') AND
T1.RefDate Between '[%0]' AND '[%1]'
```

If you noticed, the structure of this query is similar to Case 4-F1 in this category. The difference is, instead of T0.TransType IN ('13', '14'), T0.TransType IN ('24', '30') is used. T0.TransType IN ('24', '30') refers to Incoming Payment ('24') or Journal Entry transactions ('30').

Case 4-F5: Incoming payment filtering

The following query deals with customer un-deposited checks from previous post but with revision. However, the query seems to not filter incoming payments already deposited, incoming payments cancelled, or incoming payment with 'Account type'.

```
select T2.CheckKey, T0.Canceled, T0.Docnum as 'Payment no.',T0.docdate
as 'Posting date',T0.cardcode as 'Customer Code',T0.cardname as
'Customer Name',
T2.CheckDate as 'Check Date', T2.CheckNum as 'Check Number',
T2.Bankcode as 'Bank', T2.Checksum as 'Check Amount'
from orct T0
inner join rct1 T1 on T0.docentry=T1.docnum
inner join ochh T2 on T2.CheckKey=T1.CheckAbs
WHERE T2.CheckDate between %0 and %1 and T0.DocType = 'C' and
T0.Canceled= 'y' AND T0.Series = '51' or T0.Series = '12' or T0.Series
= '63' or T0.Series = '52' AND T2.CheckKey Not In (SELECT CheckKey
FROM DPS1) ORDER BY T2.CheckDate
```

The solution is:

```
SELECT T2.CheckKey,
T0.Canceled,
T0.Docnum as 'Payment no.',
T0.Docdate as 'Posting date',
T0.cardcode as 'Customer Code',
T0.cardname as 'Customer Name',
T2.CheckDate as 'Check Date',
T2.CheckNum as 'Check Number',
T2.Bankcode as 'Bank',
T2.Checksum as 'Check Amount'

FROM dbo.ORCT T0
INNER join dbo.RCT1 T1 on T0.docentry=T1.docnum
INNER JOIN dbo.OCHH T2 on T2.CheckKey=T1.CheckAbs

WHERE T2.CheckDate between [%0] and [%1] AND T0.Canceled= 'N' AND
T0.Series IN ('51','12', '63', '52') AND T2.CheckKey Not IN (SELECT
CheckKey FROM DPS1)

ORDER BY T2.CheckDate
```

The original query is almost not a problem. However, one of the conditions is not correct. Instead of looking up T0.Canceled= 'Y', it should be T0.Canceled= 'N' to get the result.

You should also notice by using the IN clause that the original condition under the WHERE clause has been trimmed much shorter. Using the first query, it is:

```
T0.Series = '51' or T0.Series = '12' or T0.Series = '63' or T0.Series
= '52'.
```

The solution is only T0.Series IN ('51','12', '63', '52'). They are equivalent. You need to replace the series from your database if you want to try it.

User query for alert

One of the important usages of SQL query in SAP Business One is for alert. SAP Business One provides a few standard alert messages after you first install. However, the numbers of built-in alerts are far from enough.

The good news is, the system provides you with the power to have your own alert by SQL query. You will find some examples here first. With the following queries, and with the ones you can create yourself, you will be able to have the right alert messages to meet your business needs at the right time with the right person. That is a great help to increase your system efficiency.

Case 4-A1: Creating a right alert without duplicated lines

Here is a rather interesting and complex scenario: a company has two physical warehouses on two different locations/cities. For transfers between warehouses/cities they created an "in-transit" warehouse for each location. Material is placed in those warehouses when it's shipped, and taken out when it reaches its destination. Since ALL of the material is taken out after each transfer, those "in-transit" warehouses are usually empty. The problem started when there were cost/price changes when material was transferred to these warehouses. So it accumulated to a significant amount on the empty warehouse account.

The user wants to create a query that gives an alert when there is zero inventory on X warehouse but with a balance different from zero on the corresponding account. In other words, whenever a warehouse is empty, it needs to be checked to see if it has outstanding balances.

A simple query created by the user gave the total stock for a specific warehouse:

```
SELECT sum(T0.OnHand)
FROM OITW
WHERE T0.WhsCode = 'X'
```

Then another query was created that listed the warehouse code, account code, on hand, and current account balance:

```
SELECT T0.WhsCode, T1.AcctCode, T2.OnHand, T1.CurrTotal
FROM OWHS T0 INNER JOIN OACT T1 ON T0.BalInvntAc = T1.AcctCode INNER
JOIN OITW T2 ON T0.WhsCode = T2.WhsCode
WHERE T0.WhsCode = 'X'
```

The problem of this query is: a single line with zero on hand and the current account balance will only be on an empty warehouse. If the warehouse is not empty, it will have multiple lines on that warehouse for each item that has stock.

By trying the SUM(T2.OnHand) function, the user got an error message.

Help is needed to create a right alert without duplicated lines that gives warning when a balance exists in an empty warehouse.

The solution query is:

```
SELECT T2.WhsCode,
T1.AcctCode,
T1.CurrTotal,
SUM(T2.OnHand) AS 'On Hand'

FROM dbo.OWHS T0
```

```
INNER JOIN dbo.OACT T1 ON T0.BalInvntAc = T1.AcctCode
INNER JOIN dbo.OITW T2 ON T0.WhsCode = T2.WhsCode

WHERE T1.CurrTotal !=0

GROUP BY T2.WhsCode, T1.AcctCode, T1.CurrTotal
Having SUM(T2.OnHand)=0
```

This query solves the problem of multiple lines for a warehouse. Actually, the last Group By clause is the ice breaker. It groups all on hands for any specific warehouses wherein `Having SUM(T2.OnHand)=0` checks the condition to ensure the warehouses are empty.

Case 4-A2: Alert for invoice without base document

Another requirement is to create an alert query to catch anyone adding anything to an invoice without a base document. This alert will inform someone in charge of the need for further action. If an invoice has no base document, that could undermine the correct accounting process.

Here is the solution:

```
SELECT T1.DocNum

FROM dbo.INV1 T0
INNER JOIN dbo.OINV T1 ON T1.DocEntry = T0.DocENtry

WHERE T1.DocNum = $[$8.0.0] AND
T0.ItemCode = $[$38.1.0] AND
T0.BaseType = -1
```

There is a system variable used in this query. The detail of its use will be explained in a later chapter for formatted search. This solution is just showing you one type of solution, which may be applied to some other types too. `T0.BaseType = -1` is the key for the solution. It means the line item has no base document. The normal invoice will have basetype = '15' for delivery or have basetype = '17' for sales order.

Case 4-A3: A/R Invoice past due alert

A very commonly required Alert Message is to get the due amount after each A/R Invoice is past due. Then this query will be used for an alert.

A simple solution is handy here:

```
SELECT T0.CardCode,
T0.CardName,
T0.DocNum,
```

```
T0.DocDate,
T0.DocDueDate,
(T0.DocTotal-T0.PAIDTODATE) 'Due Amount'

FROM dbo.OINV T0

WHERE DateDiff(DD,T0.DocDueDATE,GETDATE()) > 0 AND T0.DocTotal>T0.
PaidTODate

ORDER BY T0.CardCode
```

This query alert solution will check if the DocDueDate is already past due by `DateDiff(DD,T0.DocDueDATE,GETDATE()) > 0`. Meanwhile, another check is to see if the invoices have been paid already by `T0.DocTotal>T0.PaidTODate`. Although you can check the document status to see if they are still open, I found that this formula checking to be more efficient for the query.

If you have too many past due A/R invoices, `T0.CardName` should be taken out. Or you define a date range by adding something like `DateDiff(DD,T0.DocDueDATE,GETDATE()) < 180` to show the recent invoices only. It would probably be good enough for the alert.

Case 4-A4: Special ship to alert for Sales Order

If your company is expanding rapidly into new territories or if you have a promotion going on in specific states, you might like to have a query which shows when an order was created for a customer with ship-to address in a particular state like 'A', 'B', 'C'. Whenever this situation occurs, an alert should be triggered.

The solution is:

```
SELECT T0.DocDate,
T0.DocNum,
T0.Cardname as 'Customer Name',
T0.NumAtCard as 'Customer Ref No.'

FROM dbo.ORDR T0
INNER JOIN dbo.OCRD T2 ON T2.CardCode = T0.CardCode

WHERE
T0.Address2 like '% CA %' AND T0.DoCStatus = 'O'
```

CA here is only for an easy test. It can be changed to any state. With this simple query, you can have a template to create multiple alerts to suit specific needs.

Case 4-A5: Open Sales Opportunity alert

This alert deals with the Sales Opportunity module:

```
SELECT T0.OpprId, T0.Name, T0.CardCode, T0.CardName, T0.MaxSumLoc AS
'Potential Amt', T0.WtSumLoc AS 'Weighed Amt', T0.U_Term_Agree,T0.U_
Bus_Cat,T0.PredDate AS 'Predicted Closing Date', T1.Step_Id,
T1.DocNumber AS 'Quote No', T0.U_Bus_Cat, T0.U_new_bus,T2.SlpName AS
'Ac. Mgr.' FROM OOPR T0 INNER JOIN OPR1 T1 ON T0.OpprId = T1.OpprId
INNER JOIN OSLP T2 ON T0.SlpCode = T2.SlpCode WHERE T0.Status ='O'
```

The alert is sent out on a weekly basis to the key users of their staff. The alert identifies all open opportunities.

The problem is when this SQL query runs using the email alert, it only shows some records. However, under query manager it will show twice as many records.

The solution is:

```
SELECT T0.OpprId,
LEFT(T0.Name,20) As 'Sales Op',
T0.CardCode,
Left(T0.CardName,20) AS Customer,
T0.MaxSumLoc AS 'Potential Amt',
T0.WtSumLoc AS 'Weighed Amt',
T0.PredDate AS 'Predicted Closing Date',
Max(T1.Step_Id) 'Stage Key',
T2.SlpName AS 'Ac. Mgr.'

FROM dbo.OOPR T0
INNER JOIN dbo.OPR1 T1 ON T0.OpprId = T1.OpprId
INNER JOIN dbo.OSLP T2 ON T0.SlpCode = T2.SlpCode

WHERE T0.Status ='O'

Group By T0.OpprId, T0.Name, T0.CardCode, T0.CardName, T0.MaxSumLoc,
T0.WtSumLoc, T0.PredDate, T2.SlpName
```

This is a good example that the message from alert will cut out the query result by a fixed number of characters. The main reason why this occurs is due to the fact that Alert Messages have a limit on the number of characters which will be sent out. It is best practice for Alert Messages to have very short results per line so that complete information is provided. The solution is dependent upon reducing the number of columns which are displayed in the Alert Message. You can compare the two SQL to see what has been eliminated so that all records are displayed.

In the solution query, the first thing to reduce the query result length is through Group By clause. `Max(T1.Step_Id)` will ensure only one line for each opportunity. `LEFT(T0.Name,20)` and `Left(T0.CardName,20)` will trim all names to have a maximum 20 characters only.

User query alert guide

Because user query alert is a very good tool for getting the right information at the right time for the right user, it is necessary to show you the complete steps to build this kind of alert.

The **Alert Management** menu is easily found under the first menu category **Administration**. It is the last menu item of the said category if you do not have any third-party add-ons installed.

The following screenshot gives you a clear path. You can also select Modules from the menu item directly without going through the main menu.

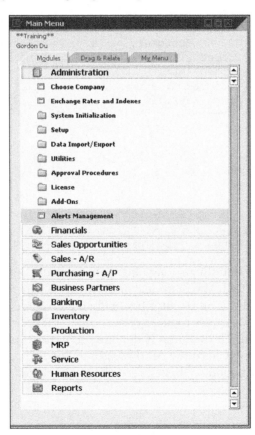

When you bring up the **Alert Management** form, it is in **Find** mode with all active user names listed. You can search for all existing alerts to manage. The screenshot is as follows:

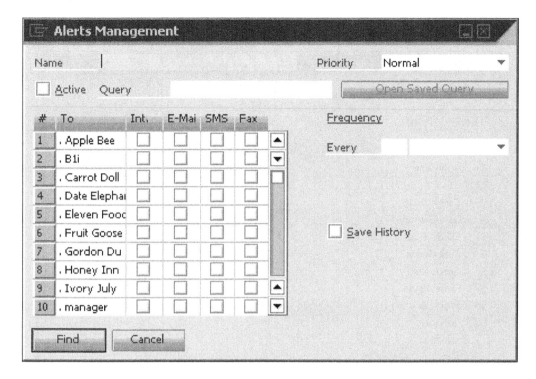

To add a new user query alert, the first thing to do is to change the form to **Add** mode as in the following screenshot. This can be done either through the toolbar, or through the shortcut key combination *Ctrl+A*.

Because alert queries have been discussed, one of the queries will be picked up to show you an example. Before clicking the alert management function, always remember alert query should be ready with sufficient tests.

The query "Invoice without base document" in the previous pages will be used to build the query alert.

A good practice many users use is to make sure they include themselves in the receipt of the Alert Message for a specific period (one month or so). This will give you the chance to review what the Alert Messages are doing in both efficiency and consistent processing.

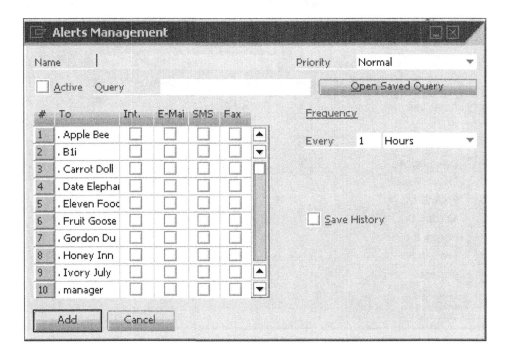

The first step to adding the user query alert is to assign a name for the alert, as shown in the following screenshot. It is better to use your query name whenever possible. Because the query name is **Invoice without base document**, we also name the alert the same way.

After the alert name put in, tab your mouse to the **query** text box. Then click **Open Saved Query**.

This will bring up the query manager window. Any saved queries can be picked up in this stage. Make sure the right one is selected. When the alert name is the same as the query name, this is guaranteed without problem. That is why it is better to keep them consistent.

The query **Invoice without base document** has been picked up by selecting the query name. Now, click **OK**. This will close the query manager and the query selected will be shown in the text box for **Query.**

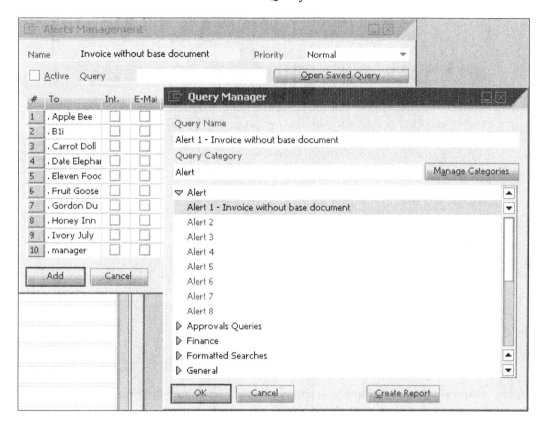

Before adding the alert, the alert frequency needs to be set up. There are five options available:

- Minutes
- Hours
- Days
- Weeks
- Months

The example has 15 minutes selected for this specific alert.

Many users like to set the alert at every minute. They hope that will give them the most updated information. However, it may not be true because this will affect system performance especially if they have more alerts set up the same way. Remember, everything needs resources. Be realistic.

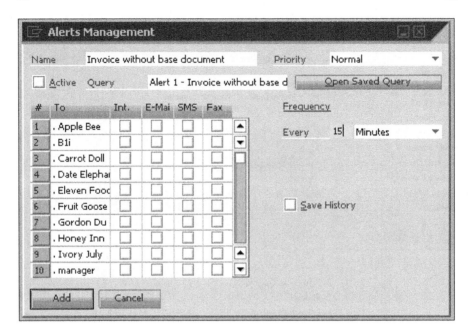

After setting up the frequency, you can click **Add**. The alert will be added. However, two things have not been completed here:

- Select the user(s) for alert to be sent
- Verify the **Active** checkbox

That is an easy fix. Just follow the steps mentioned next:

1. Find the saved alert first.
2. Select all the required users to assign.
3. Make sure the alert checked is **Active**.
4. Click on **Update**.

Now the alert is ready to be triggered.

Many users find the alert function difficult to use, especially if they want to get an email alert. This is because email alert is quite tricky. It involves more than just SAP Business One. To troubleshoot the email alert problem, the following procedure is recommended:

- Make sure the alert works by assigning both internal messages and emails
- Make sure the user who needs to receive the email alert has logged on to SAP Business One
- Check the email server error logs if the alert is received only through internal message but not email

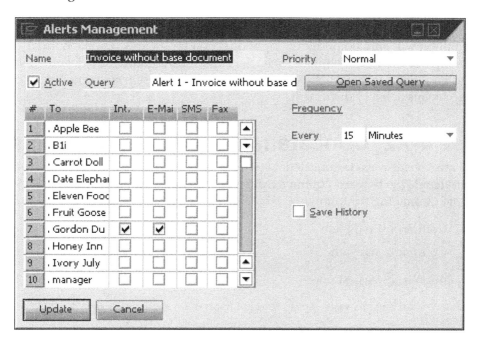

Miscellaneous query examples

Only three main categories have been covered so far. There are some other modules that also need query reports from time to time.

Besides all other query examples in the book, some of the examples do not fit in any of the categories. Here is the place for these outstanding ones.

Case 4-X1: Query related to service call

A useful query is to show items from delivery (with Serial Number or Batch Number) which is under the 'expenses' tab on the service call form. The user having this request could not find the 'expenses' tab table. Trying to find the link between DLN1 and OSCL with 'Created from Service Call' failed because the base document related columns in DLN1 are always empty.

The solution is:

```
SELECT T1.DocNum from DBO.SCL4 T0
INNER JOIN dbo.ODLN T1 on T1.DocENtry = T0.DocAbs
WHERE T0.Object = '15'
```

The solution will only point out the right direction for the link. Unlike normal marketing documents, the link between Service Call and marketing documents are always on the service call side. SCL4 table is titled "Expense Documents". `T0.Object = '15'` means delivery document.

Case 4-X2: Concatenating two text columns

There are several ways to concatenate two text columns but probably the easiest way to concatenate the two text columns from a table is to use the "+" (plus sign). For example, combining the following data fields from the table of OHEM:

- Column 1: firstName
- Column 2: lastName

This solution is the easiest one:

```
SELECT T0.firstname + ' '+ T0.Lastname AS 'Employee Names' FROM dbo.
OHEM T0
```

There are two purposes to show this very simple example here:

- Human resource module may need query too
- How to concatenate text columns

To concatenate text columns, some people with different backgrounds are used to some other string operation clauses such as CONCAT. The Print Layout Designer also uses CONCATENATE. In T-SQL, the concatenate operation is the simplest one: by + (plus sign) alone.

Summary

You saw many examples in this chapter. Those query examples are good resources for you to try. By understanding their logic, you should be able to create your own query with ease. The best way to learn something is from examples. When you get many examples to work with, you can increase the ability to create your own query with amazing speed. This is especially true for learning SQL query.

From the next chapter to the end of the book, you will get different topics related to SQL query. For example, query security and approval based on user queries will be discussed in the next chapter.

Securities and Approvals

We have learned many query examples from the previous chapter. Now it is time to check how securities can be set for SAP Business One query users. The query for approval will also be discussed in this chapter. This chapter has the following topics:

- How to handle security for query by utilizing query groups
- User query for approval procedures with some query examples

In fact, these two topics could be discussed in two chapters because they emphasize in different areas. However, there is something in common between them. That is, both topics deal with people. No matter whether it is the user security using query or the approval procedure for business processes, they focus on user rights and user restrictions.

How to handle securities for query usage

SQL query is a powerful tool to build reports. It will definitely contribute to business intelligence. In fact, you can get any information from SAP Business One if you are able to access the query. However, this power may have another side to be scrutinized. What if the users who run the query report are not supposed to run it? What if a dishonest user builds a query that can harm your database?

This is a grey area where the normal authorization for the user may not work well enough. Care must be taken when dealing with query securities. If you are not aware of this, you must read this chapter carefully.

Something needs to be done for query usage to ensure your database integrity and data confidentiality. The following list is recommended to secure your query usage:

- Give only a few users the capability to build a query report
- Create queries under different categories
- Assign different user groups for different categories

Giving only a few users the capability to build a query report

This topic may not get enough attention from many SAP Business One customers. However, it is a very important task to be carried out by every SAP Business One administrator.

In a sense, every user who can create and save a query will be deemed as a superuser. This is because SAP Business One user security is built upon windows form level. Nevertheless, the query will bypass this form level security checking.

As there are no table or record level security checkings, users with an ability to create query have the capability to access all SAP Business One tables without any restrictions. Imagine, if they know database structure very well, it won't be a secret information to them at all. They can get any critical information they want by creating related queries.

To decrease or minimize this risk, first thing to do is to analyze who can have the authorization to build a query. Usually, only the superuser is responsible for creating queries. However, there are quite a few superusers who may not have the ability or the time for this task. There are certain principles you should follow to get this job done:

1. Initially assign all users with **No Authorization** under **Reports** authorization for **Query Generator**, **Query Wizard**, and **Query Manager**. This is to ensure that no user is getting unnecessary authorization in the first place.

2. Always give Read-Only authorization first when the user needs to run a query. Do not assign more.

3. Only when users complain about their inability to create or edit query, it is high time for you to check what SQL levels they have and how much database structure they know. Based on their job title and fidelity, assign them proper authorizations. Ideally, if you have time to plan, you can create a matrix that list users and their access privilege beforehand.

4. Watch the saved queries from time to time to ensure all newly created queries fall within the scopes that they should. You can create a user alert to watch certain important queries too.

The following screenshot shows the authorization for a user under the Reports module. It can be accessed from the menu item **Administration | System Initialization | Authorizations | General Authorizations**. This screen is showing an initial assignment for all new users. Make sure all of them have to be **No Authorization**. A fresh start will keep your system safe. It is well worth to perform this task.

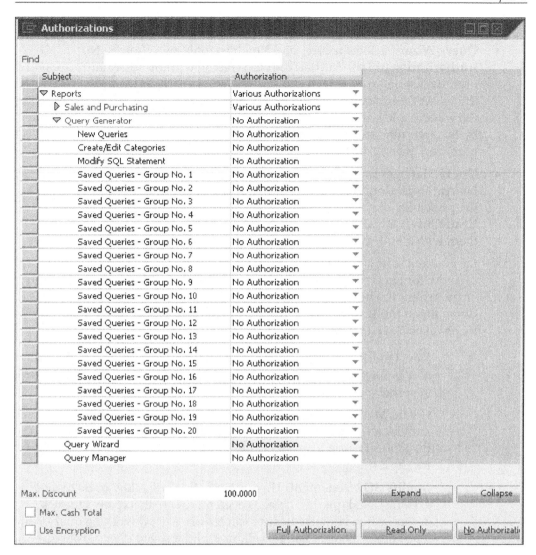

Care must be taken when you copy user authorizations. Double checking is needed, especially under query authorization. Two users with similar job titles don't guarantee that they have the same query authorizations. When you assign the same authorizations by copying from existing users, the new users may get more than they should be given.

Let's go through these three different query authorization categories, one by one:

- **Query Wizard** is the simplest one. You have only two choices: **No Authorization** or **Full Authorization**. When you grant full authorization to a user, the user may be able to run this wizard to create any queries. However, if the user has no authorization on the **New Queries** under Query Generator, the wizard still won't run. If the **New Queries** are allowed, the query created by this user may still not get saved if the user has no authorization on any of the saved query groups.

- **Query Manager** is another simpler one. There are three options available: **No Authorization**, **Read-Only**, and **Full Authorization**. As mentioned in the principles above, always assign **No Authorization** first. Then try **Read-Only**. Only if you have confidence with the users, you can assign them with a **Full Authorization**.

- Last but not least is the **Query Generator**. It should be the first authorization category for query. However, due to its complexity, explaining it last would be more logical. There are more than 20 authorization items under Query Generator authorization. The first three are discussed next. The remaining 20 items called **Saved Queries–Group XX** will be discussed later.

    ° **New Queries**: This authorization will give users the ability to create new queries. It will not only control Query Generator but also control the other query tools such as Query Wizard.

    ° **Create/Modify Categories**: This is vital to query security. Full authorization should be reserved to superusers only. Never give the authorization to anybody else unless no superusers are available for the task.

    ° **Modify SQL Statement**: This authorization will allow users to modify existing saved queries. It needs even more care than **New Queries** authorization because the user can replace a good working query with a bad one if the user has also allowed under saved query groups. If you don't have backup of the working query, it will be a disaster.

Creating queries under different categories

In Chapter 3, you learned how to create and maintain query categories. Some of the conclusions are as follows:

- Categories can resemble the module structures in the SAP Business One main menu

- Categories have to minimize any overlaps between each other

- Categories should keep the queries owned by them only

Just following these principles, you can create and maintain a good category list. However, the last one is easier to say than to do. You must take great effort to make sure the new queries are saved under the correct categories.

Some of the queries are easy to classify, such as sales and purchase. Some of them may not be that easy to tell. Take good care of each user who wrongly saved a query, especially for the new users who don't have enough knowledge about the query categories which you have created. Whenever you find something wrong, correct it immediately. Make sure you check them often.

You can use the following query to check the query list by category:

```
SELECT
T1.CatName,
T0.Qname,
T0.Qstring

FROM dbo.OUQR T0
INNER JOIN dbo.OQCN T1 ON T0.QCategory = T1.CategoryId

ORDER BY T1.CatName,
T0.Qname
```

This is an important step in query security because all securities will be handled based on the category level. Unless you have given full authorization to everyone, you need to make sure that all categories only hold those queries that supposedly belong to them.

Query Groups: a tool to assign user permissions

You have learned that there are over 20 authorization items for query generator. The first three items have already been discussed. The other 20 of them are for **Saved Queries–Groups**. The group numbers are from 1 to 20. Among them, group numbers 16 to 20 are not available to standard user interface. Therefore, we will only discuss the first 15 groups.

The last five groups may only be used when you have an add-on or through SDK coding. Unless that is the case, they do not need to be set. Keep them unchanged as shown next:

	Saved Queries - Group No. 16	No Authorization	▼
	Saved Queries - Group No. 17	No Authorization	▼
	Saved Queries - Group No. 18	No Authorization	▼
	Saved Queries - Group No. 19	No Authorization	▼
	Saved Queries - Group No. 20	No Authorization	▼
	Query Wizard	No Authorization	▼
	Query Manager	No Authorization	▼

These groups are equivalent to **Authorization Groups 1-15** under **Create/Edit Categories**. The following screenshots show you detailed setups for a few categories.

For **general** category, common practice is to assign this category to all groups. This category will be used for the queries that can be accessed to all users. For the overlap rule, it's an exception. The main purpose for this query is for "convenience". It should only keep those frequently used, non-critical queries. It will not be a good practice if many queries are saved here, because it simply means you decided to give up query security altogether.

My suggestions to save queries under this category are as follows:

- Minimize the numbers of the queries here. Unless you know it's being frequently used and it should be available to everyone, do not save the query under this category.

- Check it more often than other categories because most users with the authority to save will easily choose to save their new queries here.

- In general, finance-related queries should not be saved here.

- When naming the query under this category, the names of the queries should be clear so that everyone knows what the query results are. For example, a query of "Sales Report" does not tell you much, but when the query is named "Sales Report by Customer for Annual Commission Calculation", it is more readable as to what the query is doing.

The following screenshot shows this category as assigned to all query groups:

You can find the **Formatted Searches** category in the next screenshot. It is also assigned to all the groups. This is because most **Formatted Searches** queries cannot be run directly. However, any user may require this function. It is safe to assign this category to all the authorization groups. A detailed discussion about formatted search can be found in the next chapter. The following screenshot shows the Format Searches category assigned to all groups similar to General category.

The names of all queries under this category need to be more concise. Because it only links to Formatted Search, the query name should reflect where it will be triggered. This topic is beyond this chapter's scope. You can browse the next chapter for detailed information.

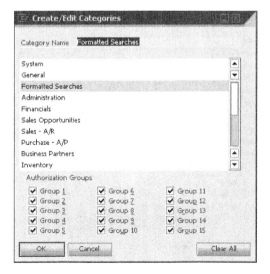

The following screenshot shows the first module **Administration**. All queries related to users can be saved here. Assigning **Group 1** would be an easy match to remember.

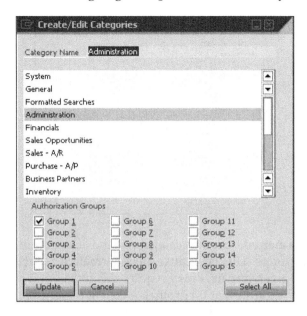

The same principle applies here: **Financials** has been assigned as Group 2 because it's the second module.

Similarly, for **Sales Opportunities**: The third module has a Group 3 assigned.

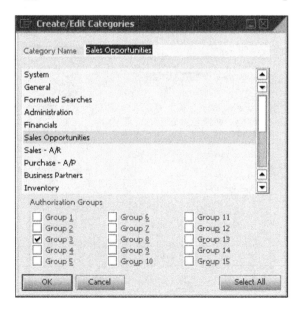

In a similar way, **Sales–A/R** has been assigned Group 4. This is the fourth module in the system.

Again for **Purchase–A/P**: The fifth module in SAP Business One with Group 5.

For Business Partners: a different approach with not only Group 6 but also Group 4 and 5.

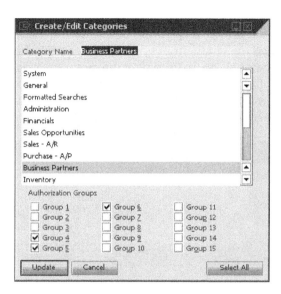

As usual for Inventory: It took Group 7 due to its occupation on the seventh module.

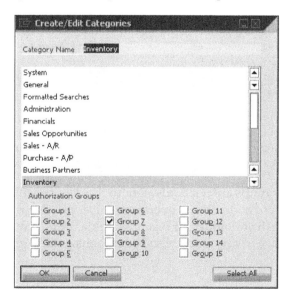

It sounds redundant for more than one screenshot to show groups' assignments. You may wonder whether it can be explained just through a few paragraphs. However, it's more effective to show you more screenshots. In this way, you can follow these suggestions easily. Remember, these are the only ways to solve the issue. You can assign any groups by using the combination of these 15 groups, as long as it meets your business needs.

After you have carefully assigned all the authorization groups, user security becomes pretty straightforward. If the users belong to the purchase department, you may assign Group No. 5 to them. As pointed out earlier, only assign Read-Only authorization first. Do not allow them to save query unless necessary. You will find out they can access both **Purchase–A/P** and **Business Partner** categories because the latter belongs to three different groups namely Group 4, 5, and 6. The following screenshot shows this concept:

Subject	Authorization	
▽ Reports	Various Authorizations	▼
▷ Sales and Purchasing	Various Authorizations	▼
▽ Query Generator	Various Authorizations	▼
New Queries	No Authorization	▼
Create/Edit Categories	No Authorization	▼
Modify SQL Statement	No Authorization	▼
Saved Queries - Group No. 1	No Authorization	▼
Saved Queries - Group No. 2	No Authorization	▼
Saved Queries - Group No. 3	No Authorization	▼
Saved Queries - Group No. 4	No Authorization	▼
Saved Queries - Group No. 5	Read-Only	▼
Saved Queries - Group No. 6	No Authorization	▼
Saved Queries - Group No. 7	No Authorization	▼

Individual users can be assigned to more than one saved queries group. For example, a sales person can be given Group 3 and 4 to use all queries under Sales Opportunities, Sale A/R, as well as Business Partner categories.

These saved queries groups are not equivalent to the department or any other user groups. It is flexible for you to design overlapped user privileges based on actual business needs; in small and midsized business, some users may have more duties. You can take advantage of this function to better manage the user security for queries.

Subject	Authorization	
▽ Reports	Various Authorizations	▼
▷ Sales and Purchasing	Various Authorizations	▼
▽ Query Generator	Various Authorizations	▼
New Queries	No Authorization	▼
Create/Edit Categories	No Authorization	▼
Modify SQL Statement	No Authorization	▼
Saved Queries - Group No. 1	No Authorization	▼
Saved Queries - Group No. 2	No Authorization	▼
Saved Queries - Group No. 3	Read-Only	▼
Saved Queries - Group No. 4	Read-Only	▼
Saved Queries - Group No. 5	No Authorization	▼
Saved Queries - Group No. 6	No Authorization	▼
Saved Queries - Group No. 7	No Authorization	▼

From these examples, you may wonder about whether you do not want the sales person to access the Business Partner category. Well, if that is the case, you have to assign a Business Partner to only one group instead of three in order to define the authorization without binding them.

 To plan for business growth, it is better to leave a couple of authorization groups without assignments. If you have assigned all 15 groups, you would not be able to deal with any future needs or growth. If the business is very stable, you can use them all.

How to use query for approval procedures

An approval procedure is a very important tool in SAP Business One for business management. It enables the management to control daily business processes. Some standard work procedures require approvals from managers or supervisors before entry level employees can generate certain documents. This is why approval procedures are needed.

The topic covering overall approval procedures may require a separate book. This book is primarily focused on SQL query. Therefore, it will not cover complete scenarios for approval procedures. However, all required steps for query approval procedures will be dealt with because you can't complete a user query approval procedure without all those steps.

The name Approval Procedure has been changed to Approval Process in version 8.8 of SAP Business One. The concept is mostly the same.

There are two steps involved in creating an approval procedure:

- Creating approval stages
- Creating approval templates

These two steps can be accessed from the **Administration** module. They are the first and second menu items under the **Approval Procedures** category. The **Approval Procedures** category lies between the **Utilities** and **License** categories.

The following screenshot shows you the path. You can also select **Modules** from the menu directly without going through the **Main Menu**.

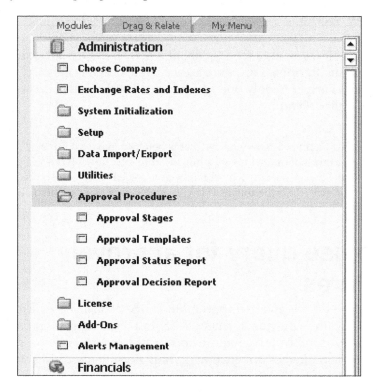

Creating approval stages

The first step in creating an approval procedure is to create an approval stage. This ensures that the persons who are in charge of approving the documents are defined first.

From the following screenshot, you can only find three textboxes that are required to be filled on the header, namely the following:

- **Stage Name**: Enter the approval stage names. It can be any name that is not more than 20 characters. The shorter, the better, as long as it can be identified. In the example, **Delivery1** is entered as the name of the stage.

- **Stage Description**: Enter the approval stage descriptions. It can be any text that's not more than 100 characters. Authorizers' names for the approval can be used here.

- **No. of Approvals Required**: This is the maximum number of authorizers required for approval. To simplify the process, only one approval is selected here. If it's more than one, it will be more complicated.

Following the header is the place to select managers or supervisors who need to approve documents. If the **No. of Approvals Required** is three, you need to select three names here. In this example, it only needs one because the **No. of Approvals Required** is only one. You can see that the manager is selected for this approval stage.

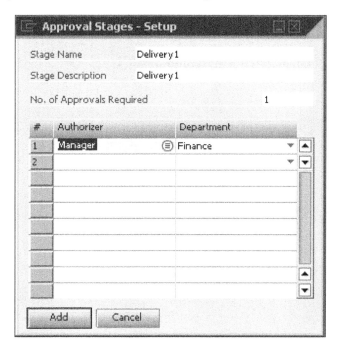

Creating approval templates

After you have created an approval stage, you can create an approval template.

There are only two textboxes and one checkbox on the header. They are listed as follows:

- **Name**: Enter the approval template's name. It can be any name and shouldn't exceed 20 characters. It should be easy to identify, and the shorter, the better. In the example, **Overdue Delivery** is entered as the name of the approval template. This is because a query with this name will be used as the base query for approval.

- **Description**: Enter the approval template's description. It can be any text that doesn't exceed 100 characters. In the example, the same text has been entered as the approval template name. It is self-explanatory, so there isn't any need for further details in the example.

- **Active**: This is a checkbox. When selected, the template becomes active. Otherwise, the template remains inactive.

There are four tabs under the approval templates header:

- **Originator**: For picking up users as originators
- **Documents**: For picking up certain types of documents
- **Stages**: For picking up approval stage
- **Terms**: The key part of the template

You will find each tab in detail in the coming pages.

Originator

The first tab is the **Originator** tab. In this tab, you can select those users who need to do the data entry. It may be one or as many as you like.

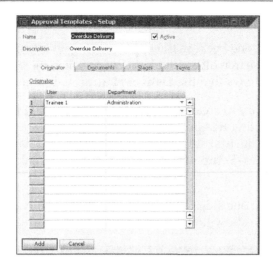

 Do not put your username under this tab. If you do, you will lose control of this template. Everything will appear grayed out to you when you browse it.

Documents

The second tab in the following screenshot is the **Documents** tab. This tab is very simple. You just need to select one or more document types here. In this example, only the delivery document type has been selected, ensuring that only the delivery document will be subjected to approval under this template. You can select more than one document here.

Stages

This tab is the simplest one because the approval stage has been set up already. You can use the *Tab* key to search all available stages to select the one you need. The following screenshot shows that the **Delivery1** approval stage is selected.

One mistake here is to try to create the approval stage during the selection process. That is not a good practice. It is problem prone. Always remember to add the approval stage during the first step. In case you forget, you have to quit from the **Approval Templates–Setup** screen. Restart only after making up for the missing stage.

There can be more than one stage as well. For simplicity, only one stage is illustrated here. It is an example to show how query approval procedure works.

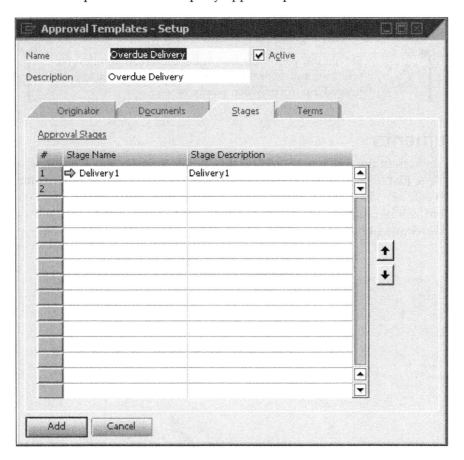

Terms

The last tab after Stage will be **Terms**. This is the most complicated one and vital for the template. There are two options to launch approval procedures:

- **Always**: Unconditional approval. If this is selected, all the documents under the selected types will be subject to approval.

- **When the following Applies**: Conditional approval based on different terms. If this is selected, some of the terms and conditions will be displayed. Query approval is under this option.

It is quite surprising that you have to select **Always** first for user query approval creation. Otherwise, you can only select system defined terms to add the approval template.

This screenshot shows that the **Overdue Delivery** approval has already been added. Otherwise, the button would still show **Add** instead of **OK**.

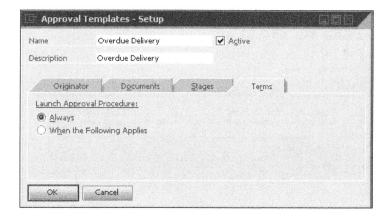

Selecting a query for the approval template

After the approval template is added to the system, you can update it immediately. Simply go to the **Term** tab directly and change the selection from **Always** to **When the Following Applies**. You can see some of the built-in terms that are displayed in the middle of the form after you have changed the selection. This is not related to user query approval. It can be ignored. There are a couple of lines close to the bottom of the screen. This is the place to put **Term Based on User Queries**.

To include a query to the template, you can highlight and double-click the first line under **Query Name**. The query manager form will pop up. You can select any prepared queries for this approval.

Remember that one of the most efficient ways for creating query approval is to use the same name for your saved query and for the approval template. In the example, you can find that it avoids having the wrong query in place.

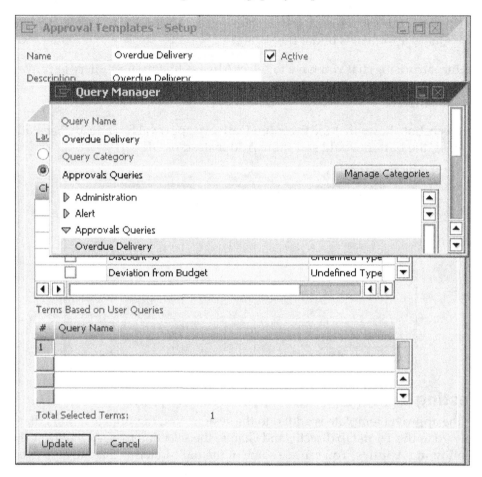

When you double-click on the query name, the query manager form will be closed. You can see that the query name **Overdue Delivery** has been selected into the first line under **Terms Based on User Queries**. You should also notice that the **Total Selected Terms** are **2** instead of **1**. This is because there is always a line in the end even though it is empty. Before you add any query, the total selected terms is already 1.

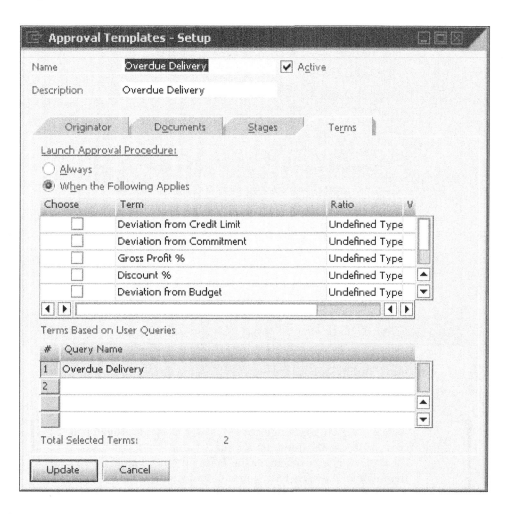

The last step is to click **Update as showed in the last screenshot**. After this action has been done, the user query approval template will be completed. You will find all delivery documents that meet the query condition are triggering approval procedures as long as the originator of the document is **Trainee1.** If the originators were someone else, the approval wouldn't trigger.

You can find the completed approval template in the following screenshot:

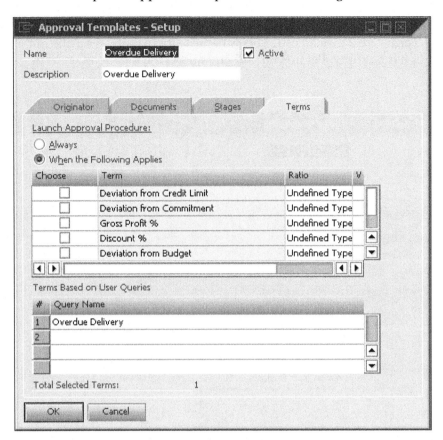

Do not forget to check the **Active** box. Otherwise, the approval template will be inactive and no approval will be triggered.

 When you plan to change query for user query approval, you have to delete the query under query name. Then you need to uncheck any boxes under the **Term** option. Change the template to **Always**. Then you can reselect the amended query.

Examples of user queries for approval

These examples will familiarize you with how to apply a user query to the approval procedure.

Case 1—Approval for adding delivery document

The first case is relatively simple. This approval in need is triggered when a user tries to add a delivery document for a customer with A/R Invoices that have overdue **DocDueDates**.

The solution to this simple request is shown here:

```
SELECT DISTINCT 'True'

FROM dbo.OINV T0

WHERE DateDiff(DD,GetDate(),T0.DocDueDate) > 0
AND T0.CardCode = $[$4.0.0]
```

This is a very simple query and is explained in the following points:

- `SELECT DISTINCT 'TRUE'` will be used for all approval queries. DISTINCT keyword can be omitted if you can make sure the query result will only return one line. When in doubt, it's always safe to leave it there. The side effect for additional DISTINCT can be ignored as even one line would be distinct from itself. Is it not? DISTINCT will ensure this query result returns only `True`. This is required by approval procedure to trigger an approval when the query result is `True`.

- `FROM dbo.OINV T0` will retrieve data from the OINV table only. You must still remember that this is an A/R Invoice table.

- `WHERE DateDiff(DD,GetDate(),T0.DocDueDate)> 0 AND T0.CardCode = $[$4.0.0]` will compare system date with the invoice document's due date as well as current customer's code for the invoice. If the query finds any invoice document due dates greater than the system date for the selected customer on the invoice, the approval will be triggered.

- `T0.CardCode = $[$4.0.0]` is using the system variable to compare with the customer code. You can find a detailed discussion of the system variable usage for formatted search in the next chapter. If the approval is needed for all customers, then this condition can be omitted.

Case 2—"On Account" outgoing payment approval

A user needs to set approval for "On Account" outgoing payment. "On Account" here means "Payment On Account". It is related to the payment screen. The following queries have been tried by the user but they aren't working:

```
SELECT (Case When (select $[ovpm.nodocsum.0]) > 0 then 'TRUE' Else
'FALSE' End) TF FROM OVPM where cardcode=convert(varchar(20),(Select
$[OVPM.cardcode.numeric]),103)
SELECT (Case When (select $[ovpm.nodocsum.0]) > 0 then 'TRUE' Else
'FALSE' End) TF FROM OVPM where cardcode=convert(varchar(20),(Select
$[OVPM.cardcode.numeric]),103) and docnum =(select $[OVPM.docnum.0])
```

Here is the solution:

```
SELECT DISTINCT 'TRUE'

FROM dbo.OVPM T0

WHERE $[ovpm.nodocsum.number] > 0 and T0.docnum = $[$3.0.0]
```

The original query has too many conversions and somehow, the logic becomes unreadable. The selective **Case** used is also not needed because we only care when the query result is True. If it is not True, then False is automatically returned. Another mistake is $[ovpm.nodocsum.0]. It will be discussed in the *Formatted Search* chapter.

The query solution is very simple. $[ovpm.nodocsum.number] > 0 checks the amount of "On Account" for the current outgoing payment. If it's greater than zero, the approval procedure will be triggered.

Actually, the last condition T0.docnum = $[$3.0.0] can be omitted because the first condition only checks the current outgoing payment.

Case 3—Approval for invoice to special customer groups

Another user tried the following query to be used for an approval procedure:

```
SELECT DISTINCT 'TRUE' FROM OINV T0 INNER JOIN OCRD T1 ON T0.CARDCODE
= T1.CARDCODE INNER JOIN OCRG T2 ON T1.GROUPCODE = T2.GROUPCODE AND
T2.GROUPNAME 'OVER SEAS CLIENTS' WHERE T0.CARDCODE = $[$4.0.0]
```

The target of the query is to check whether the customer under the customer group with the name of 'over seas clients' exists in any new invoice. If it is true, the invoice needs to go through the approval procedure. However, nothing is triggered to any invoices after assigning this query to the approval procedure.

By checking the user's query, the problem was figured out, for which the solution is listed here:

```
SELECT distinct 'true'

FROM dbo.OINV T0
INNER JOIN dbo.OCRD T1 ON T0.CardCode = T1.CardCode
INNER JOIN dbo.OCRG T2 ON T1.GroupCode = T2.GroupCode

WHERE T0.CardCode = $[$4.0.0] AND T2.GroupName LIKE 'Over seas
clients%'
```

The original query has only one mistake. The condition to check the group name in the business partner group table OCRG should be put under the `where` clause.

`T2.GroupName LIKE 'Over seas clients%'` is using LIKE instead of equal. It also has the `%` at the end. That's because it's always a weak match to make a comparison with any text string. The workaround is to make the scope bigger to increase the chance of the match.

Case 4—Approval for over booking sales order

There is another user who initially requests a formatted search query. The background is, their client usually creates Sales Order and then issues a A/R Reserve Invoice that commits certain items in certain warehouses. However, sometimes, the sales person tends to sell more than the available stock. It is even worse because the purchase order or production order quantities will also increase the available quantities. To avoid returns due to overselling, the user requests a formatted search query to check if `(In Stock - Committed - Orders) <= 0` any items for the warehouse selected are being transacted in the sales order.

After some discussion, it was found that this query is actually for triggering an approval procedure when warehouse quantity falls below the available quantity.

Here is the solution based on the actual requirement:

```
SELECT Distinct 'true'

FROM dbo.OITW T0
```

```
WHERE T0.ItemCode = $[$38.1.0] AND T0.WhsCode = $[$38.24.0]
AND (T0.OnHand - T0.IsCommited - T0.OnOrder) <= 0
```

With this query, the table to look up is the OITW—item warehouse table.

The condition is to check the sales order for the line item code and warehouse code. Using these two, we have a formula `(T0.OnHand - T0.IsCommited - T0.OnOrder) <= 0` to reflect `(In Stock - Committed - Orders) <= 0`.

This query has effectively saved one UDF and a Formatted Search. It can be used to trigger an approval directly without additional burden to the system.

Case 5—None cash outgoing payment approval

A user needs to set up an approval procedure for outgoing payments. The terms and conditions are as follows:

Documents should go for approval only when an outgoing payment is raised by choosing none cash account. Or in other words, outgoing payment from the cash account is not subject to approval.

In addition, there is another validation that has to be done when outgoing payment document series fall under any of the series in the list (`'HEA10'`, `'KEE10'`, `'GIR10'`, `'DAS10'`); the document should not be subjected to approval.

The following query is working for the above requirement.

```
Select distinct 'True' from ovpm where (select cast(BeginStr as
varchar(25)) from nnm1 where Series=(select $[OVPM.Series]) and a
approval either.
```

The previous query doesn't seem to work because all the outgoing payments are subject to approval, whether they are by cash or not.

The solution is as follows:

```
SELECT DISTINCT 'TRUE'

FROM dbo.OVPM

WHERE (SELECT cast(BeginStr as varchar(25))
FROM NNM1 where Series=(select $[OVPM.Series]) and Remark is null) in
('HEA10','KEE10','GIR10','DAS10') OR
(T0.CashSum = 0 AND T0.DocNum = $[ovpm.DocNum])
```

Only one condition `OR (T0.CashSum = 0 AND T0.DocNum = $[ovpm.DocNum])` is added. This condition ensures cash amount must not be greater than zero. If the cash amount is zero, it means it's not a cash outgoing payment. This is different from cash account checking.

The NNM1 table in the query is a row table for ONNM. This table holds all series' names.

 There is a very important limitation in user query for approval. Approvals will only check the header tables. If you need to check conditions in a row table for approval, then only the first line can be checked. All other lines will not be available to the approval terms. A workaround can be done by `SBO_SP_TransactionNotification` and a UDF. Details will be discussed in the later chapters.

Summary

In this chapter, you learned two important topics for SQL query usage in SAP Business One. First, how the security can be set to query users. The other is query used for approval procedures. All these topics are discussed in detail with many examples and multiple screenshots.

When you follow the suggestion from this book for user query security, you will be able to reduce potential problems in query usage. This will enable the users to get just the query they need without any additional risk to the system.

For the approval procedure, you can follow the examples to build your own. Because user query for approval is so flexible, you will be able to build more approval procedures to meet your specific business needs.

In the next chapter, we will discuss Formatted Search—a mystery topic for every new SQL query user.

6
SQL Query for Formatted Search (FMS)

In the previous chapter, you learned about user query security and user query for approval procedures in SAP Business One.

This chapter focuses on one of the most frequently used but error-prone processes. It is to create SQL Query for **Formatted Search** (**FMS**). This chapter covers the following topics:

- Discussing the following two terms:
    - Formatted Search
    - User-Defined Values (UDV)

- Clarification of these two terms
- The process of how to set up UDV
    - Focus is given to FMS query and issues related to FMS query, such as why there are internal error messages popping up and what a dollar sign or negative sign means in FMS query

- The last section gives you some FMS query examples

Within this chapter, the term "field" will be used if related to a table. Another term 'column' is reserved for a form-related place holder.

Formatted Search and User-Defined Values

Before going into detail of Formatted Search (FMS), User-Defined Values (UDV) need to be discussed in detail. These two concepts are closely related.

Formatted Search has been replaced by User-Defined Values with the 2007 version. However, these two terms co-existed until version 8.8. There seem to be no stop signs in using the term Formatted Search. Actually, this term is more popular than UDV.

The rationale behind this is that UDV is an overall concept to describe the ability for users to define values in both system and user-defined fields. It covers both the values from a predefined value list and the values from FMS user query results. To use it as a menu item, UDV fits perfectly. However, Formatted Search emphasizes how the value has been obtained. This term is more meaningful for user query generated values. These two terms have different scopes. Formatted Search may never be replaced by User-Defined Values completely.

The official explanation of the User-Defined Values can be found next.

The User-Defined Values function enables SAP Business One users to enter values, originated by a predefined search process, for any field in the system (including user-defined fields).

Examples of using this function include:

- Entering values into fields using a predefined list
- Automatic entering of values into fields via user-defined queries
- Creating dependence between fields in the system, for example, the value in field X influences the value in field Y
- Displaying fields that are only available to queries, for example, User Signature, Creation Date, Open Checks Balance for business partner, and so on

In short, this function enables the user to enter data more efficiently and – perhaps most importantly – more accurately. In fact, the concept is sort of a "Workflow Light" implementation. It can both save user time and reduce data double entries.

How to work with User-Defined Values

To access the User-Defined Values, you can choose menu item **Tools | User-Defined Values**. You can also use the shortcut key *Shift+Alt+F2* instead. Another option is to access it directly from a non-assigned field by using *Shift+F2*. This will be discussed later.

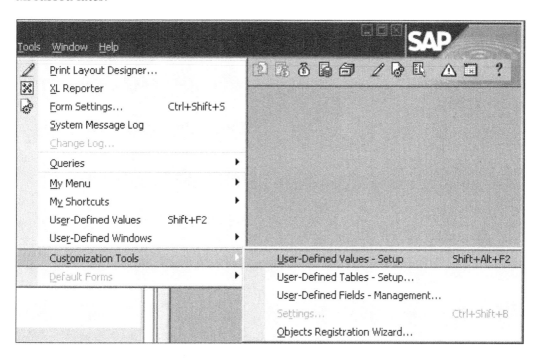

You must notice that the option will not be available until you brought up at least one form. This is because the UDV has to be associated with a form. It can't stand alone.

The following screenshots are taken from A/R Down Payment Invoice. It is one of the standard marketing documents. From the UDV point of view, there is no big difference between this and the other types of documents, namely, Sales Order, Purchase Order, Invoice, and so on.

After a form is opened, a UDV can be defined. We will start from an empty screen to show you the first step: bringing up a form.

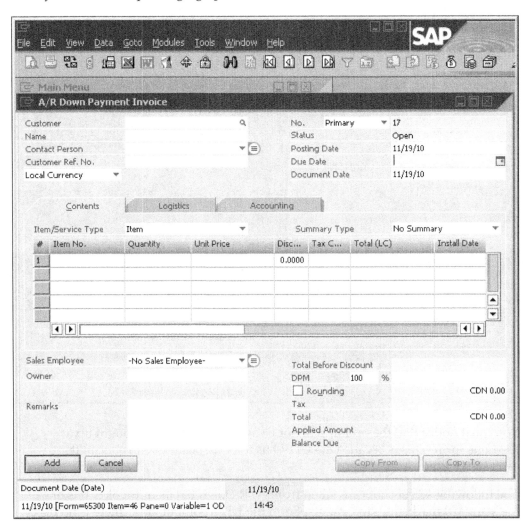

When a form is opened, you can define or change any UDV. In this case, we stop our cursor on the **Due Date** field and then enter *Shift+F2*. A system message will pop up as shown in the following screenshot:

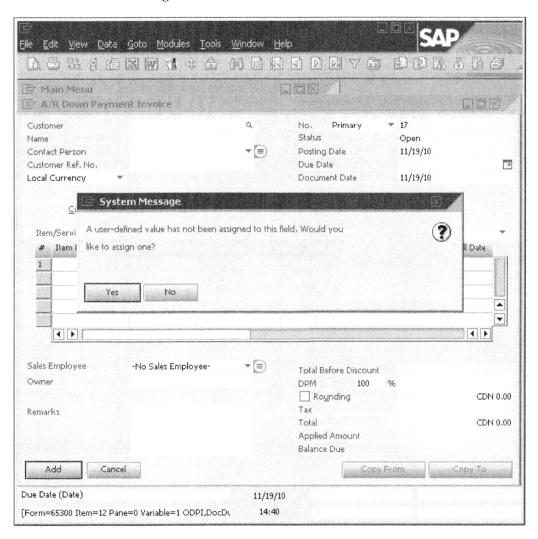

If you click **Yes**, it will bring up the same window in the manner you select the menu item mentioned earlier from the **Tools** menu or press *Shift+Alt+F2*.

When you get the **User-Define Values-Setup** screen, you have three options. Apart from the default option: **Without Search User-Define Values**, you actually have only two choices:

- **Search in Existing User-Define Values**
- **Search in Existing User-Define Values according to Saved Query**

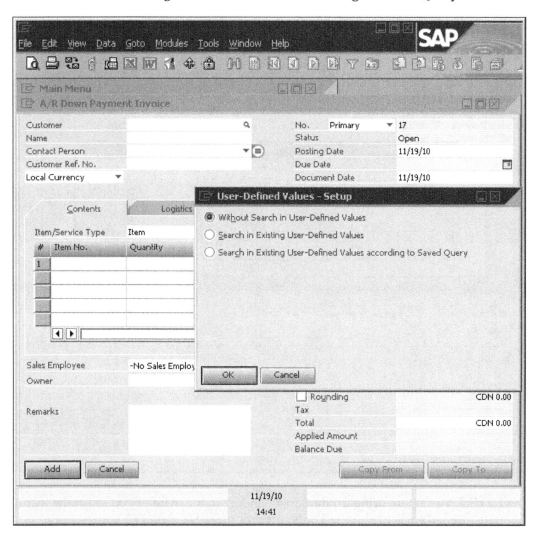

Let's go through the last option first: **Search in Existing User-Define Values according to Saved Query**. This book is focused on queries. Therefore, the topic related to query will always be assigned with the top priority. There are quite a few screenshots that will help you understand the entire process.

Search in existing User-Defined Values according to the saved queries

The goal for this example is to input the due date as the current date automatically.

The first thing to do for this option is to click on the bottom radio button among three options. The screenshot is shown next:

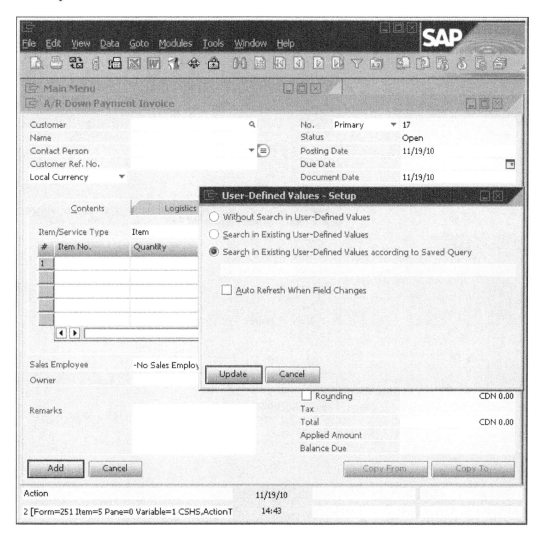

After you have clicked the **Search in Existing User-Defined Values according to Saved Query** radio button, you will find a long empty textbox in a grey color and a checkbox for **Auto Refresh When Field Changes** underneath. Don't get confused by the color. Even though in other functions throughout SAP Business One, a gray colored field normally means that you cannot input or enter information into the field. That is not the case here. You can double-click it to get the User-Defined Values.

When you double-click on the empty across-window text box, you can bring up the query manager window to select a query.

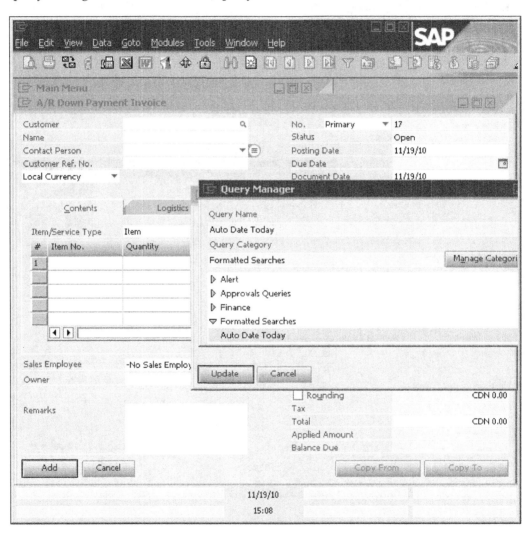

You can then browse the query category that relates to Formatted Searches and find the query you need. The query called **Auto Date Today** in the showcase is very simple. The query script is as simple as this:

```
SELECT GetDate()
```

This query returns the current date as the result.

You need to double-click to select the query and then go back to the previous screen but with the query name, as shown in the following screenshot:

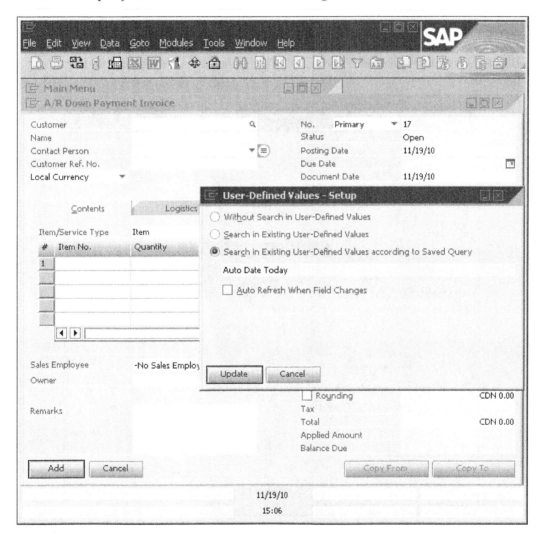

It may not be good enough to select only query because if you stop here you have to always manually trigger the FMS query run by entering *Shift+F2*.

To automate the FMS query process, you can click on the checkbox under the selected query. After you check this box, another long text box will be displayed with a drop-down list button.

Under the text box, there are two radio buttons for **Auto Refresh When Field Changes**:

- **Refresh Regularly**
- **Display Saved User-Defined Value**

Display Saved User-Defined Values will be the default selection, if you do not change it.

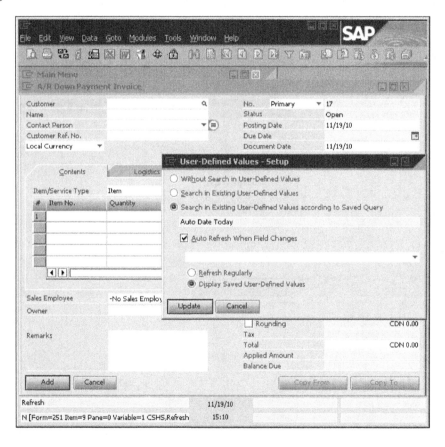

When you click on the drop-down list arrow button, you will get a list of fields that are associated with the current form.

You can see in the following screenshot that **Customer/Vendor Code** field has been selected. For header document UDV, this field is often the most useful field to auto refresh the UDV.

In theory, you can select any fields from the list. However, in reality only a few fields are good candidates for the task. These include **Customer/Vendor Code**, **Document Currency**, **Document Number**, and **Document Total** for document header; **Item Code** and **Quantity** for document lines. Choosing the correct data field from this drop-down list is always the most difficult step in Formatted Search, and you should test your data field selection fully.

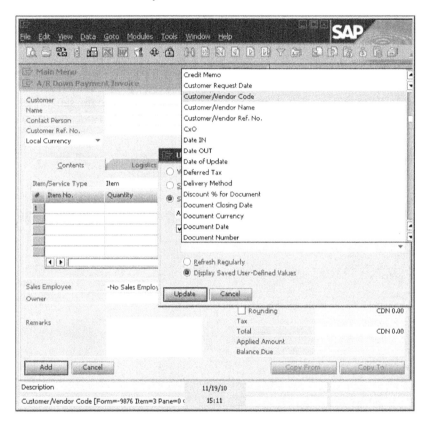

Now, the text box is filled with **Customer/Vendor Code** for automatically refreshing the UDV.

Between two options, this query can only select the default option of **Display Saved User-Defined Value**. Otherwise, the date will always change to the date you have updated the document on. That will invalidate the usage of this UDV. The **Refresh Regularly** option is only suitable to the value that is closely related to the changed field that you have selected.

In general, **Display Saved User-Defined Value** is always a better option than **Refresh Regularly**. At least it gives the system less burden. If you have selected **Refresh Regularly**, it means you want to get the UDV changed whenever the base field changes.

The last step to set up this UDV is by clicking **Update**. As soon as you click the button, the **User-Defined Values–Setup** window will be closed. You can find a green message on the bottom-left of the screen saying **Operation Completed Successfully**.

You can find a small "magnifying glass" added to the right corner of the Due Date field.

This means the Formatted Search is successfully set up. You can try it for yourself.

 Sometimes this "magnifying glass" disappears for no reason. Actually, there are reasons but not easy to be understood. The main reason is that you may have assigned some different values to the same field on different forms. Other reasons may be related to add-on, and so on.

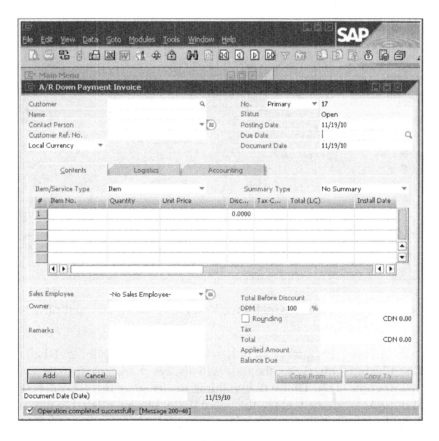

In order to test this FMS, the first thing to try is to use the menu function or key combination *Shift+F2*. The other option is to just click on the "magnifying glass". Both functions have the same result. It will force the query to run. You can find that the date is filled by the same date as posting date and document date.

 You may find some interesting date definitions in SAP Business One, such as Posting Date is held by the field DocDate. Document Date however, is saved under TaxDate. Be careful in dealing with dates. You must follow the system's definition in using those terms, so that you get the correct result.

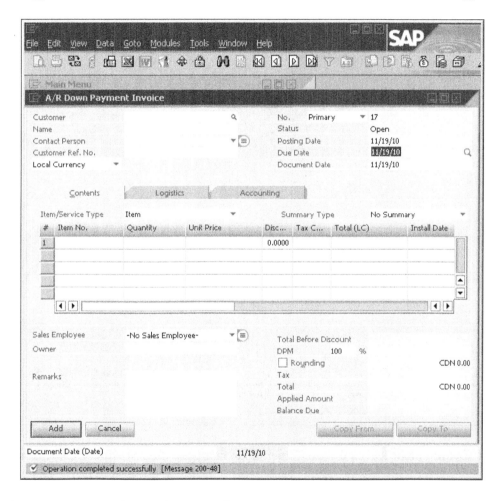

A better way to use this FMS query is by entering the customer code directly without forcing FMS query to run first.

The following screenshot shows that the customer code OneTime has been entered.

Please note that the **DueDate** field is still empty.

Is there anything wrong? No. That is the system's expected behavior.

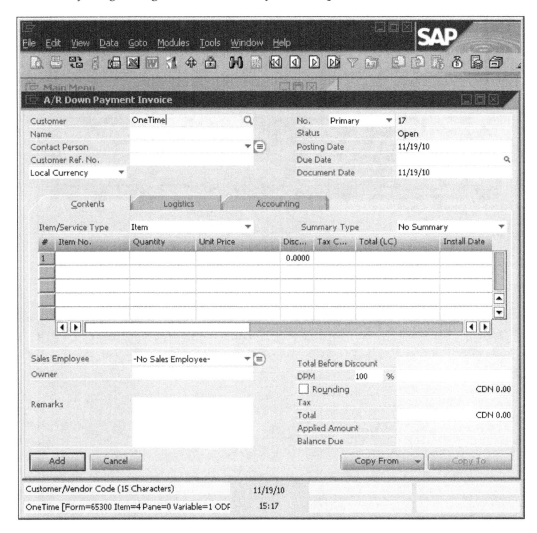

Only if your cursor leaves the Customer Code field, can the FMS query be triggered.

That is a perfect example of **When Field Value Changes**. The system can only know that the field value is changed when you tab out of the field. When you are working with the field, the field is not changed yet.

Be careful to follow system requirements while entering data. Never press *Enter* in most of the forms unless you are ready for the last step to add or update data. If you do, you may add the wrong documents to the system and they are irrevocable.

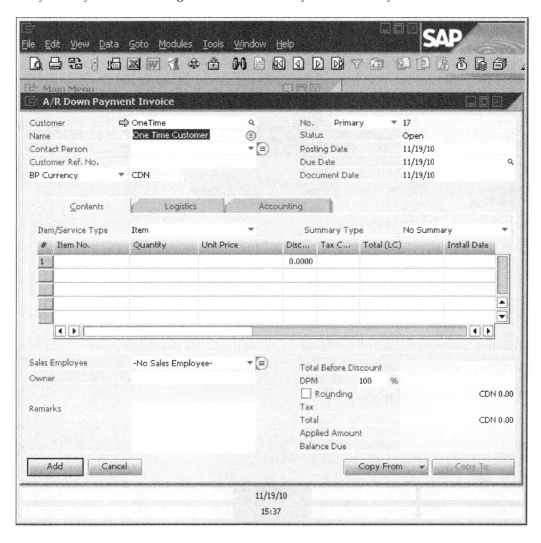

The previous screenshot shows the complete process of setting up search in **Existing User-Define Values according to Saved Query**. Now it is time to discuss the $ sign field.

Where do the $ values come from?

Many users have this question when they first read a FMS query script with system variables, because not all users have the chance to access SAP's formal document.

A $ sign in the query means a system variable. There are few variables available all the time such as $[user]. This is the variable to represent the current log in user sign. However, most variables will be form dependent. To get detailed information regarding the variable, you need to activate the **System Information** function as shown in the next screenshot:

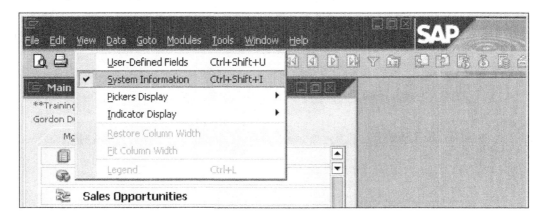

This menu option is under the **Views** menu. You can use the shortcut key *Ctrl+Shift+I* to get the same result. This menu option is an On/Off switch. You can change it from off to on or from on to off if you select it. A check in front of the **System Information** means it is on.

When the system information switch is on, all system information related to the current mouse position will be shown on the status bar at the bottom left of the screen. It is irrelevant to the cursor position.

The following example shows that the mouse is over the top first field **Customer**. The information related to it is as follows:

[Form=65300 Item=4 Pane=0 Variable=1 OPDI,CardCode]

This is a header field so only two parts are useful to the FMS query:

- The first one is Item=4. Item here means form element; it has nothing to do with item master data.

- The second one is OPDI, CardCode. It is the table and field name for this item.

In the FMS query, the usages can be either of the following:

- `$[$4.0.0]` that reflects `Item=4`
- `$[OPDI.CardCode]` that only adds `$[]` to the field name

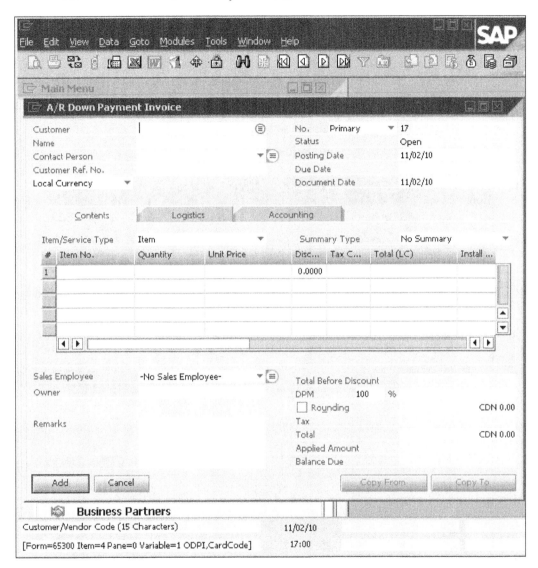

The other similar screenshot, as follows, looks exactly the same but the mouse is over the **Item No**. field in the line detail of the form.

The information that relates to this field is:

[Form=65300 Item=38 Pane=1 Column=1 Row=1 Variable=11 PDI1,ItemCode]

This is a line field and three parts are useful to the FMS query:

- `Item=38`: This item stands for the whole matrix of the line detail
- `Column=1`: This refers to the field in the table
- `PDI1,ItemCode`: Again it is table and field name

In the FMS query, the usages can be in two equivalent formats:

- `$[$38.1.0]` that reflects `Item=38` and `Column=1`
- `$[PD1.ItemCode]` that only adds `$[]` to the field name

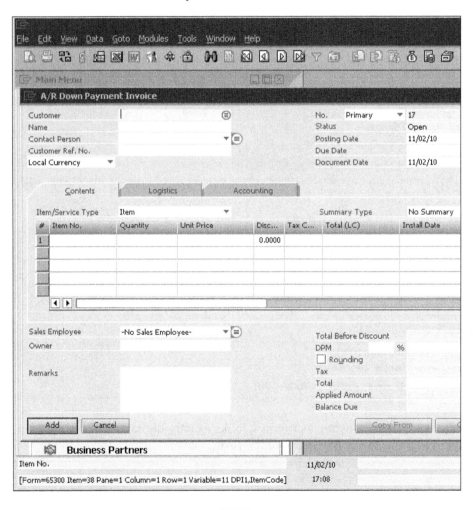

The syntax for a form based line level variable is $[$Item.Column.Type].

For header items, columns are always zero because all items on the header represent a field in a table if it has a datasource. Column is only useful for line details.

The last portion is the Type. It is not related to system information found on the screen. It is the type of value you need to return, and can be any of the following:

- 0-String(text)
- Number
- Currency
- Date

For example, a value returned by $[$22.0.0] as N'USD 100' when a marketing document total is 100 US Dollars. If by $[$22.0.number], it will return 100. It returns only N'USD' if you use $[$22.0.currency]. As a default selection of type 0, it can often be omitted.

While in the form based variable, the column represents the order number of the column in the form. For example, $[$38.11.number] stands for quantity field in the marketing document. It is the eleventh column within the line detail matrix.

The syntax for a table based variable is $[Table.Field.Type].

The field in this syntax is the actual field code within the table. It is the last part of the system variables. It can be a UDF starting with U_. If you use a table based variable, the form based variable $[$38.11.number] is equivalent to $[RDR1.quantity.number].

In general, you can always use a form based variable to reduce the trouble for one query that has to be written multiple times based on the different tables for different forms.

How to get the value you need from, and for, the FMS query

To get any values from the FMS query, the first thing to remember is: only the first field can be returned to the field if you select more than one field in your query. All fields from the second one will be ignored no matter how many fields you have selected for the query. The additional fields can only be functioned as references.

To assign any values to a FMS query, the principle is: only a table available to the current form can be based to set a variable. If you open a new form, the base form variable will become inaccessible. For example, all variables on the main form of the marketing document will not be available to a freight form and vice versa.

If you create a query using the $ variables and have a form open that uses the variables then the query replaces the $ values with the current values in the form. This is an important step to test FMS query before assigning. Make sure you save the query first. Otherwise, the variable will become a hard value. You cannot get it back to $ variable.

Can you run FMS queries directly?

Can you run FMS query directly under query manager? The answer is partially yes and partially no. It depends on whether you have form variables or dollar sign field values.

If a FMS query has a variable, then this query must be saved under one of your categories. Preferably, you create an exclusive folder with the name related to Formatted Search. It is considered as the best practice.

You will get an error message if you select run query from query manager or user queries directly without any related form open. This is due to the undefined form. A $ sign will be meaningless without current form support. You will get a red "Internal error" message immediately on the status bar.

What is the negative sign's function in FMS query?

We often find that certain FMS queries have a negative sign for variables. For instance:

$[$-4.0.0]

What does the negative sign stand for?

A negative sign for a form variable means your FMS query is related to header level User-Defined Fields. The form number will have the same value as the main form but with the opposite sign.

For example, form 139 is a sales order form. UDF form for a sales order will be -139. Form 142 is a purchase order form. UDF form for a purchase order will be -142. The difference between those two related forms is only a negative sign.

When we refer the main form variable to the UDF form, a negative sign is always needed. The actual form number is not important to FMS query. Only the negative sign matters. $[$-4.0.0] refers to the BP code in the main document form. It will be used for a FMS query assigned to the UDF form.

Search in existing User-Defined Values only

The simplest form of a search for UDV is to define a list of values, which the system proposes as input values. These input values are triggered when the user selects *Shift+F2* in the relevant field. The procedures to define this simplest search will be shown next.

Although this function may not be directly linked to SQL query, it is worth going through the detailed process to get one more options under the same menu function with FMS query for UDV.

The same process will be discussed as from the breaking point that showed the **Without Search User-Define Values** option previously. With one exception: the cursor is not on the DueDate but the Remarks field.

Instead of selecting the bottom option, the middle option, **Search in existing user-define values only**, will be selected as follows:

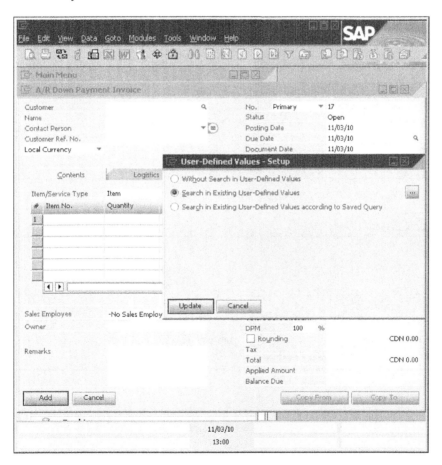

In the right-most screen of this middle selection, you can find a button with three dots. It is the access path for predefined values.

This button needs to be clicked to assign a list of predefined values. There is nowhere else you can find it.

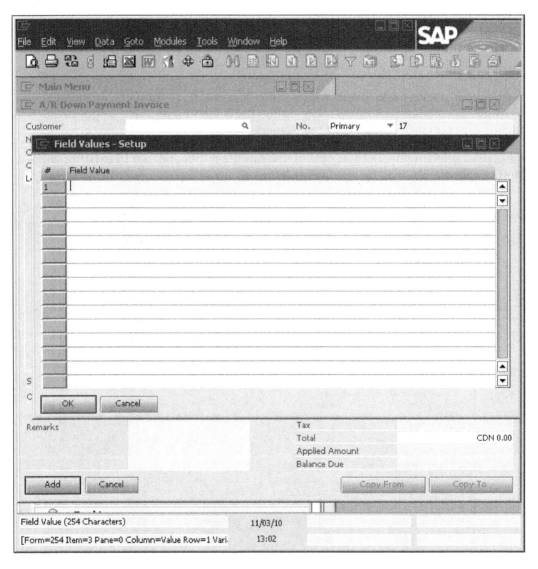

After clicking on the button, a new form will pop up with the title: **Field Values–Setup**. There is only one field in the form. The field title is **Field value**. Your cursor will remain on the first line.

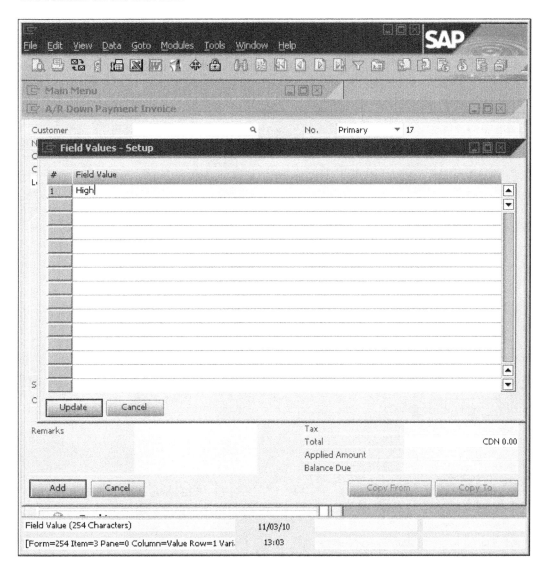

You can input any letter or number here. In the example, **High** is inputted on the first line. You will notice the button **OK** has changed to **Update**. This **Update** is not only for the form but for every line. You only need to press *Enter* to move to the next line. It acts as a click on the **Update** button.

After pressing *Enter*, the cursor moves down to the second line. The button becomes **OK** again. A green message is shown on the bottom-left of the screen: **Operation Completed Successfully**. You can input any characters just like in the first line.

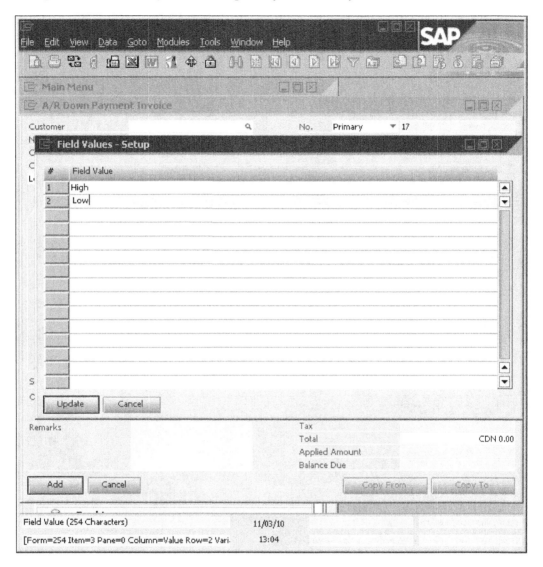

Low is entered on the second line. The button now changes from **OK** to **Update**. As before, you just need to press *Enter* to move the cursor down again.

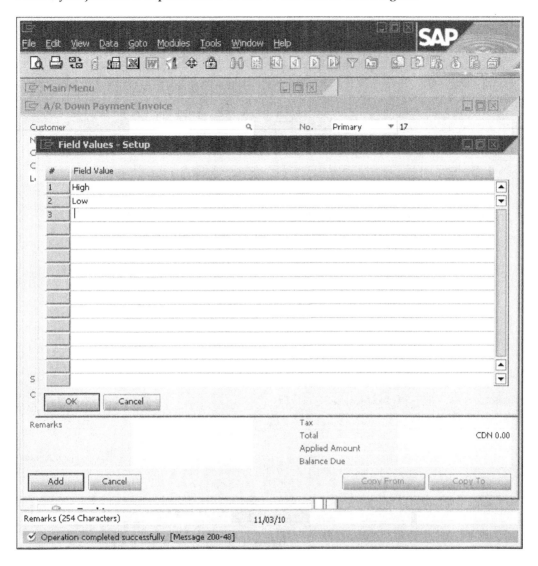

When the line is empty and the button is **OK**, you can close the form by pressing *Enter* or clicking on the **OK** button. This will complete the value list input. You can always go back to **Update** or add new lines to the list.

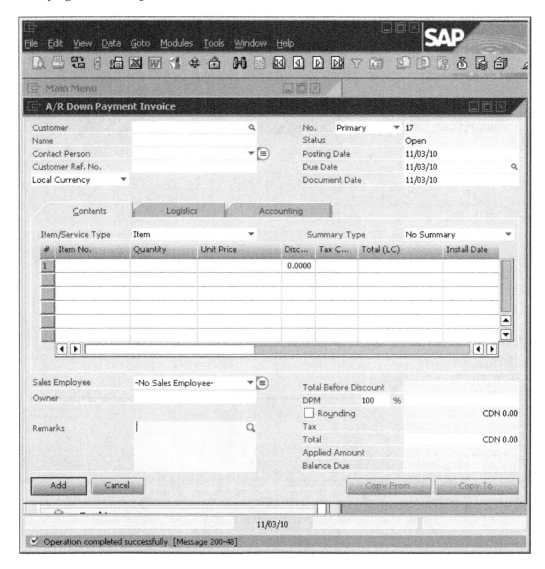

Just like the other example, you should find that the magnifying glass has been added to the right corner of the **Remarks** field from the last screenshot. This means that the UDV has been assigned successfully.

When you press *Shift+F2*, a list of values will pop up. All values that were entered on the list will be available.

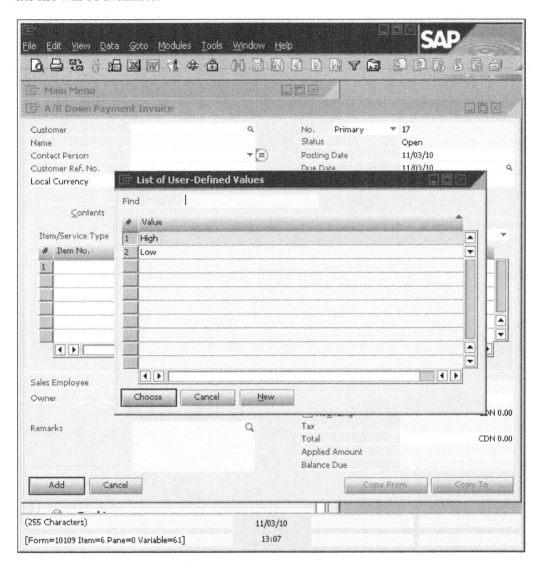

You can select any line from the list. Then press *Enter* to select one of the values required or click the **Choose** button. Click the **Cancel** button if you do not want to assign any values from the list. There is an additional button besides these two buttons. It is the **New** button. This button allows you to edit or to add values on the list.

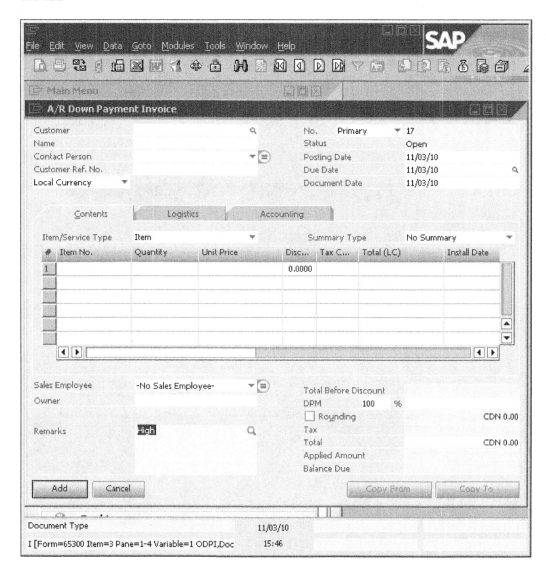

As you can see, since the value selected is that of the first line, **High** has been returned to the field. This value can be very long. That may save you a great amount of time.

The previous screenshots conclude the process to set up **Search in existing user-define values only** function. Next, you will learn some FMS query examples to help you build your own query quickly.

A typical FMS query application: auto code creation

The first kind of examples for FMS query will be the typical ones.

FMS query is a very good tool to facilitate auto code generation to maintain a cleaner database. It is a good practice to create code without human intervention.

The code creation required is the BP code generation. The others will be for new item code. Some special requirements can be user document numbers or line numbers auto code.

Let's take a look at BP auto code generation first, then item code creation, and finally a special code-related issue will be discussed briefly.

BP code auto generation

When adding BP code, auto generation can save time and reduce certain problems. First, classify BP to three categories, namely: Lead, Customer, and Vendor. In common practice, the first letter will be reserved to BP type. We use **L** for **lead**, **C** for **customer**, and **V** for **vendor**.

Here is an example code to auto generate the BP code:

```
SELECT
CASE $[$40.0]
When 'C' then 'C'
When 'L' then 'L'
When 'S' then 'V'
END
+Isnull(Substring(Str(100000+Max(Right(T0.
CardCode,5))+1,6),2,5),'00001')

FROM OCRD T0

WHERE T0.CardCode like '%[0-9][0-9][0-9][0-9][0-9]'
AND T0.CardType = $[$40.0]
```

The previous example defines a BP code with one letter for BP type and five digits for auto code. It is better to keep the same length code for consistency. If you have more BP to be set up, you can increase one digit to six numbers. Usually 99,999 customers or vendors are more than enough for a SME to handle.

Item code auto generation

When creating new item code, it is also a good idea to automate the process.

There is a common wrong perception that a number must mean something in order to manage the item by those codes easily. However, this is wrong in many cases. Unless your business has very few items that need to be set up, autogenerated item codes will always supersede the manual item code that fails to imitate the complicated business process.

One way to adapt to both needs is by using an initial letter for item group or item category. Other than that, all additional code should be by auto number.

An example of the item code auto creation FMS query is as follows:

```
SELECT
CASE $[$39.0.number]
When 101 then 'I'
When 102 then 'J'
When 103 then 'K'
END
+Isnull(Substring(Str(1000000+Max(Right(T0.
ItemCode,6))+1,7),2,6),'000001')

FROM OITM T0

WHERE T0.ItemCode like '%[0-9][0-9][0-9][0-9][0-9][0-9]'
AND T0.ItmsGrpCod = $[$39.0.number]
```

If you check between this example and the BP code example, you will find the differences are easy to tell. This FMS query assumes all items under item group 101 will start with **I**. While item group 102 will start with **J** and item group 103 will start with **K**, you can define any kinds of naming convention according to your convenience.

The item code includes one letter and six digits. You will get 999,999 items for one item group. This would be more than sufficient for any business. You can reduce the digits to be less. However, it should not be too short in case the business grows.

Special code auto generation

A user has requested to know if it's possible to have a value in a UDF in the invoice rows automatically increase with each line entered.

This request is not normal because Linenum field holds autoincrement value in invoice row already. By clarifying the requirement, it turned out the actual need is to increment another document number, which will not necessarily follow the same numbering as the row numbers.

The solution is very simple:

```
SELECT U_special_number + $[inv1.linenum.number] + 1
```

This FMS query satisfied the user's needs. The last part of + 1 is to keep the line number starting with one instead of zero.

General FMS query examples

Other than the auto code FMS query, the other types will be difficult to classify. The name general is chosen for all other queries. To be able to create a good FMS query, a good practice is to try more whenever you have the opportunity. The examples covered in this chapter will give you a solid foundation to start building your own FMS query.

Case 1—Double quotes should be avoided

A user created a very simple query. It gave an error message when assigned to FMS. The query is as follows:

```
IF (2500 < $[ORDR.DocTotal.number] or $[ORDR.CardCode] like "C99%")
SELECT 'Pre Pay No Charge'
ELSE
SELECT 'Pre Pay and Bill'
```

The logic is so simple that it should be correct. Where is the problem? Here is the solution:

```
IF (2500 < $[ORDR.DocTotal.number] or $[ORDR.CardCode] like 'C99%')

SELECT 'Pre Pay No Charge'

ELSE

SELECT 'Pre Pay and Bill'
```

The difference between two queries may not be easy to identify. They are only using different quotation marks. It is so simple but has often been neglected. Usually, we can use both double quotes and single quotes within query without any issue. However, it will not work in the FMS query. A good practice in creating SQL query in SAP Business One is not using double quotes for any kinds of queries. Wherever a pair of quotation marks is required, always use single quotes as a safe harbor.

Case 2—Price value validation on line level

A user is trying to do a user input validation on the price field. A new UDF on marketing document lines named U_price_validation has been created for the task. Whenever the price field on the given row is greater than 100, the U_price_validation should be set to 1.

The following search query format has been tried:

```
SELECT TOP 1
CASE WHEN $[$38.14.N] > 100 THEN 1 ELSE NULL END AS Value
FROM OPDN T0
```

However, it is not working.

Here is the solution:

```
SELECT CASE WHEN $[$38.14.number] > 100 THEN 1 ELSE NULL END
```

This query can be set on U_price_validation. It will return value 1 to the field when you set autorefresh based on the price field.

Case 3—Populating a UDF from OITM in a UDF on quotation

A user created a query that can be run under query manager:

```
SELECT T1.U_NPS_QD FROM OITM T1 INNER JOIN QUT1 T2 ON T1.ItemCode =
T2.ItemCode WHERE T1.ItemCode = T2.ItemCode
```

The user wants to use the previous query to populate the query result to a user-defined field U_NPS_D2 on Sales Quotation. Whenever an item is added to quotation or an item is changed, the field U_NPS_D2 should be changed accordingly. It is expected that U_NPS_D2 updating would be done automatically without the user entering *Shift+F2*.

The question is: how do we convert the previous query to a FMS query with the right syntax?

This is a very straightforward query for FMS. Here is the solution:

```
SELECT T0.U_NPS_QD

FROM dbo.OITM T0

WHERE T0.ItemCode = $[$38.1.0]
```

This query should be assigned on U_NPS_D2 field and set autorefresh on the ItemCode field. The field can then be automatically populated by FMS query and there is no need for users to press *Shift+F2*.

You can see the solution query is simpler than the original query. This is because there is no need to join any tables anymore. The original query also has the redundant statement T1.ItemCode = T2.ItemCode. The variable $[$38.1.0] is equivalent to QUT1.ItemCode in current form. Whenever the item is changed in the sales quotation, the UDF U_NPS_D2 will be updated automatically with U_NPS_QD value from OITM.

Case 4—Difference between two UDFs into another UDF

A user made three UDFs in row level of GRPO named U_AS_PER_CHALLAN, U_Rec_Qty, and U_APPROVE_QTY to represent per Challan (a term used in Asia which means receipt for payment or delivery), Received Quantity, and Approved Quantity.

An FMS query needs to be calculated using the following formula:

As per challan-Received Quantity = Approved Quantity

The final Value should be returned to the third UDF's.

Here is the solution:

```
SELECT $[PDN1.U_AS_PER_CHALLAN.number] - $[PDN1.U_Rec_Qty.number]
```

The query is again a simple one. It is almost the same as the original formula. You only need to add the table name PDN1, which stands for Goods Receipt PO, two letters U_ for the UDF, and a number to convert the result to numeric values.

Case 5—Displaying warehouse name beside warehouse code

A user wants to add a new field or just "display" the warehouse name besides the warehouse code field in the Goods Receipt PO form. What is the FMS query for the job?

This is the simplest request and the solution query is as follows:

```
SELECT T0.WhsName

FROM dbo.OWHS T0

WHERE T0.WhsCode = $[$38.24.0]
```

This query can be assigned to a UDF and the UDF can be moved to just beside the warehouse code.

Case 6—Showing purchase order due date on sales order

A user created a line level UDF called U_PO in the sales order documents to record the purchase order number the particular item is ordered on.

There is another line level UDF called U_XMill, which will be used for the corresponding PO document due date.

The user created a query wherein, only one part needs to be corrected:

```
SELECT T0.DocDueDate
FROM OPOR T0
WHERE T0.DocNum=$[$38.44.0]
FOR BROWSE
```

The user knows "38.44" in the query is wrong but has difficulty getting the UDF U_PO value into the query.

Here is the solution:

```
SELECT T0.DocDueDate

FROM dbo.OPOR T0

WHERE T0.DocNum=$[RDR1.U_PO]
```

This is a very simple one because all UDF needs is to get the table name in front, such as this: `$[RDR1.U_PO]`. In the original query, `FOR BROWSE` is unnecessary and can be omitted. FMS query will disable all Linked Arrows by default.

Case 7—Auto populating the profit center code

A user is trying to use a FMS query to autopopulate the profit center but it is not working. The query is as follows:

```
select t0.ocrcode
from OOCR t0
where t0.ocrname like '%% $[ordn.cardcode]'
```

The profit center description (name) has been set up that includes the customer code in the end as part of the description. An example name is "Customer ABC C00022", wherein C00022 is the customer code and Customer ABC is the customer name. They use the same length customer code for all their customers.

The user's FMS query is intended to read the customer code from the AR invoice screen and pull the profit center based on the customer code that is included in the profit center name. The query failed to reach the goal.

Here is the solution:

```
SELECT T0.ocrcode

FROM dbo.OOCR T0

WHERE $[$4.0.0] LIKE RIGHT(T0.ocrname,6)
```

There is only one difference with the original query. The original query tried to compare the whole name with the customer code from sales return screen. The solution query uses generic BP code in the marketing department, that is, `$[$4.0.0]` to compare with the last six characters in the profit center description. This will ensure it works for A/R invoice profit center description.

Case 8—Calculation by three user-defined fields

A user set up three UDFs in the title level of Marketing Document and named them as Cost1, Cost2, and Gross Profit.

The goal is to calculate the Gross Profit for sales order by assigning a formatted search using a formula: Document Total - Cost1 - Cost2.

The query has been tried without success.

Here is the solution:

```
SELECT $[$29.0.number] - $[ordr.U_cost1.number] - $[ordr.U_cost2.
number]
```

Within the query, $[$29.0.number] stands for Document Total. The other UDFs are straightforward; all three fields with `.number` as type because the values are all numeric.

Case 9—Open order reminder in new order

When adding a new sales order for the customer, the user wants to have a reminder or a pop-up block/notice. That will tell if the customer has open orders in the system.

The business background is: sometimes orders shipped out without notice that another order had shipped a day before to the same customer.

The main goal is to give a notice or reminder whenever adding a new order to a customer that already has some orders open. This is not in order to block any customer from adding new orders; the more, the better.

This is only to remind clerks or the stock keepers to merge the orders into one package in order to save shipping costs and not send two different packages to the same address on different days.

Apparently, this pop up can be done only through SDK. However, based on the need, I have suggested the user to use FMS query.

Instead, to show "Attention-client has open orders!", the FMS query can actually show open order numbers if they exist.

Here is the solution:

```
SELECT T0.DocNum, T0.DocDate

FROM dbo.ORDR T0

WHERE T0.DocStatus = 'O' AND T0.CardCode = $[$4.0.0]
```

The query is very simple. It compares the current customer code against the ORDR table. Then it lists all open order numbers with a posting date for the selected customer.

Case 10—Commitment checks for warehouse in stock

A user has an initial request. Their client usually creats a sales order and then an A/R Reserve Invoice, which creates a commitment for certain items in certain warehouses. Sometimes, they tend to sell more than the available stock.

They are also quite misled when there is an ordered quantity because it will also be added to the available quantity. To avoid returns due to overselling, a FMS query is required with the formula: In Stock - Committed - Orders <= 0 to show items' availability in certain warehouses selected in the sales order.

Here is the solution:

```
SELECT (T0.OnHand - T0.IsCommited - T0.OnOrder)

FROM dbo.OITW T0

WHERE T0.ItemCode = $[$38.1.0] AND T0.WhsCode = $[$38.24.0]
```

This query will calculate the item commitment based on item code and warehouse for each line item in the sales order. Then check the OITW table for those three fields.

Finally, another solution is to create an alert directly based on the calculation. It can be calculated on the fly. And it can reduce one UDF for holding the query result.

Case 11—Multiplying a field from OITM with a field on order line

A user needs to multiply two fields. One is weight, located in the **Purchase** tab from OITM, and the other is quantity from order lines. The user has tried with the following query but got an error:

```
SELECT $[oitm.BWght1Unit.number]*$[por1.Quantity.number]
```

Here is the solution:

```
SELECT T0.BWeight1*$[$38.11.number]

FROM dbo.OITM T0

WHERE T0.ItemCode = $[$38.1.0]
```

Again, the problem is the use of the form variable. Order lines are in the marketing documents. OITM is not opened. A $ sign should not be used for any fields from OITM because Item master is not the current table in the form.

Case 12—Multiplying two UDF values from two tables

A user has a user-defined field on sales order row level called U_DEPFEEAMT.

The user would like this field multiplied by a field from OITM UDF called U_DepositFeeON.

The details of the field for U_DEPFEEAMT are:

Form=139, item=38, pane=1, column=10002117, and row=1

Here is the solution:

```
SELECT T0.U_DepositFeeON*$[$38.10002117.number]

FROM dbo.OITM T0

WHERE T0.ItemCode = $[$38.1.0]
```

The column number in this example is special. Because it is a UDF, the number is much larger than usual. However, the same concept still applies. The second component in the variable always represents a column in the matrix on a form.

Case 13—Last sales price for a customer

A user wants to get the last price on the unit price field.

The correct FMS query to satisfy the need is as follows:

```
SELECT TOP 1 T0.Price

FROM dbo.RDR1 T0
INNER JOIN dbo.ORDR T1 ON T1.DocEntry = T0.DocEntry

WHERE T0.ItemCode = $[$38.1.0] AND T1.DocNum != $[$8.0.0]

ORDER BY T1.DocDate DESC
```

The last price normally refers to the last purchase price. However, the user didn't require that price but instead the sales price that applied to the last sales order before. The TOP function is used to get the latest price for the item. The query looked up for reversed date range sorting by using the "DESC" in the last line. The top one would be the latest sales price.

Case 14—Calling a UDF value in the BOM to Production Order

A user wants to know how to call a value in a user-defined field at row level in the BOM (Bill of Material or Production Tree) to Production Order.

The detail requirement is: as soon as a BOM item code entered on the production order header, the values defined in a column in the line details of BOM should be displayed in a user-defined field in the Production Order line level.

Here is the solution:

```
SELECT T0.U_UDF

FROM dbo.ITT1 T0

WHERE T0.Father= $[$6.0.0] and T0.Code= $[$37.4.0]
```

This is an easy Formatted Search query. You only need to know two screen variables. One is on the production order header. The other is on the production order lines.

Case 15—Multiplying a UDF value with a system field value

A user is trying a formatted search for Receipt from Production transaction. The request is to multiply the system field Quantity with a user-defined field called UOMinSale and display it in another UDF. UOMinSale is a numeric field.

The user knows the first part, that is, $[IGN1.Quantity] but not the UDF part.

Here is the solution:

```
SELECT $[IGN1.Quantity.number] * $[IGN1.U_UOMinSal.number]
```

This is another simple example. UDF is treated the same as a system field with one exception. A U_ will always be needed in front of UDF. The last part, .number, should also be used to return a numeric value.

Case 16—Eliminating the duplicate lines returned by FMS query

A user created a UDF on the service call table to identify the billing and shipping information for that specific service call. The intent is to create a Return Goods Authorization from this UDF with that information.

The problem is with the following query. The query can return the addresses for the BP but it will be repeated many times if there are multiple Service calls for that BP. How do we limit it to only show the address once?

```
SELECT T2.Address, T2.Street, T2.City, T2.State FROM OSCL T0 INNER
JOIN OCRD T1 ON T0.customer = T1.CardCode LEFT OUTER JOIN CRD1 T2 ON
T1.CardCode = T2.CardCode WHERE T2.AdresType ='S' AND
$[OSCL.CUSTOMER] = T1.CardCode
```

Here is the solution:

```
SELECT Distinct T2.Address,
T2.Street,
T2.City,
T2.State

FROM dbo.OCRD T1
LEFT JOIN dbo.CRD1 T2 ON T1.CardCode = T2.CardCode

WHERE T2.AdresType ='S' AND $[OSCL.CUSTOMER] = T1.CardCode
```

From the solution, the duplicated lines will be eliminated by double insurances. The first one is takes out the unnecessary table OSCL from the original query. This will reduce most of the duplicates. The second one is the keyword Distinct. Even if there are duplicates returned by the query result, it will never be shown.

Case 17—Getting the sales rep code assigned to an activity form

A user gave the following case:

Sales Operations Department schedules appointments for the Sales Representatives.

Currently, this is how the schedule appointment works:

- Sales Opportunity Module
- 'Stages' tab

- 'Activities' Column
- Click the orange arrow

When clicking the orange arrow, an **Activity** form opens up.

On the **Activity** form, the **Assigned To** field populates as the user who is logged in.

However, the **Assigned To** field should be pointing to the Sales Representative for that account. (Sales Reps do not schedule their own activities. It is the Sales Operations Department's job). In other words, a FMS that puts OOPR.SlpCode into OCLG.AttendUser is needed.

The following query has been tried with no success:

```
SELECT $oopr.slpcode as $oclg.AttendUser
SELECT
T0.slpcode
as $oclg.AttendUser
FROM dbo.OOPR T0
```

Here is the solution:

```
SELECT DISTINCT T0.SlpCode

FROM dbo.OOPR T0

WHERE T0.CardCode = $[$9.0.0]
```

The user's query will not work because the current form cannot have both OCLG and OOPR tables. Since the OCLG is associated with Activity form, the query only needs one variable, which is $[$9.0.0] that represents OCLG.CardCode.

Case 18—FMS query for User-Defined Table (UDT)

A user created a user table with three fields. The table name is @Nor_VBN. As you can see, @ is the first character in the table name. That indicates it's a UDT.

- Itemcode
- ItemDesc
- Qty

A formatted search is needed in ItemDesc field. Whenever the Itemcode has a value entered, the description field should be displayed automatically from item master.

An internal error is returned by the following query:

```
select ItemName
from OITM
where ItemCode=$[@NOR_VBN.ItemCode]
```

A careful examination of the previous query gave the following solution:

```
SELECT ItemName

FROM dbo.OITM T0

WHERE T0.ItemCode=$[@NOR_VBN.U_ItemCode]
```

There are two mistakes in the original query:

- Alias is mandatory when the query has a conditional statement to compare with certain variables.
- All UDFs need two letter initials as U_. These include all fields within user-defined tables.

After correcting these two errors, FMS can return values as expected.

Summary

You have learned about a very important tool for SAP Business One in this chapter: Formatted Search.

This tool can save the company a fortune comparing with developing customized solution by using SDK programming. Combined by User Defined Field, Formatted Search will be very useful in getting the information to the right place without double entries.

You have learned about User Defined Value and the relationship with Formatted Search. You have learned the $ sign variable as $[$item.column.type] and $[table.field.type].

With the large amount of real world examples of FMS queries in this chapter, you will be able to create your own with ease.

7

SQL Query for Reporting Tools

The standard usage of the SQL query for SAP Business One has been discussed in previous chapters. You have quite a few query examples to work with.

In this chapter, the focus will be on some additional usages of SQL query, which are applicable to SAP Business One. This chapter discusses the following two topics on usage in some reporting tools:

- The first topic illustrates **Query Print Layout Designer (QPLD)** including:
  - Simple query report printing
  - Working with a QPLD report
  - Creating/Editing/Deleting a QPLD report
  - Working with Print Layout Designer for a QPLD report

- The other topic explains the SQL query usage within **Crystal Reports**. It focuses on **Command** in the database expert selection of Crystal Reports. This includes:
  - Direct query for Crystal Reports (Command)
  - Working with Standard Report Wizard
  - Creating a new database connection
  - Adding a Command to a report
  - Working with a Command
  - Basic formatting for a Crystal Report

Query Print Layout Designer (QPLD) and its usage

Query creation and examples are important. However, as a query report, it may not be good enough to only view it on the screen. Quite often you need to print it out.

The most common practice to create a report is by using SAP Business One's "Export to Excel" function to export the query results to an Excel Spreadsheet and then reformat the data into the report required. It is a time consuming task. Another easy method to print out a query result is to choose **Print** from the **File** menu directly, or to use the keyboard shortcut *Ctrl+P*. However, the result of this simple print method yields a different report from ones generated by the QPLD. In order to show you the differences between a report by this simple print and a report by Query Print Layout Designer, the results from the simple print method will be shown first.

One simple query to make attachment statistics has been created for this chapter. All query results are returned as numbers. This is designed to reduce the reliance on the data but is focused on the report format. The query script is as follows:

```
SELECT T0.CntctDate,
Max(T0.atcentry) As 'AttachID',
T0.Closed,
Count(T0.CntctDate) AS 'No. of Attach',
Min(T0.UserSign) 'User'

FROM dbo.OCLG T0

WHERE T0.Atcentry > 0 and
T0.CntctDate> [%0] and T0.CntctDate< [%1]

GROUP BY T0.CntctDate, Closed

ORDER BY T0.CntctDate Desc
```

As shown in the following screenshot, the query is saved under the general category:

The query is named **Attachment Statistics**. By pressing *Enter* key or double-clicking on the query name, the query can be opened from the menu:

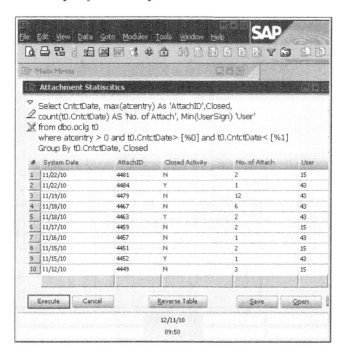

Simple query report printing

You can print the query in the previous screenshot by selecting **Print** from the **File** menu, or by using the shortcut *Ctrl+P*. A **Print preferences** window will then pop up. You have two **Printing options** to choose from:

- Window
- Table

Table would be a natural selection for the query report. You will have the option to change the report title so that it can be different from your query name. By default, the user name and date will be added to the report. If you don't want them, you have to uncheck those checkboxes.

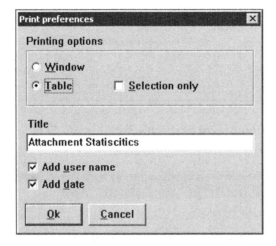

After clicking on **OK**, a query report will be printed out with the table option as follows:

#	System Date	AttachID	Closed Activity	No. of Attach	User
1	11/22/10	4481	N	2	15
2	11/22/10	4484	Y	1	43
3	11/19/10	4479	N	12	43
4	11/18/10	4467	N	6	43
5	11/18/10	4463	Y	2	43
6	11/17/10	4459	N	2	15
7	11/16/10	4457	N	1	43
8	11/15/10	4451	N	2	15
9	11/15/10	4452	Y	1	43
10	11/12/10	4449	N	3	15
=					

The page header and report title are omitted here due to space constraints. All reports will look similar to the format as shown in the previous screenshot when you print this way.

You have another option to print out by **Window** instead of by **Table**:

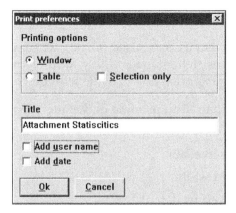

Using this option, the report looks similar to a screenshot plus a title. That is why this option is not normally used. The majority of users select the **Table** option and also another check box **Selection only**. By checking this option, only the selected area of the table will be printed. But for an example of how the "Window" option printout looks see the results in the next screenshot:

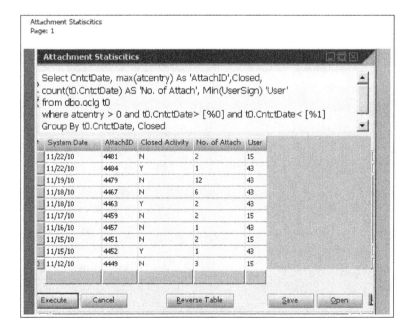

Query Print Layout Designer

Compared with regular query printing, a better option is to use a system tool called Query Print Layout Designer. It is usually abbreviated to Query PLD or QPLD. The term **Print Layout Designer (PLD)** represents a printing tool exclusively developed for SAP Business One. PLD will not be discussed here since it is out of the scope of this book. If you have further interest in PLD, you can refer to related documents.

QPLD has the advantage that it can be used quickly whenever you need to show your query results in a consistent manner with your preferred styles. It can either be printed out to a printer or exported as a PDF file with much better readability.

QPLD has more options than plain printing of the query. Some of these options include:

- More text formats available
- Customizable field width
- Parameter displayed by default
- Logo, picture, or formula fields to be added

There are many other options that are omitted and not listed here. In general, most functions supported by PLD will be available to QPLD.

QPLD is available through the following menu item shown in the next screenshot. The full menu path can be found from the **Tools | Queries | Query Print Layout...**.

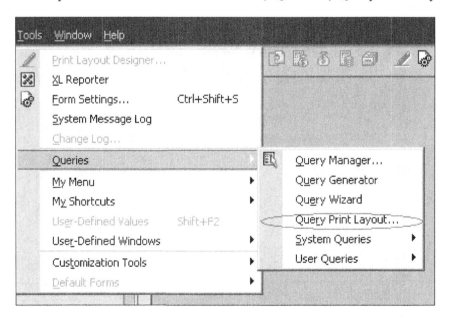

When the QPLD form is opened, you will find two tabs:

- **Reports**
- **Templates**

The **Reports** tab holds all QPLD reports that you have saved.

The **Templates** tab saves all QPLD templates that can be used as a base for your report.

You can get two screenshots for one tab, each illustrated as follows.

The following is the screenshot for the **Reports** tab:

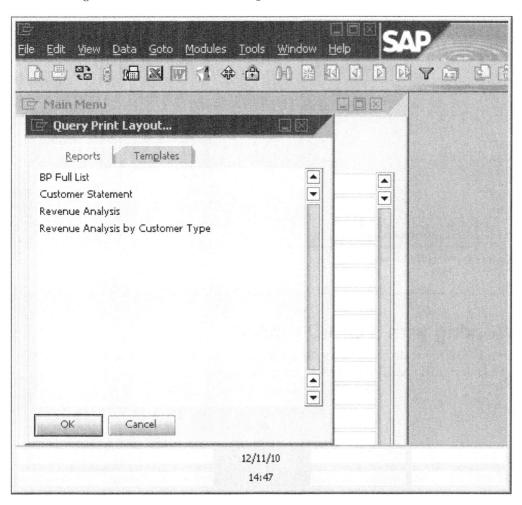

The following is the screenshot for the **Templates** tab:

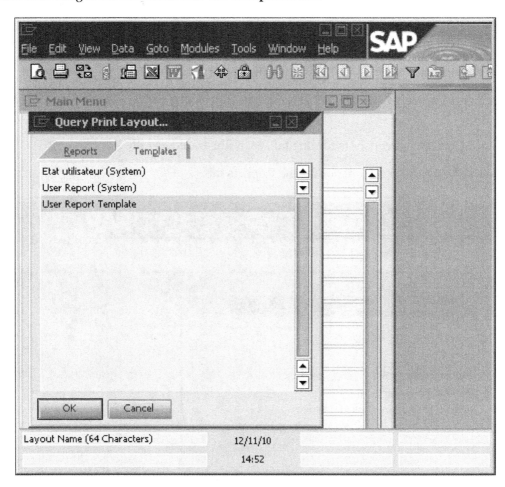

Working with a QPLD report

If you want to create a QPLD report for the queries, each query will require its own QPLD designed specifically for this individual query.

Creating a QPLD report

We start with the same query "Attachment Statistics", which was used for simple query printing in the previous section.

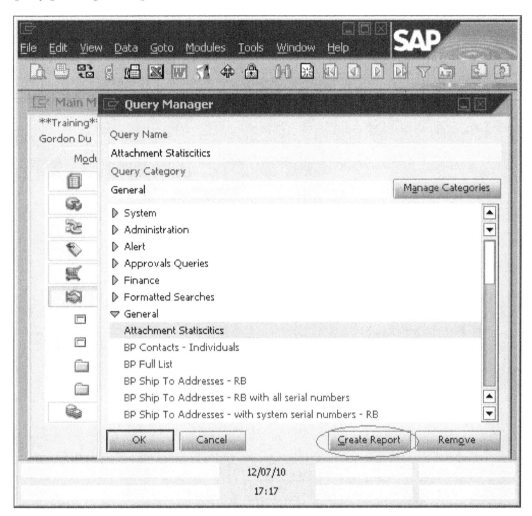

Notice the **Create Report** button under the query manager form, as shown in the previous screenshot. When you click on this button, a QPLD form will be opened similar to the one found in the next screenshot. The form title is: **Create User Report.** The upper part of the form is for inputting or modifying the **Name** of the report. You can accept the query name as the report name or change it to any name you like. The lower part is **Base Template** for you to choose from and start a new report. You must select one template; it is mandatory.

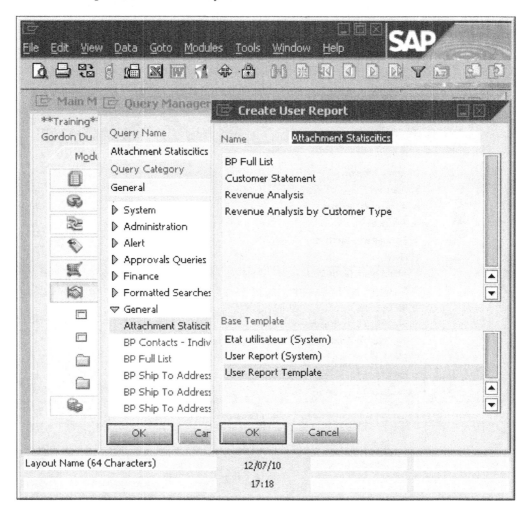

A default name that is the same as the query name has been accepted. And the base template has been selected as **User Report template**. After you click **OK**, the QPLD is added to the system. You are then taken back to the query manager screen. The next screenshot shows the newly created QPLD on top of the list.

The best practice is to add a version number, or possibly a date, to the end of the report name in case additional report layouts from the same data are required in the future.

Editing a QPLD report

To edit the newly created QPLD, you can go to the menu or use key combination *Alt+TQR*. Your newly created QPLD name is ready for you to pick.

 Base template is nothing but a special QPLD report where you can make a special style to fit your need. The editing of the template is exactly the same as editing a normal QPLD report. In order to maintain your report with the same style, you need to create a well-designed template first.

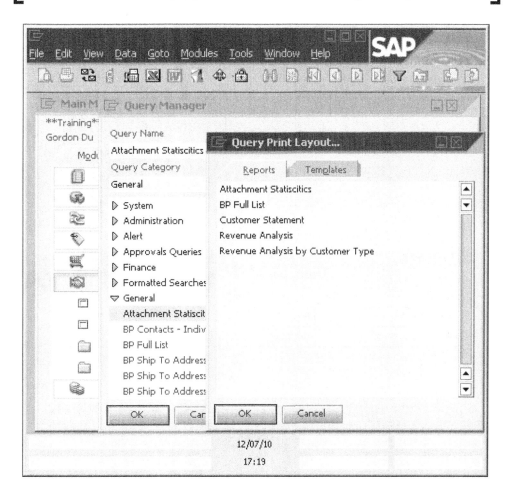

Working with Print Layout Designer for a QPLD report

When you double-click the selected QPLD report name, the QPLD opens. This action changes the toolbar at the top of the screen so that you can use either the Print Layout Designer top menu or the icons from the toolbar to access PLD functions.

The QPLD report selected from the previous screen is the one created from the last action. This QPLD contains three forms:

- QPLD layout—in this case, **Attachment Statistics**.
- Field Index
- Property

The whole screen is too large to fit in the book page. I have squeezed these forms into smaller sizes so that you can have them in one place with much larger text size.

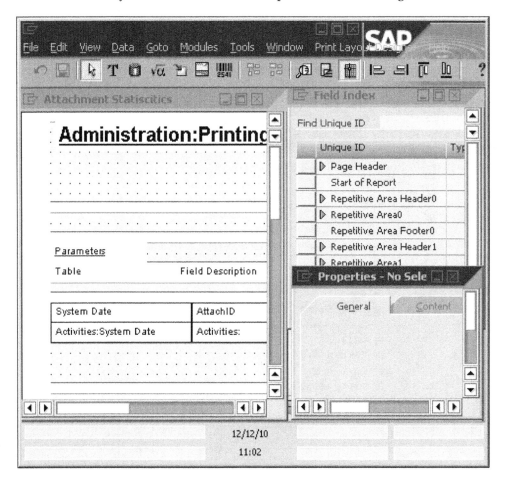

Working with a property form when editing QPLD

Suppose you need to change one of the default fields on the **Page Header** from a database field **Administration: Printing Header** to a static text field that just shows your query report title, the first thing you need to do is to select the field.

You may click on the area in the QPLD to select the field or go to the **Field Index** form to browse each field. The first method is always the preferred option as long as you don't have too many fields in the query report, especially any hidden fields.

After you have selected the area, the **Properties** form shows the **General** tab with information regarding the **Unique ID**, **Height**, and a checkbox to decide if the area or fields need to be visible or not.

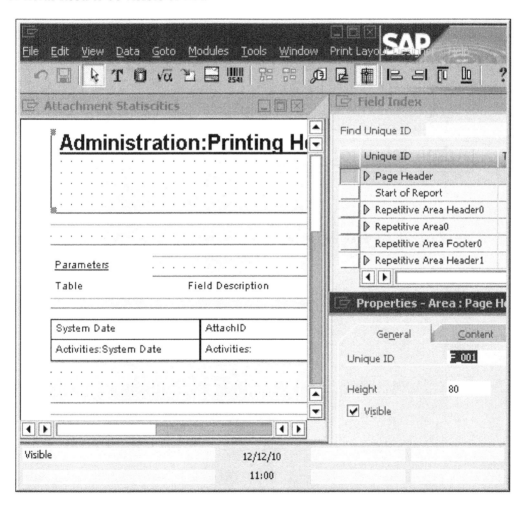

For the selection in this example, the **Page Header** area is selected. You can see that the **Page Header** is highlighted under the **Field Index** form. The **Unique** ID for this field is **F_001**. **Height** is 80, which stands for the pixels of the entire area. The **Visible** check is selected by default. If you want to hide any areas or fields, you can simply uncheck this box.

Editing QPLD field content and the limitation in editing

Only selecting an area is not sufficient. To change any field, make certain that you have selected an individual field and not just an area on the print layout. An example here is to click on the text of **Administration: Printing Header** to select this field. When you have selected this field, the **Page Header** section under **Field Index** is expanded. From the **Index** form, you can find the unique ID of this field, which is F_007.

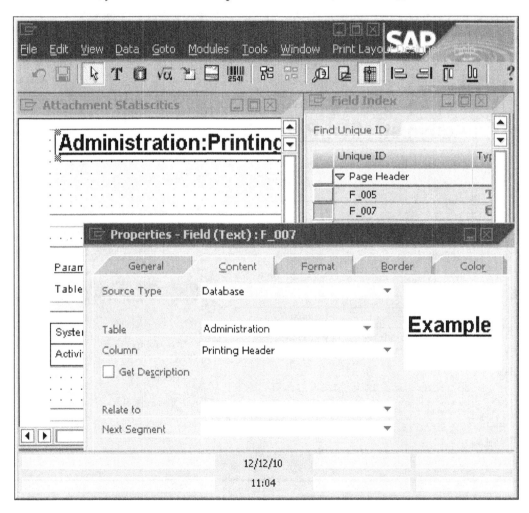

To change this field, the first thing to do is select the second tab, which is **Content**. The first option under content is **Source Type**. There are four source types available:

Source Type	Description
Free Text	Any free entered strings or numbers
Database	A database table field from a preselected table list
Formula	A formula from build in function within PLD
System Variable	A variable defined by the system but not available to QPLD

The fourth source type option **System Variable** is only available to documents or master data PLD. It is not available to QPLD. Type option is also very limited to a few number of tables and fields. They do not link to your query. Avoid wasting your time on this. Refer to the previous screenshot to find out.

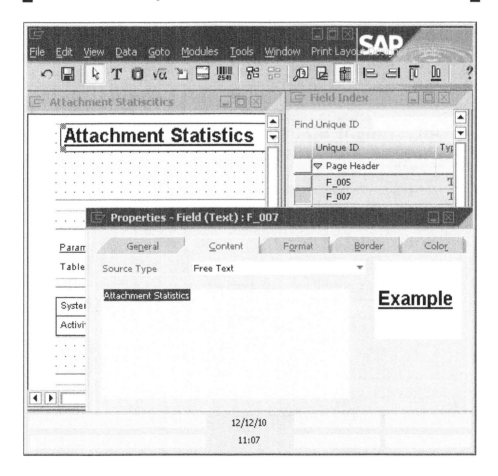

If the selected field type is the database type, there are more options available because there are more properties. You need to select **Table**, **Column**, **Relate to**, and **Next Segment**. However, this type is not good for QPLD use. It is mainly for normal PLD.

Changing field type of QPLD

To change this field to a text field, you can select the **Free Text** field type. When the source type is selected as **Free Text**, the text area below the source can be used to write any free forming texts. In this example, **Attachment Statistics** is typed in to reflect the name of QPLD.

On the right side of the **Content** tab of the properties form, you can find a small square box. This box is used for field format preview. All settings under the **Format** tab will be shown here such as font, style, color, border, and shade. If you are not satisfied with the result the system provides, you can change the settings under the **Format** tab.

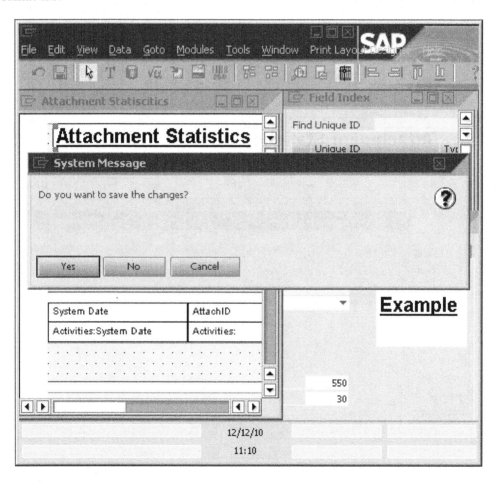

Saving a QPLD report

When the field change is completed, you can click on the close window icon (a boxed-cross at the top right corner of the QPLD).

The system then pops up a message: **Do you want to save the change?** Click **Yes** to change. If you select **Save** from the PLD menu without closing it, you will get the same message.

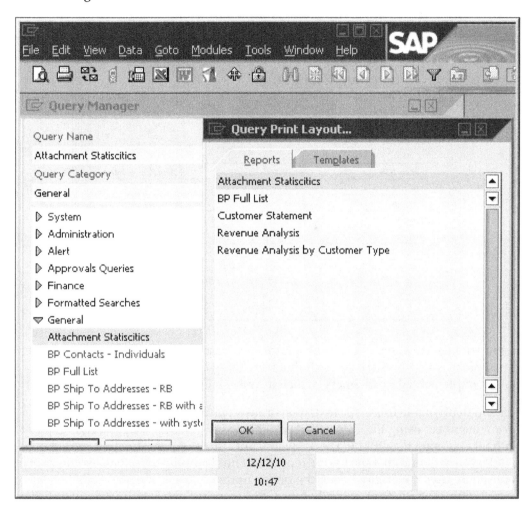

Printing a QPLD report

To print out the QPLD report, select the report you want to print out or preview from the QPLD menu. Then select the toolbar icons or file menu items **Print** or **Print Preview** to complete the task. A print preview screenshot can be found next:

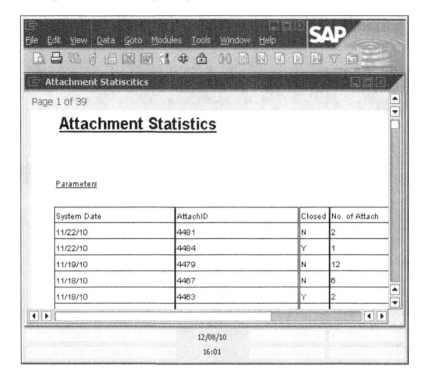

In the print preview, the page count sounds incorrect. If you have gone through the actual process step-by-step, you will find something is wrong. The 'where clause' is not yet implemented in the query, which means the QPLD is still using the old query.

I intentionally made this error to demonstrate an important point often asked by forum members using the QPLD: Is it possible to only change the underlying query without changing the QPLD? The answer is unfortunately: "No". If you keep the QPLD, you will find that the QPLD report will not be updated to the new query. The report only uses the original query before an update. This is one reason to have a version number or date at the end of the QPLD report.

Deleting a QPLD report

As a matter of the fact, the QPLD always uses a copy of the query during QPLD report creation. There is no link between the query under query manager and the QPLD created.

The only solution is to delete and recreate the QPLD. To save time, make sure you update the template to retain the customized contents and formats.

The function to delete QPLD can be found on the PLD menu. A system message: **Delete Document?** pops up after you select the delete PLD option.

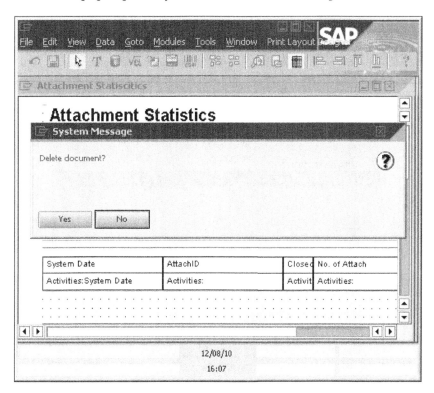

When you click **OK** to allow deletion, the old QPLD will be deleted. You are able to add new QPLD based on the updated query that includes the missing where clause.

Recreating the QPLD report

You can still use the same name as the old QPLD when you create a new QPLD for the newly edited query. A new template from the first QPLD can be used as a base template, so that you do not need to repeat what you have done for the old QPLD.

After making the correction, you will find the correct query running behavior because the **Query — Selection Criteria** window pops up before the print preview. This is the expected result because there are two parameters set up in the sample to restrict the date range for the report. Two **System Dates** are shown in the following screenshots with two input boxes to the right.

Some users have questions regarding the parameter descriptions. Sometimes they are not satisfied with the way descriptions are displayed. Unfortunately, all those descriptions are built into the application. It is not possible to change them. You need to properly train your users regarding the query. Let users know what parameters are expected.

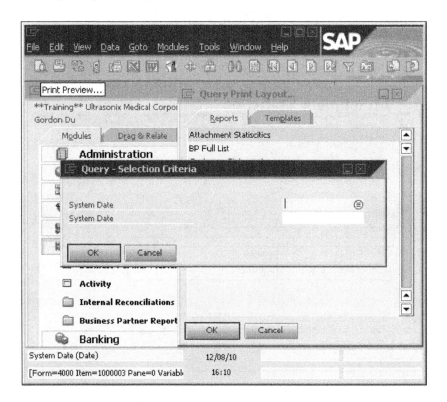

To input the parameters, there are two options:

- Select the existing value from the list by clicking on the button to the right of the box
- Input manually

The first option is normally the preferred option because the input box only accepts the correct values from the list. Manual input is a good choice when the parameter is set up as a fuzzy value, such as %[%0]%.

In this example, two fixed dates are needed to be used as the "from date" and "to date". Any valid dates can be used. You can save some keystrokes by typing in a number that is less than 31 to get the date in the current month, or by typing in any letters to get the current date.

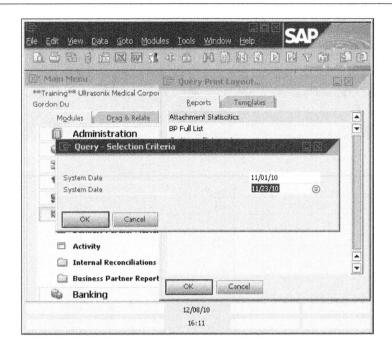

After filling in with two dates, you can click on **OK** to bring up the report to the screen. The screenshot is as follows. You will notice the page number shows **1 of 1**.

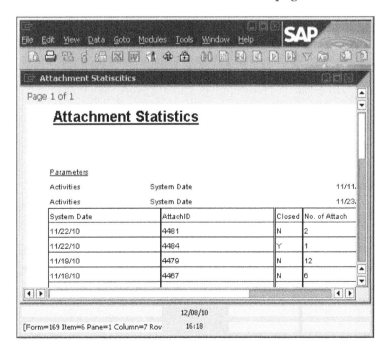

You can then move around in the report by using the *Page Down*, *Page Up*, or scroll bar. The following screenshot shows the movement within report:

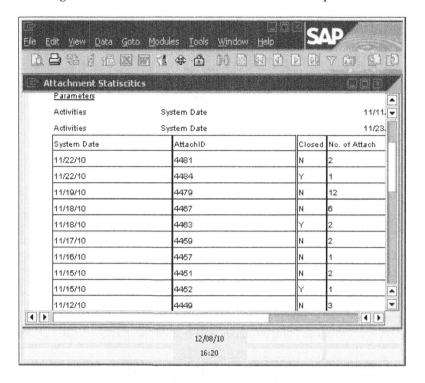

Before starting a PLD, ensure that you have reviewed the SQL results with the person who requested the report. This is a critical step in ensuring you can use everyone's time effectively.

Direct query for Crystal Reports (Command)

Crystal Reports, a SAP product, is a business intelligence application used to design and generate reports from a wide range of data sources.

Since version 8.8, Crystal Reports became an integrated reporting tool for SAP Business One. Prior to this version, there is a "Crystal Reports Integration for SAP Business one" add-on available. In both situations, you can use **Crystal Reports Designer**.

The following section contains query-related functions in Crystal Reports. This is called Command for Crystal Reports. This tool ensures that the query can function as the kernel for a crystal report without worrying about the complicated links if you build a report from multiple tables directly. You can reuse some queries under user query category directly to get better formatted reports. Crystal Reports is much more powerful than QPLD. If you need a professional final touch for the report, Crystal Reports should be selected first.

For this section, the assumption is that you have Crystal Reports Designer installed and ready to run. Otherwise, the topic would be extremely difficult to understand. All screenshots in this section are generated from Crystal Reports Designer.

Working with Standard Report Wizard

We start from the **Standard Report Creation Wizard** form as shown next. You will get two windows within the form. The **Available Data Source** window is on the left side while the **Selected Tables** window is on the right side.

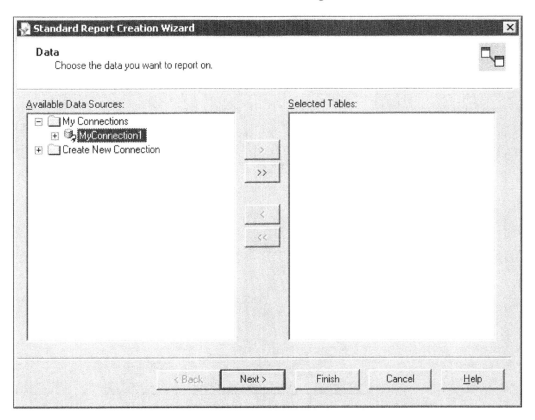

To show you this function, the initial screens and some other parts of Crystal Report Designer screens are omitted. If you are not familiar with how to run Crystal Reports in general, you need to check some other resources.

To create a crystal report, the first thing to do is choose a suitable data source. The wizard shows you all available data sources from the operating system.

There are two items under **Available Data Sources**:

- **My Connections**
- **Create New Connection**

Creating a new database connection

Creating new connection is the initial step for any reports. As soon as you create a new connection, it is shown under **My Connections**. You can expand **Create New Connection** by clicking the Expand icon to the left of the text.

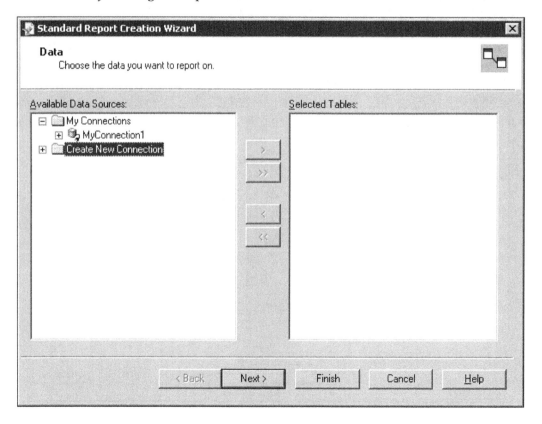

You will get some available data sources from the connected SQL server. The next two screenshots show some of the data sources. For SAP Business One database, you can use ODBC, OLE DB (ADO), or other compatible sources. Both ODBC and OLE DB are acceptable sources. In this sample, we select OLE DB (ADO).

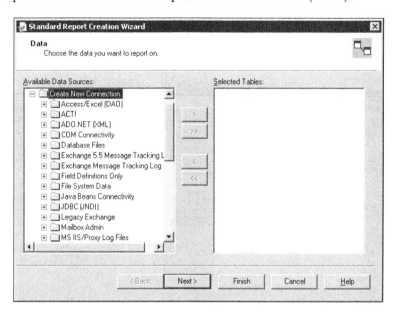

The next screenshot shows the same available data source after scrolling down a few lines of the list:

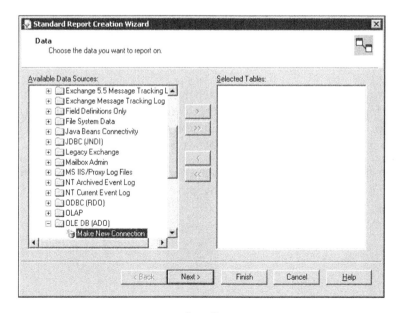

After expanding OLE DB (ADO) data source, you will get an option to **Make New Connection**. You need to double-click on the link. This action brings up another window that lists all OLE DB Providers. You have an additional option to **Use Date Link File** in this window as well.

Within a dozen of OLE DB providers, SQL Native Client is normally at the bottom of the list because of the alphabetical order. SQL Native Client is selected for this sample report.

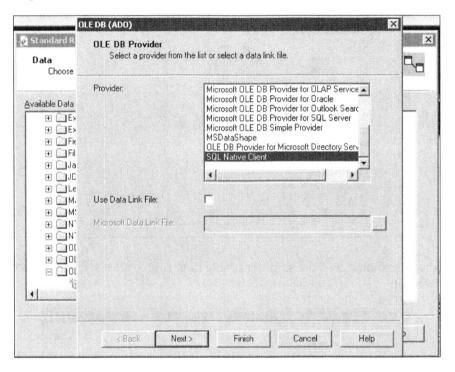

There is a **Use Data Link File** option under the **Provider**. It actually requires a file (.udl), which provides connection (string) to an **ActiveX Data Objects** (**ADO**). Every time the report runs, it retrieves the connection string from the file, which could affect system performance and that is why we will not select this option.

After the selection, you will get two **Next** buttons. You have the option to click on **Finish** whenever you are satisfied with the system default or if you plan to complete it later.

Upon the first **Next** button click, the window proceeds to the **Connection Information** form. Under this form, you need to fill in the following:

- **Server**
- **User ID**
- **Password**
- **Database**

There is another check box: **Integrated Security**. If this box is checked, the **User ID** and **Password** are greyed out. In this case, only server and database need to be selected. Integrated security uses the current Windows identity established on the operating system thread to access the SQL Server database. You can then map the Windows identity to a SQL Server database and permissions. That is why those boxes are greyed out.

If **Integrated Security** is not checked, you must enter a valid **User ID** and **Password** to connect to the database. The root user for a SQL Server — **sa** is usually entered here.

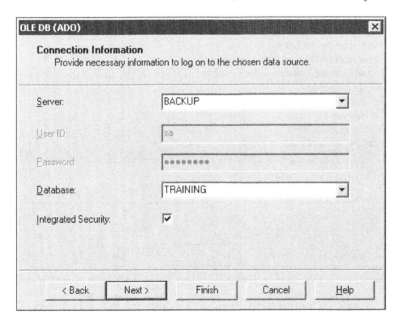

The second **Next** will show you the **Advanced Information** form. Under this form, you have three options:

- **Add Property**
- **Edit Value**
- **Remove Property**

These properties are so advanced that normally only a database administrator would be able to differentiate them. They do not need to be touched for a regular report.

The **Back** button allows you to go to the previous step at any given point.

Clicking on the **Finish** button is needed in order to complete the connection selection.

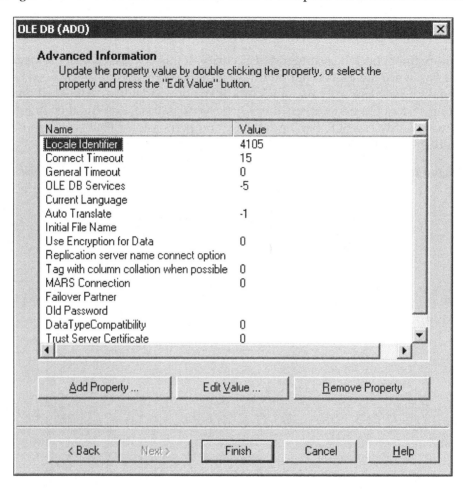

As soon as you click on **Finish** in the **Create New Connection** stage, your new connection is shown under My Connections. You can have more than one connection.

Under any of these connections, there are also two options:

- **Add Command**
- **Database Connected that is expandable**

Adding a Command to a report

From here you can go to the normal route to select any table directly. However, that is not the topic for this book. Add Command is all you need.

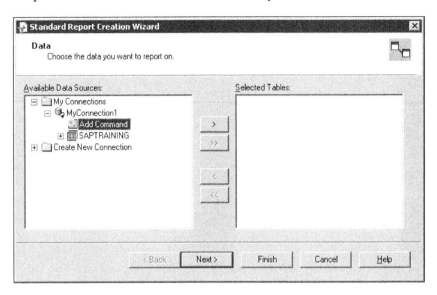

By double-clicking on **Add Command**, a new form pops up. The title of the form is: **Add Command to Report**. You can enter or copy any SQL queries here in the large text box area to the left side of the form. The box has a clear title: **Enter SQL Query in the box below**. The right-side box is for maintaining a parameter list. It is not tightly related to the query, so it will not be discussed in the book.

Two screenshots are shown next to illustrate two different views. One is only with an empty text box and the other shows a SQL query filled box. The query is the same query found on the first page of this chapter except one minor change in the Where clause.

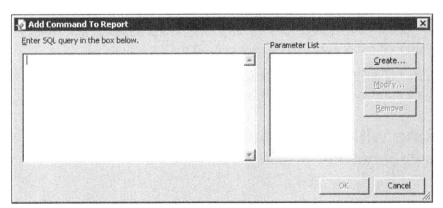

`T0.CntctDate> [%0]` and `T0.CntctDate< [%1]` in the original query is not a valid statement for Crystal Reports. It has to be dropped off.

Examining the empty box, you will find that the **OK** button is disabled if nothing has been entered. As long as you have entered a valid SQL query script, you can click **OK** to add the command to the report.

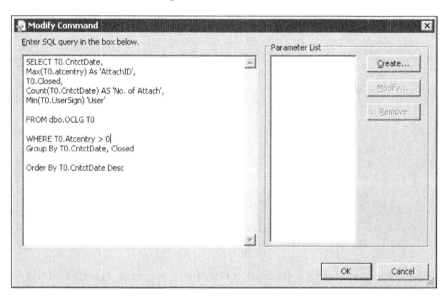

The system validates the query after you click **OK**. If the query has problems, you will receive appropriate error messages and the add command will fail. A valid query is mandatory. The best way to minimize this error would be to run the query first under query manager or SQL Server management studio, and make sure it is working. The only restriction here is that you are not allowed to use [%] as a parameter. You can add parameter fields to the report itself. It is much more convenient.

After validation, the **Command** is displayed on the right side of the form. It is treated as one of the **Selected Tables**. You can still select some other normal tables if the **Command** does not cover everything you need for the report.

To simplify the illustration of the **Command** function, you will only get this particular **Command** under the **Selected Tables**.

Working with a Command

After you have created a Command, you can work with it.

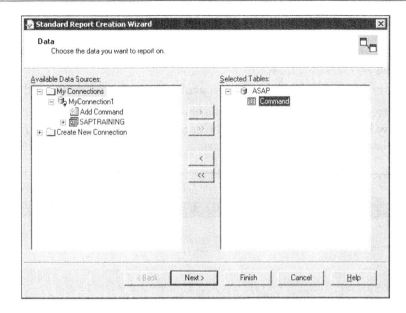

Click **Next**, and you will open up the **Fields** form. Under the left-side box, all **Available Fields** in the **Command** will be listed. The right side of the form is for **Fields to Display**.

Selecting fields from a Command

The first task to work with a Command is selecting fields from it.

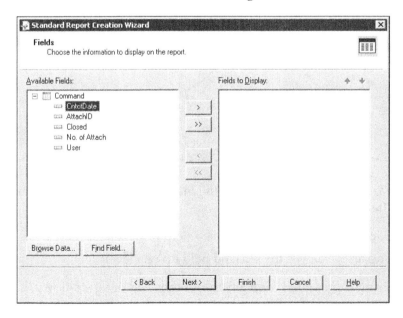

There are four buttons in the middle of the form:

- The top button with a single left arrow is used for selecting one field to display.

- The next button with a double left arrow is used to select all fields to display.

- The two right arrow buttons under these two top buttons reverse the left arrow buttons' functionalities. You can take out one or all fields from the display by using these two buttons.

For simplicity, we chose them all by clicking on the double left arrow.

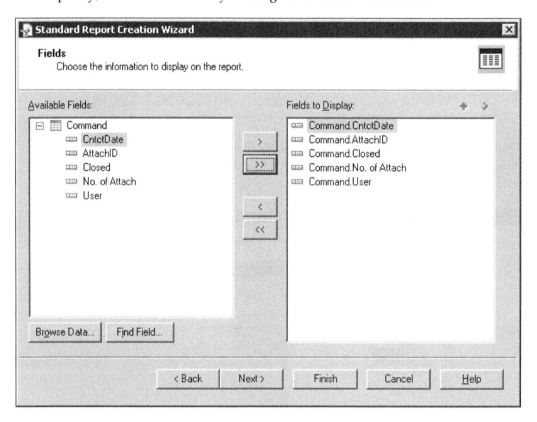

There are two arrows at the top right of the **Fields to Display** box that can be used to reorder the fields:

- The down arrow moves the selected field down one level

- The up arrow moves the selected field up one level

The actual result is presented from left-to-right instead of top-to-down, if you accept default report layout for detail records.

Under the **Available Fields** box, there are two buttons:

- Browse Data
- Find Fields

These two buttons are only useful if you have too many available fields to select from. In that case, to find a field quickly, you need to use either the **Browse Data** or **Find Fields** function. The usage of these functions is not elaborated here.

Working with two optional forms—records selection and templates

Click **Next** from here, and you will get the **Records Selection** form.

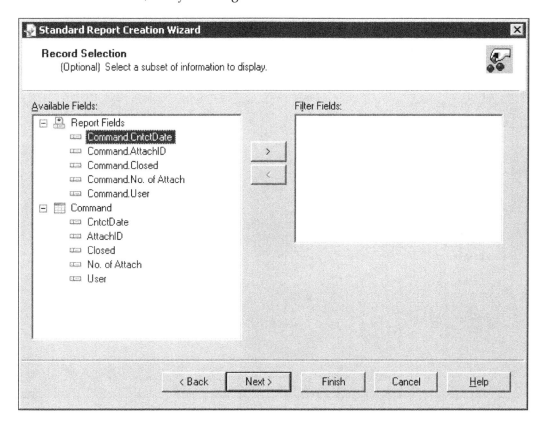

This is an optional form. Using this form you can select a subset of information to display. First is selecting the **Filter Fields** from command fields or report fields. Then set the filter condition to restrict the scope of the records.

The form acts as a WHERE clause in SQL query. Any conditions listed here are treated as permanent filters. Only records that meet all filter conditions can be returned.

Since we can use the WHERE clauses in the query script directly, this function may not be needed for Command. It is mostly used by a report with table data source only.

Now we can click on **Next** to bring up the last optional form.

The last optional form is used for selecting report format. The default selection is **No Template**.

After accepting the default selection, you can click on **Finish** to finish this **Standard Report Creation Wizard**.

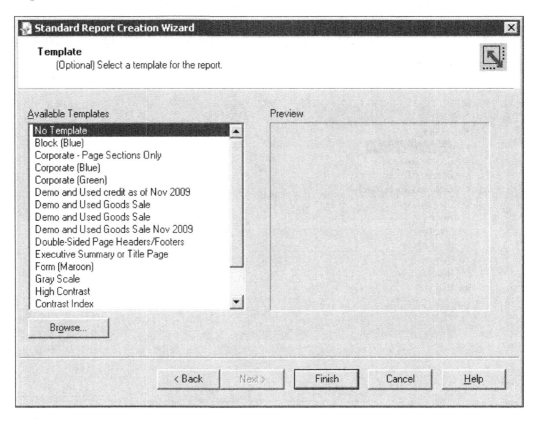

No template means the report only has very simple output. It looks like the default QPLD report with little formatting.

Basic formatting for a Crystal Report

From the first report output, the date format and number format seems odd. In order to resolve this issue, you can select the field and change the field format.

```
16/12/2010

CntctDate                    AttachID  Closed  No. of Attach
22/11/2010  12:00:00AM         4,481   N               2
22/11/2010  12:00:00AM         4,484   Y               1
19/11/2010  12:00:00AM         4,479   N              12
18/11/2010  12:00:00AM         4,467   N               6
18/11/2010  12:00:00AM         4,463   Y               2
17/11/2010  12:00:00AM         4,459   N               2
16/11/2010  12:00:00AM         4,457   N               1
15/11/2010  12:00:00AM         4,451   N               2
15/11/2010  12:00:00AM         4,452   Y               1
12/11/2010  12:00:00AM         4,449   N               3
11/11/2010  12:00:00AM         4,447   N              14
11/11/2010  12:00:00AM         4,429   Y               2
10/11/2010  12:00:00AM         4,433   N               2
```

For a date field, there are dozens of formats to choose from. An mm/dd/yyyy format is selected instead of the default date format with the time included.

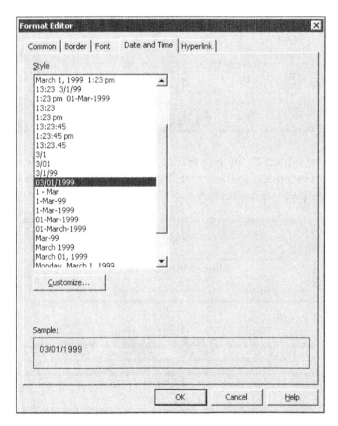

For the number field, because the report field AttachID is not a regular number but an identifier, it can be changed to No Thousand's separator.

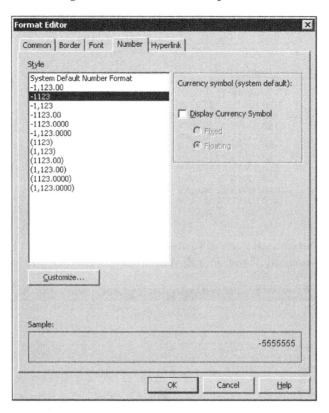

A report title can be added to the **Report Header** or to the **Page Header**. For this report, the title can be added to the report header so that the title does not get displayed on every page of the report.

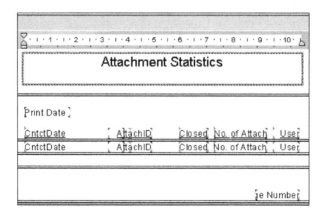

After all these changes, you can get a better looking report as follows:

Attachment Statistics			
16/12/2010			
CntctDate	AttachID	Closed	No. of Attach
11/22/2010	4,481	N	2
11/22/2010	4,484	Y	1
11/19/2010	4,479	N	12
11/18/2010	4,467	N	6
11/18/2010	4,463	Y	2
11/17/2010	4,459	N	2
11/16/2010	4,457	N	1
11/15/2010	4,451	N	2
11/15/2010	4,452	Y	1
11/12/2010	4,449	N	3
11/11/2010	4,447	N	14
11/11/2010	4,429	Y	2

The template function is very powerful. If you decide to try other templates, that's always possible. The default look of the report is based on the selected new template.

In the following example, the **Table Grid Template** has been selected instead of **No Template**:

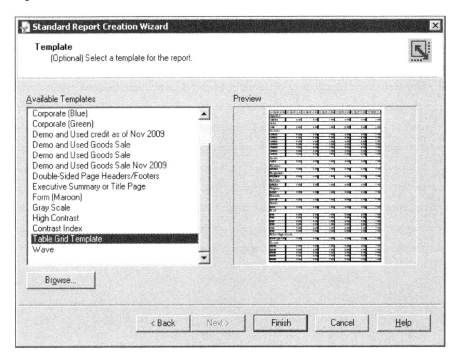

The manually edited date and number field formats need to be applied again:

CntctDate	AttachID	Closed	No. of Attach	User
22/11/2010 12:00	4,481	N	2	15
22/11/2010 12:00	4,484	Y	1	43
19/11/2010 12:00	4,479	N	12	43
18/11/2010 12:00	4,467	N	6	43
18/11/2010 12:00	4,463	Y	2	43
17/11/2010 12:00	4,459	N	2	15
16/11/2010 12:00	4,457	N	1	43
15/11/2010 12:00	4,451	N	2	15
15/11/2010 12:00	4,452	Y	1	43
12/11/2010 12:00	4,449	N	3	15
11/11/2010 12:00	4,447	N	14	43
11/11/2010 12:00	4,429	Y	2	43

After the second edit, you can get a better looking report as follows:

CntctDate	AttachID	Closed	No. of Attach	User
11/22/2010	4481	N	2	15
11/22/2010	4484	Y	1	43
11/19/2010	4479	N	12	43
11/18/2010	4467	N	6	43
11/18/2010	4463	Y	2	43
11/17/2010	4459	N	2	15
11/16/2010	4457	N	1	43
11/15/2010	4451	N	2	15
11/15/2010	4452	Y	1	43
11/12/2010	4449	N	3	15
11/11/2010	4447	N	14	43
11/11/2010	4429	Y	2	43

Summary

In this chapter, we discussed two main areas of SAP Business One reporting tools to increase the query's usage. You learned Query Print Layout Designer and Command for Crystal Reports.

By using these tools, you can generate user-friendly reports.

Query Print Layout Designer (QPLD) has the advantage of being used quickly whenever you need to show your query results in a consistent manner using your favorite style.

You learned how to create, edit, and delete QPLD.

Command for Crystal Reports ensures that the query can be the kernel for a Crystal Report with no need to worry about the complicated links if you build the report from multiple tables directly.

You leaned how to create data connections. Last but not least, you learned how to add Command for Crystal Reports as well as some Report formatting and presentation.

In the next chapter, you will have another tool to master: the only legitimate store procedure allowed for SAP Business One — SBO Transaction Notification.

8
SQL Query for a Stored Procedure

In the previous chapter, we learned about two printing tools for SQL query: Query Print Layout Design and query for Crystal Reports. This chapter focuses on one of the very special cases for SQL query usages. It is regarding the query used in a special **Stored Procedure (SP)** called **SBO_SP_TransactionNotification**. The chapter focuses on the following:

- Why this Stored Procedure is included in the book
- SBO_SP_TransactionNotification overview
- How to work with this SP
- Multiple examples for the SP including its core SQL queries

Why Stored Procedure is included in this book

Stored Procedure is a subroutine available to applications accessing a relational database system. In the case of SAP Business One, the database accessed is Microsoft SQL Server. Stored Procedures are mainly used to simplify the database development process by grouping Transact-SQL statements into manageable blocks.

It might sound like this topic does not fit with this book. However, if you examine the query usages within SAP Business One carefully, query for this SP usage is never a trivial part to be ignored. This SP can turn out to be extremely useful. Based on some example data, I have analyzed the distribution ratio of the query usages by the following chart:

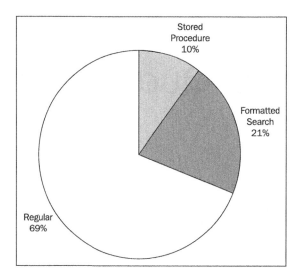

I have broken down 100 random queries by normal users into three categories:

- Stored Procedure
- Formatted Search
- Regular

There are no overlaps between each category. Queries for stored procedure and queries for formatted search are easily identifiable. If none of them apply, the query will be categorized as regular.

In the statistics, the percentage for stored procedure may not be exactly right. This ratio should be close to formatted search. The smaller percentage is due to the fact that I have answered many more questions on the formatted search query as opposed to stored procedures. I have only counted what I have answered.

SBO_SP_TransactionNotification overview

The SBO_SP_TransactionNotification is the only legal way in SAP Business One to do a validation with this stored procedure.

It is mainly used to prevent the user from performing an action if the validation condition failed. The mechanism of this SP works by receiving notification of data-driven events from the system.

This stored procedure is created automatically with each database. A simple skeleton to show this SP structure is as follows:

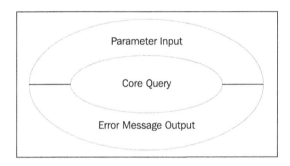

A default empty SP is shown as follows:

```
SET ANSI_NULLS ON
SET QUOTED_IDENTIFIER ON
GO

ALTER proc [dbo].[SBO_SP_TransactionNotification]

@object_type nvarchar(20),    -- SBO Object Type
@transaction_type nchar(1),   -- [A]dd, [U]pdate, [D]elete, [C]ancel,
C[L]ose
@num_of_cols_in_key int,
@list_of_key_cols_tab_del nvarchar(255),
@list_of_cols_val_tab_del nvarchar(255)

AS

begin

-- Return values
declare @error int            -- Result (0 for no error)
```

```
declare @error_message nvarchar (200)   -- Error string to be
displayed
select @error = 0
select @error_message = N'Ok'



----------------------------------------------------------------
----------------------------------------------------------------


-- ADD  YOUR  CODE  HERE

----------------------------------------------------------------
----------------------------------------------------------------


FINISH:
-- Select the return values
select @error, @error_message

end
```

The first two sets of clauses are only meaningful for the database administrator. We do not need to discuss them in this book.

There are five input parameters and two output values.

The five input parameters are as follows:

- **@object_type nvarchar(20)**: This stands for the object type in SAP Business One; the complete object type list can be found in the appendix of this book.
- **@transaction_type nchar(1)**: Five valid transaction type values allowed are:
  - A for add
  - U for update
  - D for delete
  - C for cancel
  - L for close
- **@num_of_cols_in_key int**: Numbers of key columns in the table.
- **@list_of_key_cols_tab_del nvarchar(255)**: Key column name.
- **@list_of_cols_val_tab_del nvarchar(255)**: Value in the key column. This is the most useful parameter to link the current transaction by this SP.

As you can see, the structure for all samples remain the same and only the inside query or logic changes.

Beginning with the 2007 version, there are four related Stored Procedures for SAP Business One:

- SBO_SP_PostTransactionSupport
- SBO_SP_TransactionSupport (since SAP Business One 2007)
- SBO_SP_PostTransactionNotice (since SAP Business One 2007)
- SBO_SP_TransactionNotification

Let us see what these Stored Procedures' functions are:

The first two encoded Stored Procedures named SBO_SP_TransactionSupport and SBO_SP_PostTransactionSupport cannot be edited by the user. They are database notification stored procedures, which can be used by SAP support only. They are used to add diagnostic code, so they are of no use for the customer's daily work. Due to this reason they are removed in SAP Business One Version 8.8.

SBO_SP_PostTransactionNotice and SBO_SP_TransactionNotification are the only Stored Procedures where a user can add SQL code to be a part of the notification process. The functionalities of both are the same. The only differences are when they are triggered and the ability to use the @error functionality of SBO_SP_TransactionNotification to rollback transactions.

SBO_SP_PostTransactionNotice is triggered at the end of an action (transaction committed). It is preferable to use SBO_SP_PostTransactionNotice. However, because this occurs after the transaction, the @error rollback functionality can not be used. SBO_SP_TransactionNotification is the main SP that most companies can use to help SAP Business One fit their business process without investing a lot of time and money in the SDK development. The ability to rollback transaction by this SP can effectively help business rule enforcement.

How to work with SBO_SP_ TransactionNotification

This SP cannot be accessed or maintained within a SAP Business One application. You need to directly access Microsoft SQL Server Management Studio to work with it.

There is a simple way to access and maintain this SP

1. To open up the management studio. This is usually done by clicking a shortcut if you have standard SQL Server installation. Or you may go through **Start | All Programs | Microsoft SQL Server** to find the application to run.

2. To locate the database that you need to work with. Be careful with this step if you have multiple databases under one SQL Server. Each SP will only work within one specific database. Wrong database selection could cause serious problems. Always handle it with care.

 A good practice is to always work with this SP under a test environment. When you are fully satisfied with the SP results, you can then open up production database to insert your tested code.

The following screenshot displays the first screen after you run SQL Server Management Studio. There are two panels under menu and toolbars:

*   **Object Explorer**
*   **Object Explorer Details**

Object Explorer displays categorized objects for the entire SQL Server. **Object Explorer Details** shows the details of the selected objects.

The first objet under **Object Explorer** is **Databases**. This object is our main interest in this chapter. It needs to be expanded.

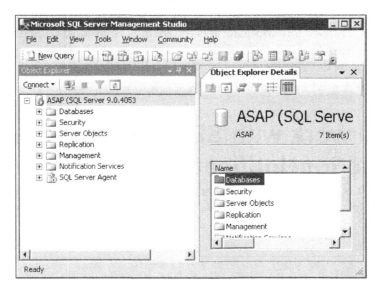

Object Explorer works very similar to Windows Explorer. You can browse the database list by expanding the category. Then you can locate the database you prefer. Once you locate the database, you can open up the selected database. The following objects can be found under the databases category:

- Database Diagrams
- Tables
- Views
- Synonyms
- Programmability
- Service Broker
- Storage
- Security

The **Programmability** category is the one that contains the required object. The first object under **Programmability** is the one you need:

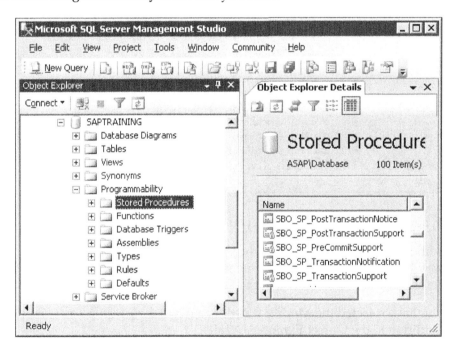

By expanding **Stored Procedures**, you can locate this SBO_SP_ TransactionNotification SP through an alphabetical order.

Under this SP, there is only one subobject. It is **Parameters**. You can get five parameters and a returns integer under parameters.

The details of the parameters have already been explained in the overview section of this SP. You may refer to the previous section if you have skipped that part.

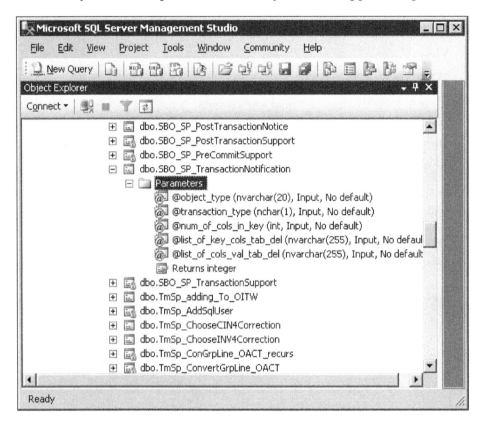

To add your own SQL code to this SP, you need to modify it.

The modified function can be found when you right-click on this selected SP. A window will pop up. Click the second item to choose **Modify**. The alternative is using the shortcut key *y* when you get the pop-up window.

When you have selected the **Modify** function, a new window pops up from the right side in addition to the **Object Explorer Details**.

The SP is editable now. You can copy the code you have written to the section that reads: **Add your code here.** You can also write directly under this window if you have confidence and a tight schedule.

It is recommended to click on the Parse or check mark icons to verify the grammar of your code. If you get the message: **Command(s) completed successfully**, it means the SP has no error in terms of grammar.

If you get an error, you can always check the line number indicated by the error message. Troubleshoot your SP until it passes the test. There are different methodologies to do the testing. However, it is beyond the scope of this book.

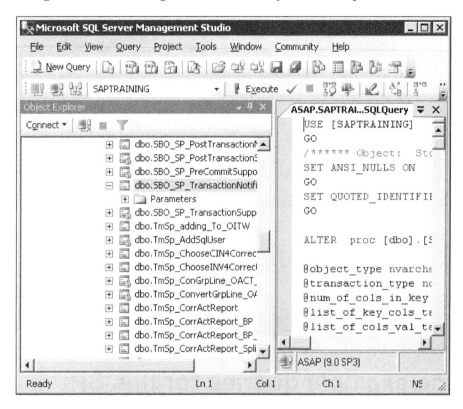

 You might want to copy the successfully tested stored procedure into a word processing document to ensure that you have a sound back up. If the test environment is refreshed or overwritten before you get a chance to insert it into the production environment, you will have saved a good amount of time and effort.

The final step is to save the modification. This can be done by closing this window. When you close it, the system will pop up a smaller window like the following screenshot. The message is clear: **Save changes to the following items?**

In the window, you can find all the edited SPs that need to be saved. If you know they are the right SPs, click **Yes**. If they should not be saved, click **No**. Or click **Cancel** if you still want to continue working with the SP.

In the screenshot, you can see only one SP inside the window. The name is **SQLQuery1.sql**. That is a temporary SP name before you save. If you have modified more than one SP in one session, you can get SQLQuery2.sql, SQLQuery3.sql, and so on. Do not work with more than one SP if you are not familiar with it.

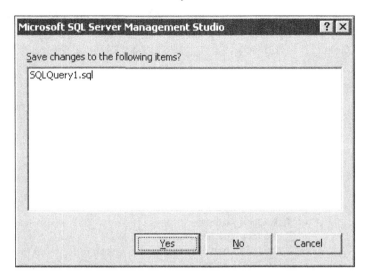

This concludes the procedures on how to work with this SP. As for how to write a correct SP, the following examples should give you some guidelines.

Some example queries for this SP

Within this book, you have already found quite a few example queries. There is no exception in this chapter. I do believe query by example is one of the most efficient ways to learn queries.

Case 1—Blocking an outgoing payment for a specific BP

A user is trying to block outgoing payments (Object 46) for a specific Business Partner for some reason by using the following SP:

```
IF (@Object_Type = '46') AND (@transaction_type in (N'A', N'U'))
BEGIN
```

```
IF EXISTs (SELECT T0.[DocEntry] FROM OVPM T0 WHERE
T0.[DocEntry] = @list_of_cols_val_tab_del and T0.CardCode = 'V0271')
BEGIN
  SET @error = 10
  SET @error_message = N'Block BP'
END
END
```

However, this SP blocks all outgoing payments for all BP Codes. What is the problem with this SP?

Check the following solution:

```
IF (@Object_Type='46') AND (@transaction_type in (N'A', N'U'))

BEGIN

IF Exists (SELECT T0.DocNum

FROM OVPM T0

WHERE T0.DocEntry = @list_of_cols_val_tab_del and
T0.CardCode = 'V0271')

Begin
SET @error = 10
SET @error_message = N'Blocked BP'
End

END
```

The problem for this user's SP is quite simple. A condition like `T0.DocEntry = @list_of_cols_val_tab_del` or similar is always required to identify the current transaction being processed. Otherwise, SP will look through the entire table. As long as there is one transaction in history, the condition will be satisfied. That is why all outgoing payments for all BP codes had been blocked by the user's SP.

For all sample SPs within this chapter, you will notice that two BEGIN and END pairs have a different format. The outer pairs are all capitals as BEGIN and END. The inner pairs are in proper format as Begin and End. This is not mandatory but can help reduce errors. This is considered a "best practice" as a way to ensure the SP is properly completing and closing its intended function. The format also eliminates confusion on which "begin" belongs with each "end". They function like different brackets as {[]}. You can easily find the right level begin with the corresponding end.

Case 2—Restricting outgoing payments above 20,000

The same user from Case 1 wants to restrict outgoing payments in which the cash transactions for cash account above 20,000 should not be added.

An approval procedure is not suitable for them. The payment has to be stopped from being created.

The solution is:

```
IF (@Object_Type='46') AND (@transaction_type in (N'A', N'U'))

BEGIN

IF EXISTs (SELECT T0.DocNum
FROM OVPM T0

WHERE T0.DocEntry = @list_of_cols_val_tab_del and
T0.CardCode = 'V0271' and
T0.CashSum > 20000)

Begin
SET @error = 10
SET @error_message = N'Cash amount >20,000 is Not allowed'
End

END
```

The difference between Case 2 and Case 1 is in one condition only. It is: `T0.CashSum > 20000`.

Case 3—Blocking goods receipt entry

A user has been trying to block a new goods receipt from creation if the entered total quantity of all the line items is greater than the quantity on the header UDF U_nQty.

For example, if header UDF U_nQty has quantity 4 and row level has two items:

- Item A with quantity 2
- Item B with quantity 3

Then the system will block the goods receipt because the sum of row level quantity is 5 (2+3). It is greater than the header level UDF U_nQty quantity 4.

This user created an SP as follows but it was not working:

```
if @object_type='59' and @transaction_type='A'
BEGIN
If Exists
(SELECT *
FROM OIGE T0 INNER JOIN IGE1 T1
ON T0.DocEntry=T1.DocEntry
WHERE T0.DocEntry = @list_of_cols_val_tab_del
Group By T0.U_nQty
Having Sum(T1.Quantity) <=T0.U_nQty)
Begin
SELECT @error = 1,
@error_message = 'error'
End
END
```

The solution is:

```
IF @object_type='59' and @transaction_type='A'

BEGIN

If Exists
(SELECT T0.DocEntry

FROM OIGE T0

INNER JOIN IGE1 T1 ON T0.DocEntry=T1.DocEntry

WHERE T0.DocEntry = @list_of_cols_val_tab_del

Group By T1.DocEntry
Having Sum(T1.Quantity) <=T0.U_nQty)

Begin
SELECT @error = 1, @error_message = 'error'
End

END
```

Actually, the original SP by the user is almost correct. If you do not check the two SPs very carefully, you may hardly notice the differences.

The most important correction is for the Group By clause. Group By T1.DocEntry can return the right result. The original Group By T0.U_nQty cannot work. Because the grouped data is in IGE1, only DocEntry for IGE1 or T1 in query can be the field to return the correct result.

Another correction is SELECT *. Although it may still work, it is not recommended in the query for SP because one field is good enough to show that the document meets the conditions. Selecting all fields is not a good idea. The intent of the query for a Stored Procedure is to create a "trigger" or to check for very specific conditions in the processing of business transactions. Only one field should be selected in the SP. Selecting all fields should be avoided at all costs.

Case 4—Blocking a sales quotation if no value in row level UDF

Another user created the following SP with the intention to block the addition of a sales quotation if there is no value in row level UDF U_Lot1. There are a few more UDFs such as U_lot2 and U_lot3 with the same requirement. A question arising from the user: "Is it possible to get all these UDFs in the same SP so that there is no need to write a different SP for the other UDFs?" The following SP is a working SP for U_Lot1 created by this user:

```
IF @transaction_type IN (N'A', N'U') AND
(@Object_type = N'23')

BEGIN

If exists(select T.docentry

From QUT1 T

where T.docentry = @list_of_cols_val_tab_del and
T.[U_Lot1] IS NULL)

Begin
SET @error = 14
SET @error_message = N'Please enter Lot Numbers for Item'
End

END
```

The solution is:

```
IF @transaction_type IN (N'A', N'U') AND
(@Object_type = N'23')

BEGIN

If EXISTS (SELECT T.docentry

FROM QUT1 T

WHERE T.docentry = @list_of_cols_val_tab_del and
(T.[U_Lot1] IS NULL or T.[U_Lot2] IS NULL or T.[U_Lot3] IS NULL)

Begin
SET @error = 14
SET @error_message = N'Please enter Lot Numbers for Item'
End

END
```

The solution mentioned earlier clearly answered the user's question. There is no need to create any other SP. The same logic can be put in to the same query easily. The only addition is the extra **OR** conditions enclosed by parentheses. Remember, all those conditions need to be put into one parenthesis only to get the correct result.

Case 5—Blocking invoice based on GL account and project

A user gave a detailed case for A/R invoice validation.

The requirement is to block any other GL Accounts from using the Intercompany Project Code except for the Intercompany Loan accounts.

Intercompany loan accounts range from 125100 to 125950 and the project code for intercompany is 105000.

The solution SP is as follows:

```
IF @transaction_type='A' AND @Object_type = '13'

BEGIN

IF EXISTS
```

```
(SELECT T0.DocEntry

FROM dbo.INV1 T0

WHERE T0.Account NOT LIKE '125%' AND
T0.Project = '105000' AND
T0.DocEntry = @list_of_cols_val_tab_del)

Begin
SET @Error = 13
SET @error_message = 'The Accounts are not allowed for this project.'
End

END
```

This validation is to block addition of the documents. So the @transaction_type = 'A' is the only type that needs to be checked. To exclude account codes ranging from 125100 to 125950 is equivalent to: T0.Account NOT LIKE '125%'.

Case 6—Blocking GRPO if quantity is more than PO quantity

A user had created the following SP to block the Goods Receipt PO if Goods Receipt PO quantity is more than Purchase Order quantity. The SP seems to be working but the cursor shows a busy icon. It would not return to a normal cursor.

```
IF @transaction_type IN (N'A', N'U') AND
(@Object_type = N'20')
begin
if exists (SELECT T0.BaseEntry, SUM(T0.Quantity)
FROM dbo.PDN1 T0 INNER
JOIN dbo.POR1 T1 ON T1.DOCENTRY =
T0.BASEENTRY
WHERE T0.BaseType = 22 AND T0.ItemCode =
T1.ItemCode AND T0.BaseLine = T1.LineNum
and T0.DOCENTRY = @list_of_cols_val_tab_del
GROUP BY T0.BaseEntry
HAVING (SUM(T0.Quantity) > SUM(T1.Quantity)) or sum(t0.quantity) >
sum(t0.BaseOpnQty))
begin
select @Error = 10, @error_message = 'GRPO quantity is greater than PO
quantity'
end
end
```

The solution is:

```
IF @transaction_type IN (N'A', N'U') AND
(@Object_type = N'20')

BEGIN

IF EXISTS (SELECT T1.BaseEntry

FROM dbo.OPDN T0
INNER JOIN dbo.PDN1 T1 ON T1.DOCENTRY = T0.DocEntry
INNER JOIN dbo.POR1 T2 ON T2.DOCENTRY = T1.BaseEntry

WHERE T1.BaseType = 22 AND
T1.ItemCode = T2.ItemCode AND
T1.BaseLine = T2.LineNum AND
T0.DOCENTRY = @list_of_cols_val_tab_del

GROUP BY T1.BaseEntry
HAVING SUM(T1.Quantity) > SUM(T2.OpenQty))

Begin
SELECT @Error = 10, @error_message = 'GRPO quantity is greater than PO
open quantity'
End

END
```

Comparing these two SPs, you can find the following differences:

1. The first difference can be found after SELECT. The original SP has two fields to return. Actually, one field is good enough and has fewer errors.

2. The second difference is an addition of another table OPDN. This is not mandatory. However, it is clearer for the logic.

3. The last but obviously not the least is the HAVING clause. HAVING (SUM(T0. Quantity) > SUM(T1.Quantity)) or sum(t0.quantity)>sum(t0. BaseOpnQty)) in the original query is not correct. The correct one is to compare the summary of PDN1 quantity against the summary of the corresponding POR1 open quantity directly by HAVING SUM(T1.Quantity) > SUM(T2.OpenQty).

These differences make the solution SP work without any problem.

Case 7—Blocking, adding, or updating an order for duplicated BP ref

One of the users had some troubles in getting SP working. The goal is to stop an order from adding or updating if the same BP reference number value exists in NumatCard field on another order from the same customer.

The following SP has been tried by the user but it is not working as expected:

```
DECLARE @PORef nvarchar (100)
DECLARE @BPCode Nvarchar (35)

IF @transaction_type in('A','U') AND @object_type = '17'
BEGIN
Set @PORef = (Select T1.NumAtCard
FROM ORDR T1
WHERE T1.docentry = @list_of_cols_val_tab_del)

Set @BPCode = (Select T1.CardCode
FROM ORDR T1
WHERE T1.docentry = @list_of_cols_val_tab_del)

IF @PORef, @BPCode In (Select T0.NumatCard, T0.CardCode
From ORDR T0)

BEGIN
SET @error = 11
SET @error_message = N'Customer PO is already in the system'
END
END
```

The solution is:

```
DECLARE @PORef nvarchar(100)
DECLARE @BPCode Nvarchar(35)

IF @transaction_type in ('A','U') AND @object_type = '17'

BEGIN

Set @PORef = (Select T1.NumAtCard

FROM ORDR T1

WHERE T1.docentry = @list_of_cols_val_tab_del)
```

```
Set @BPCode = (Select T1.CardCode

FROM ORDR T1

WHERE T1.docentry = @list_of_cols_val_tab_del)

IF @PORef IN
(Select T0.NumatCard

From ORDR T0

WHERE T0.docentry != @list_of_cols_val_tab_del and
T0.CardCode = @BPCode)

Begin
SET @error = 11
SET @error_message = N'Customer PO is already in the system'
End

END
```

Again, the difference between these two SPs is not significant. All you need is the addition of T0.docentry != @list_of_cols_val_tab_del, so that the condition of comparison can be based on other records in the table that does not include the current one.

Case 8—Blocking sales documents based on dates

A user wants to block the creation of the sales order, the delivery, and the return of previous months after the fifth of the current month.

The solution for sales order is as follows:

```
IF @object_type = '17' and @transaction_type = 'A'

BEGIN

IF EXISTS (SELECT T0.DocEntry

FROM dbo.ORDR T0

WHERE DateDiff(MM,T0.DocDate,GetDate())>1 AND DatePart(DD,GetDate())>4
AND
```

```
            T0.DocEntry = @list_of_cols_val_tab_del)

     Begin
     select @error = 99, @error_message = 'You are not allowed to post to
     previous month.'
     End


     END
```

The month of the document date has been checked first. Then the current date has been checked to see if it is after the fifth. These two conditions satisfy the user's request. All other types of documents can be easily added by the same logic.

For delivery, @object_type needs to be changed to '15' and table name would be ODLN. For sales return, @object_type is '16' and table name is ORDN.

Case 9—Validation service type A/R credit memo

A user wants to restrict the creation of service type A/R credit memo. SP had been created to try to block certain users. The following SP by the user is not working to serve this purpose:

```
     declare @usersign as INT
     SELECT @usersign=USERSIGN FROM ADOC WHERE DOCENTRY=@list_of_cols_val_
     tab_del AND ObjType=14
     If @transaction_type IN ('A','U') And @object_type = '14'
     Begin
     If exists (SELECT DocNum FROM ORIN WHERE DocEntry = @list_of_cols_val_
     tab_del
               AND DocType = 'S' and @usersign not in (1,2,3))
         Begin
           Select @error = -1, @error_message = 'Access not allowed'
         end
     END
```

The solution is:

```
     If @transaction_type IN ('A','U') and @object_type = '14'

     BEGIN
     declare @user int

     SELECT @user=SELECT usersign2 FROM ORIN WHERE DocEntry = @list_of_
     cols_val_tab_del
```

```
If @user in (1,2,3)
 Begin
 If EXISTS
(SELECT DocNum
FROM ORIN
WHERE DocEntry = @list_of_cols_val_tab_del AND
DocType = 'S')
  begin
  SELECT @error = 14, @error_message = 'Access not allowed'
  end
 End
END
```

The difference between the two queries is the variable definition. In the solution, the variable is reduced to only one. Declaration of the variable is moved to the section after initial condition: If @transaction_type IN ('A','U') and @object_type = '14'.

Instead of checking if users are not in a specific list, the solution checks if users are in a list. This is good for system performance if the number of users in the list is not too many.

Case 10—Blocking goods issue for none super user

A user successfully managed to apply a transaction notification on a goods issue document to give an error when WhsCode = '02'. The reason to block issuing from this warehouse is because it has been defined as warehouse for scrap.

```
If @transaction_type = 'A' And @object_type = '60'
Begin
If Exists (Select T0.itemcode from dbo.IGE1 T0, dbo.OIGE T1 Inner Join
dbo.OUSR T2
On T1.userSign=T2.UserId where T0.docentry = @list_of_cols_val_tab_del
and T2.USER_CODE != 'manager2' And T0.whscode = '02')
Begin
select @error = 1, @error_message = 'You are not allowed to issue from
Warehouse 02'
end
end
```

However, this SP is blocking all users to add the goods issue document. The intended result should only stop all other users but not super user 'manager2'. The code added to the SP T2.USER_CODE != 'manager2' is not working.

The solution is:

```
IF @transaction_type = 'A' And @object_type = '60'

BEGIN
If Exists (SELECT T0.itemcode

From dbo.IGE1 T0
INNER JOIN dbo.OIGE T1 ON T1.DocEntry = T0.DocEntry
Inner Join dbo.OUSR T2 On T1.userSign=T2.UserId

WHERE T1.docentry = @list_of_cols_val_tab_del AND
T2.USER_CODE != 'manager2' AND
T0.whscode = '02')

Begin
SELECT @error = 1, @error_message = 'You are not allowed to issue from
Warehouse 02'
End

END
```

The difference is that the solution linked all tables but the original one used a comma between IGN1 and OIGN. OUSR (T2) is only linking to OIGN (T1). But OIGN has not been bound to IGN1 (T0). That makes `T0.docentry = @list_of_cols_val_tab_del` without binding of OIGN. All records on OIGN will return. It effectively nullifies the condition put in to OUSR.

Case 11—Blocking Goods Receipt PO if no based PO

A user wants to block Goods Receipt POs that are not based on Purchase Orders.

The solution is simplest as follows:

```
IF @transaction_type = 'A' AND @object_type = '20'

BEGIN

IF exists (Select ItemCode from dbo.PDN1 T0

Where T0.BaseType=-1

AND T0.DocEntry=@list_of_cols_val_tab_del)
```

```
Begin
SELECT @error = 20, @error_message = 'GRPO without Purchase Order!'
End

END
```

This is a typical solution for a similar requirement. For example, you can change @ object_type from '20' to '15' and PDN1 to DLN1 to block delivery if delivery has no base document.

Summary

Throughout this chapter, you have learned an important application for SQL query in SAP Business One. This chapter presented a thorough overview of query writing for SBO_SP_TransactionNotification.

You also received an explanation of the important parameters showing you how to work with the processing of Stored Procedures. It also sheds light on query writing skills and query optimization technicalities.

By reading and testing a portion of the entire sample SPs within this chapter, you should now be able to create your own core query for SBO_SP_ TransactionNotification.

The next chapter is the last chapter. It focuses on more complicated query topics and conditions for your use in writing advanced functionality into your queries.

9
More Complicated SQL Query Topics

This is the last chapter of the book and we will have an extended discussion, which will give you some of the most complicated examples of SQL query in SAP Business One. This chapter will bring you closer to introducing even more Business Intelligence into SAP Business One. The main topics include:

- The Case expression usage
- Working with subquery
- Using PIVOT to simplify a cross tab style queries
- Database query for Excel

In addition, this last section will give you some advice on the pitfalls and mistakes to be avoided in query writing.

These topics are more suitable to the users who have extra interests to extend their capabilities to create more complicated queries. Although the previous examples can be revisited, I would like to show more query examples to cover more areas.

Please refer back to the the preface for more information on the specific naming conventions of the query examples in this chapter.

The Case expression usage

In *Chapter 3*, you have learned the grammar of Case and If expressions. Furthermore, you should have noticed these expressions have been used quite a few times in the sample queries of previous chapters. However, those examples are mainly focused on the business processes. There were no extended discussions on how to use those expressions. CASE has a similar function to what most individuals understand as "IF/THEN" conditions often used in flowcharts and other programming languages. However, in SQL query, the IF expression can only be used outside the SELECT statement. On the contrary, CASE can be used within SELECT statement. Therefore, it is used more frequently. You can find some more queries using the CASE expression. We will only discuss this expression and won't go into the other.

Case 9-C1—Displaying Transtype as code instead of a number

A user had written a query to display the number of each type of journal entry created by users during a specific period:

```
SELECT COUNT(*) AS 'Created', T0.TransType, T0.UserSign, T1.U_NAME
FROM OJDT T0 JOIN OUSR T1 ON T0.UserSign = T1.USERID
WHERE T0.RefDate >= '20100301' AND T0.RefDate <= '20100331' GROUP BY
T0.TransType, T0.UserSign, T1.U_NAME
```

However, this query returns the origin number (TransType value), which is not intuitive.

The user wants to replace those numbers with names or codes of where that journal entry originated (Invoice, Credit Memo, etc).

Here is the solution:

```
SELECT COUNT(*) AS 'Created',
CASE T0.TransType
WHEN 13 THEN 'IN'
WHEN 18 THEN 'PU'
WHEN 19 THEN 'PC'
WHEN 20 THEN 'PD'
END as TransType,
T0.UserSign,
T1.U_NAME

FROM DBO.OJDT T0
JOIN DBO.OUSR T1 ON T0.UserSign = T1.USERID

WHERE T0.RefDate >= '20100301' AND T0.RefDate <= '20100331'

GROUP BY T0.TransType, T0.UserSign, T1.U_NAME
```

This is a perfect example to show how CASE expression can be used to solve such a problem. It is one of the simplest CASE usages. As the values returned by **T0.TransType** are within a known list and are predictable, it is easy to translate those values with a standard CASE statement:

```
Case FieldName
When Value1 Then Result1
When Value2 Then Result2
```

```
......
When ValueN Then ResultN

End
```

Here, N can be any limited integer. If you prefer the natural language instead of code, you can replace those codes with a description such as "A/R Invoice" instead of N. All those codes can be found in the *Appendix* of this book. Using code in query is recommended because it matches the display in the system. The complete list for TransType is very long. As for this specific query, you do not need to put in all code. Only the pertinent types should be included. They are good enough.

END is always needed for CASE expression. CASE.....END acts as a parenthesis. Do not forget the END clause to terminate CASE.

Case 9-C2—Combining two queries with a Case expression

There is a simple request from a user, which is to combine two similar queries:

Query 1:

```
SELECT T0.[U_empName], T0.[U_NetAmt] 'EPF Amt',
FROM [dbo].[@BIZ_SALLOG] T0
WHERE T0.[U_Code] = 'EPF' And T0.[U_MthID] Like '%[%0]%'
```

Query 2:

```
SELECT T0.[U_empName], T0.[U_NetAmt] 'ESI Amt',
FROM [dbo].[@BIZ_SALLOG] T0
WHERE T0.[U_Code] = 'ESI' And T0.[U_MthID] Like '%[%0]%'
```

To combine these two queries, the solution is as follows:

```
SELECT T0.U_empName,
CASE WHEN T0.U_Code = 'EPF' THEN T0.U_NetAmt ELSE 0 END 'EPF Amt',
CASE WHEN T0.U_Code = 'ESI' THEN T0.U_NetAmt ELSE 0 END 'ESI Amt'

FROM [dbo].[@BIZ_SALLOG] T0

WHERE T0.U_Code in ('EPF','ESI')
And T0.U_MthID Like '%[%0]%'
```

This solution is different from the previous example. Two case expressions are needed because two columns have to be returned. Notice that there is only one WHEN after CASE; also, the field name is not in front of WHEN but behind it. Although you can still use something like CASE T0.[U_Code] WHEN 'EPF' THEN, it is common practice to put T0.[U_Code] after WHEN. This sounds more natural.

ELSE is an optional word in CASE expression. Only if you want to assign a specific value other than the listed value when all conditions fail, you do not need to include it in the query. For this example, it is necessary because zero needs to be assigned to all records if U_Code is not equal to the value under the WHEN condition. However, though the output results are usually predictable, using ELSE statement is an extra measure to reduce the chances of errors.

Case 9-C3—Showing discount percentage for each interval

A user has the following condition to be applied on the field discount percentage.

A percentage should be automatically calculated based on the document total of each invoice as follows:

- 500,000 – 750,000: 3 percent
- 750,000 – 1,000,000: 5 percent
- 1,000,000 – 1,250,000: 8 percent
- 1,250,000 – 1,500,000: 10 percent
- 1,500,000 – 1,750,000: 13 percent
- 1,750,000 – 2,000,000: 15 percent

What would be the query syntax with conditions for each interval?

The solution is:

```
Case
WHEN (DocTotal >= 500000 AND DocTotal < 750000) THEN .03
WHEN (DocTotal >= 750000 AND DocTotal < 1000000) THEN .05
WHEN (DocTotal >= 1000000 AND DocTotal < 1250000) THEN .08
WHEN (DocTotal >= 1250000 AND DocTotal < 1500000) THEN .1
WHEN (DocTotal >= 1500000 AND DocTotal < 1750000) THEN .13
WHEN (DocTotal >= 1750000 AND DocTotal < 2000000) THEN .15
END
```

This example is almost the same as the first one. The only difference is the conditions following WHEN. A complete formula or statement is needed whenever one value cannot be directly returned under the WHEN condition. The pattern is:

```
CASE
WHEN Condition1 THEN Value1
WHEN Condition2 THEN Value2
......
WHEN ConditionN THEN ValueN
END
```

This is the standard usage of the CASE expression. It is used more often than the first example. In the example, one part is missing. There is no definition for document total > 2,000,000. So it may not be a complete list.

Case 9-C4—Item wise subtotal in a goods receipt

A user got a query to display a Goods Receipt. The query works fine but it is not summarized. It needs to add subtotal item wise.

```
Select t0.docdate,(t1.itemcode),sum(case (t0.comments) when 'P' then
t1.Quantity else 0 end) 'P',
sum(case (t0.comments) when 'S' then t1.Quantity else 0 end) 'S'
From oign t0 inner join ign1 t1 on t0.docentry = t1.docentry
inner join oitm t2 on t2.itemcode = t1.itemcode
where T0.Docdate >= %0 and T0.docdate <= %1 and t2.itmsgrpcod = 138
and (t0.comments like '%PAT%' or t0.comments like '%SAN%')
Group by t0.docdate,t1.itemcode
```

Output from this query looks like the following:

Posting Date	Item	P	S
1/12/10	1	7116	
2/12/10	1	7104	
1/12/10	2	19632	16632
2/12/10	2	19680	16608

The expected results are as follows:

Posting Date	Item	P	S
1/12/10	1	7116	
2/12/10	1	7104	
		14220	
1/12/10	2	19632	16632
2/12/10	2	19680	16608
		39312	33240

The solution is as follows:

```
Select '' 'Total',(t1.itemcode),t0.docdate,sum(case (t0.comments) when
'P' then t1.Quantity else 0 end) 'P',
sum(case (t0.comments) when 'S' then t1.Quantity else 0 end) 'S'
From oign t0 inner join ign1 t1 on t0.docentry = t1.docentry
inner join oitm t2 on t2.itemcode = t1.itemcode
where T0.Docdate >= [%0] and T0.docdate <= [%1] and t2.itmsgrpcod =
138 and (t0.comments like '%PAT%' or t0.comments like '%SAN%')
Group by t1.itemcode,t0.docdate

UNION ALL

Select 'Subtotal',(t1.itemcode),'',sum(case (t0.comments) when 'P'
then t1.Quantity else 0 end) 'P',
sum(case (t0.comments) when 'S' then t1.Quantity else 0 end) 'S'
From oign t0 inner join ign1 t1 on t0.docentry = t1.docentry
inner join oitm t2 on t2.itemcode = t1.itemcode
where T0.Docdate >= [%0] and T0.docdate <= [%1] and t2.itmsgrpcod =
138 and (t0.comments like '%PAT%' or t0.comments like '%SAN%')
Group by t1.itemcode

UNION ALL

Select 'Grand Total','','',sum(case (t0.comments) when 'P' then
t1.Quantity else 0 end) 'P',
sum(case (t0.comments) when 'S' then t1.Quantity else 0 end) 'S'
From oign t0 inner join ign1 t1 on t0.docentry = t1.docentry
inner join oitm t2 on t2.itemcode = t1.itemcode
where T0.Docdate >= [%0] and T0.docdate <= [%1] and t2.itmsgrpcod =
138 and (t0.comments like '%PAT%' or t0.comments like '%SAN%')
ORDER by t1.itemcode
```

This example has something special because the CASE expression is after the SUM clause. This is to show you how each CASE ……END pair can be treated as a normal value to be part of any formula.

Case 9-C5—Updating UDF with different dates

A user has made a UDF in the sales order header. This UDF needs to be updated automatically with the next day's date through a formatted search.

A special requirement is that if the next day is Friday or Saturday then the date should be Sunday because these two days are their days off.

The solution is:

```
SELECT
CASE WHEN DatePart(DW,$[ORDR.DocDate.Date])=6
THEN DateAdd(DD, 3, $[ORDR.DocDate.Date])
WHEN DatePart(DW,$[ORDR.DocDate.Date])=7
THEN DateAdd(DD, 2, $[ORDR.DocDate.Date])
ELSE
DateAdd(DD, 1, $[ORDR.DocDate.Date])
END
```

In the solution, these three kinds of possible dates based on the dates in the week are covered by three cases. The Weekday (DW) in DatePart function stands for the number of the day in the week, for example: Sunday = 1, Saturday = 7. It can distinguish the required conditions easily. Apply this formatted search query to the UDF; the date in the UDF should be updated automatically.

Working with a subquery

A subquery is a very useful tool to solve certain special problems. It can return values to form a condition or to add a column. There are mainly three different usages:

- Subquery under a Where clause
- Subquery as a standalone column
- Subquery within a subquery

Although you can add a subquery within a subquery and the level for subquery can be more than two, it is not recommended. The more sublevels that exist in your query, the more trouble you may end up with. It is not worth the effort to create such a monster-like query unless you do not have any other choice.

The following query example cases belong to the first two categories. No subquery within a subquery is shown here due to the obvious reason just mentioned.

Case 9-S1—Item groups not in use

A user needs a query to show which item groups do not contain any items.

The solution is by a simple query:

```
SELECT T0.ItmsGrpCod,
T0.ItmsGrpNam

FROM dbo.OITB T0

WHERE T0.ItmsGrpCod Not IN
(SELECT Distinct ItmsGrpCod FROM dbo.OITM)
```

Even though the query is simple, a subquery is needed here. This is the case when returned records have no link between two tables. A subquery is a good technique to bridge the gap. Returned values from the subquery include all groups with the items. Therefore, if nothing can be found from the list, it means the group does not contain any items.

This subquery is under the Where condition. It is one of the simplest cases for subquery. A subquery should always have a parenthesis to make a clear boundary from other SQL statements.

Case 9-S2—YTD sales for two years

A user would like to add 2009 and 2010 YTD sales for each of the customers to the following query:

```
SELECT T0.CardCode, T0.CardName, T0.Phone1, T1.Name, T1.E_MailL, T0.U_
ORDN
FROM dbo.OCRD T0
LEFT JOIN dbo.OCPR T1 ON T1.CardCode=T0.CardCode AND T1.Name ='A/P'
```

The solution is:

```
SELECT T0.CardCode,
(SELECT SUM(T2.Debit) - sum(T2.Credit) FROM JDT1 T2
INNER JOIN OJDT T4 ON T4.TransID = T2.TransID AND Year(T4.Refdate) =
2009
WHERE T2.ShortName = T0.CardCode AND T2.TransType in ('13','14')) AS
'Sales 2009',
(SELECT SUM(T2.Debit) - sum(T2.Credit) FROM JDT1 T2
INNER JOIN OJDT T4 ON T4.TransID = T2.TransID AND Year(T4.Refdate) =
2010
WHERE T2.ShortName = T0.CardCode AND T2.TransType in ('13','14')) AS
'Sales 2010'

FROM DBO.OCRD T0
WHERE T0.CardType = 'C'
```

This solution is showing you two subqueries as two columns. It is often used when you need to get values from the same table with different conditions. If you can use the JOIN and GROUP BY clauses to achieve the same result, it can greatly boost the performance of the query.

Case 9-S3—Checking only the similar records

A user has created a query to show service and contract.

The requirement is to show only those records which have more than one "internalSN" code (Serial Number). This is to know whether the same equipment is coming in for service more than once during a certain period. The following query needs to be changed to get the desired result:

```
SELECT T0.[callID], T0.[customer], T0.[custmrName], T0.[manufSN],
T0.[internalSN], T0.[itemCode], T0.[itemName], T0.[createDate]
FROM OSCL T0 INNER JOIN OCTR T1 ON T0.contractID = T1.ContractID INNER
JOIN CTR1 T2 ON T1.ContractID = T2.ContractID
WHERE T0.[createDate] >=[%0] and T0.[createDate] <=[%1] and T2.[U_
Afdeling] LIKE 'meetin%'
```

The solution is:

```
SELECT Distinct T0.callID,
T0.customer,
T0.custmrName,
T0.manufSN,
T0.internalSN,
T0.itemCode,
T0.itemName,
T0.createDate

FROM dbo.OSCL T0
INNER JOIN dbo.CTR1 T2 ON T0.ContractID = T2.ContractID

WHERE T0.createDate >=[%0] and T0.createDate <=[%1]
AND T2.U_Afdeling LIKE 'meetin%'
AND T0.internalSN IN
(SELECT T0.internalSN

FROM OSCL T0

WHERE T0.createDate >=[%0] and T0.createDate <=[%1]

GROUP BY T0.internalSN

HAVING COUNT(T0.internalSN) > 1)
```

This query also has a subquery under the WHERE clause. You can see that a subquery itself may also be a complicated query. That is one of the reasons why multiple level subqueries should be avoided. Under the subquery, the condition to filter more than one identical internalSN is achieved with the following:

```
GROUP BY T0.[internalSN]
HAVING COUNT(T0.[internalSN]) > 1
```

Case 9-S4—Showing the last A/P invoice document date for items

A user needs to link items with their 'last A/P invoice document date' and 'last A/P Invoice BP name'.

The solution is:

```
SELECT Distinct T0.ItemCode,
T2.TaxDate,
T2.CardName

FROM dbo.PCH1 T0
INNER JOIN dbo.OPCH T2 ON T2.DocEntry=T0.DocEntry

WHERE T2.TaxDate > '[%0]' AND
T0.DocEntry in
(SELECT MAX(T1.DocEntry)
FROM dbo.PCH1 T1
WHERE T0.ItemCode = T1.ItemCode
GROUP BY T1.ItemCode)
```

This solution may not exactly meet the original requirement, but it is accepted by the user. Instead of checking the document date, the subquery checks the document entry. The document entry is a primary key of the table. It always increases automatically. To me, it is a more reliable way to check the last record.

If your system has many manual date changes during document creation, you need to revise the query to add more conditions. If you find a non logical answer that way, don't be surprised. Different period selections may cause a reversed result sometimes. For example, when you select an earlier date as the duration, you may get a more recent invoice date instead.

Using PIVOT to simplify a cross tab style queries

The Pivot function is introduced in MS SQL Server 2005. If you are still using SQL Server 2000 or lower (unlikely), you may skip this section. Pivot table is a common term. I have used it in Excel extensively. If you are not familiar with it, run a sample query here.

Even if your SQL server version is equal or higher than 2005, you may still get an error message because the compatibility level of the server has to be 2005 or higher. You can change this level under SQL Server Management Studio if the compatibility level is low.

Pivot function is a very useful tool to simplify long repeating queries.

Case 9-P1—Monthly sales by geography

A user would like to get a listing of each state's sales by month. They are using the first two characters of a BP's account code to represent their states.

The query would be similar to the one under the *Case 4-M14 of Query for marketing document* recipe in *Chapter 4*.

The solution is as follows:

```
SELECT P.[STATE],
   [1]  as [Jan],
   [2]  as [Feb],
   [3]  as [Mar],
   [4]  as [Apr],
   [5]  as [May],
   [6]  as [Jun],
   [7]  as [Jul],
   [8]  as [Aug],
   [9]  as [Sep],
   [10] as [Oct],
   [11] as [Nov],
   [12] as [Dec]

FROM
(SELECT Left(T0.CardCode,2) as [State],
T0.DocTotal as [DocTotal],
MONTH(T0.docdate) as [month]
FROM dbo.oinv T0
```

```
WHERE Year(T0.docdate)=2010
UNION
SELECT Left(T0.CardCode,2) as [State],
-T0.DocTotal as [DocTotal],
MONTH(T0.docdate) as [month]
FROM dbo.orin T0
WHERE Year(T0.docdate)=2010) S

PIVOT (SUM(DocTotal) FOR [month] IN
([1],[2],[3],[4],[5],[6],[7],[8],[9],[10],[11],[12])) P

ORDER BY P.[State]
```

You can see in the example that I am using the **Left** function in combination with a **2** to read the first two characters of the Business Partner code, which, in turn, gives me the state code for each BP based on the user's data.

If you compare this query with the one in *Chapter 4*, you will find Pivot function can simplify so much to get the same job done in less than 50 percent of the query size.

One thing needs to be pointed out here, the query example in *Chapter 4* has only queried one table. This example queries two tables.

Pivot function requests two parts. The first part is the main data including all logic. You can find this part with alias as S table right after FROM. The S table acts as a temporary table. The following part is P table that feeds in all data from S table into different branches. All columns after SELECT are coming out of the P table. Alias S and P can be changed to any other words. I just find it is convenient to keep them this way.

Case 9-P2—Complete list of all items with/ without sales

A user needs to find the quantity sold per month for each of their styles. The styles have multiple color and sizes. Each style is indicated by the first four characters of the Item Code.

The user has a query already. The query also resembles the one in *Case 4-M14* mentioned in *Chapter 4*. The beginning and the end of the query looks like the following:

```
SELECT LEFT(T0.ITEMCODE,4) AS 'Style', (SELECT SUM(T1.QUANTITY)
FROM INV1 T1 with (NOLOCK) WHERE MONTH(T1.DOCDATE) = 1 AND
LEFT(T1.ITEMCODE,4) = LEFT(T0.ITEMCODE,4) AND YEAR(T1.DOCDATE) =
YEAR(GETDATE())) AS 'JAN Amt'
......
```

```
(SELECT SUM(T1.QUANTITY) FROM INV1 T1 with (NOLOCK) WHERE MONTH(T1.
DOCDATE) = 12 AND LEFT(T1.ITEMCODE,4) = LEFT(T0.ITEMCODE,4) AND
YEAR(T1.DOCDATE) = YEAR(GETDATE())) AS 'DEC Amt'
FROM dbo.OITM T0 LEFT JOIN dbo.INV1 T1 ON LEFT(T1.ITEMCODE,4) =
LEFT(T0.ITEMCODE,4) WHERE T0.SellItem = 'Y' GROUP BY LEFT(T0.
ITEMCODE,4),YEAR(T1.DOCDATE) HAVING YEAR(T1.DOCDATE) = YEAR(GETDATE())
ORDER BY LEFT(T0.ITEMCODE,4)
```

One change is needed for the query to show a complete list of all styles. No matter if there are sales for any month or not, this query only shows items that have sales.

The solution is as follows:

```
SELECT P.[Style],
  [1] as [Jan],
  [2] as [Feb],
  [3] as [Mar],
  [4] as [Apr],
  [5] as [May],
  [6] as [Jun],
  [7] as [Jul],
  [8] as [Aug],
  [9] as [Sep],
  [10] as [Oct],
  [11] as [Nov],
  [12] as [Dec]
FROM (SELECT LEFT(T0.ITEMCODE,4) AS 'Style', T1.QUANTITY, MONTH(T1.
Docdate) as [month]
FROM dbo.oitm T0
LEFT JOIN INV1 T1 ON T1.ItemCode=T0.ItemCode AND YEAR(T1.DocDate) =
YEAR(GETDATE())) S

  PIVOT (SUM(QUANTITY) FOR [month] IN
([1],[2],[3],[4],[5],[6],[7],[8],[9],[10],[11],[12])) P

ORDER BY P.[Style]
```

The original query has only listed two months instead of twelve and is still very long. The new query takes advantage of the Pivot function. You can see how much length difference there is between the solution and the original query.

Database query for Excel

Database query for Excel is a built-in function of Microsoft Excel. It is available from early versions of Excel. Once I started to use it, I found this function to be very powerful. It can be used for almost all queries you are running under Query Manager. The format of the report can be done quickly and attractively. To me, it is an alternative to a simple Crystal Report.

The screenshots in the book all come from Excel 2003. If you are using Excel 2007 or higher, you may need to from a similar menu but not an identical user interface. The functionality has no significant changes.

Import External Data is the menu item you need to locate. It is under the **Data** menu. The first thing to do is to create a **New Database Query**. This is one of the submenu items for **Import External Data**. You can select this menu to get to the next screenshot.

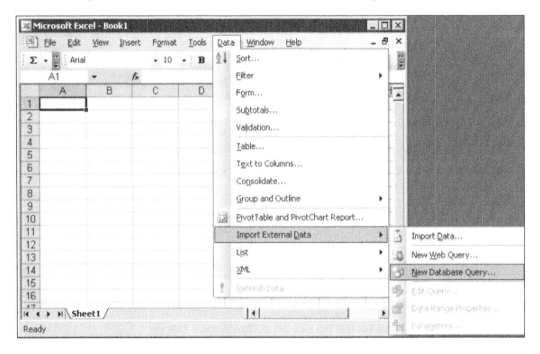

Creating a new data source

The first task in creating a new database query is to **Choose Data Source**. If it is the first time you are trying to use this function, you will probably not have many data sources to select from. In fact, you may not find any data source that is related to your SAP Business One system.

New data source added within Excel

You can select the first entry there: **<New Data Source>.** This is a clear name to lead you into the right direction.

Make sure the check under the bottom of **Choose Data Source** form is in its default position. You can take advantage of **Use the Query Wizard to create/edit queries**.

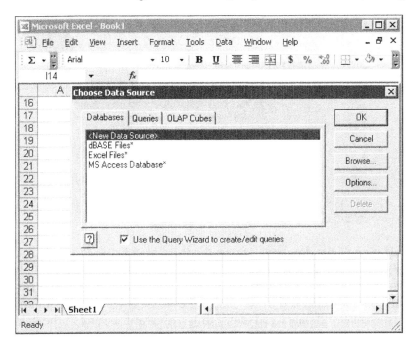

The following screenshot will pop up: **Create New Data Source**. There are four steps in creating a new data source:

1. Name your new data source.
2. Select a database driver.
3. Test the data connection.
4. Select a default table for the data source (optional).

The first step as shown in the following screenshot is the name given to the data source — **ASAP**.

For the second step, since the database driver for SQL server is usually located at the bottom, **SQL Native Client** is selected as the right data driver in order to connect to the SAP Business One database.

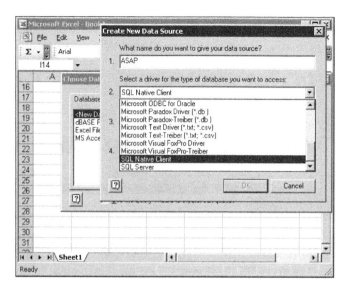

After the selection of the database driver, the third step is the connection. Click **Connect**. **SQL Server logon** form pops up. You can select from the available SQL servers the right one that holds SAP Business One database. **Use Trusted Connection** is usually checked in order to log in to SQL server without any need to put in the username and password every time you want to refresh the data.

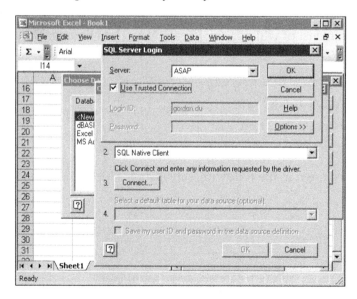

In the previous form is the **Options >>** button. By clicking on it, this form can show more options:

- **Database**
- **Language**
- **Application Name**
- **Workstation**

Under the SQL server selected, you must have more than one database. Select the one you need SAP Business One data for. If you need access to more than one SAP Business One database, multiple data sources are necessary.

Language is usually left as **(Default)**, which usually gives you the right language version based on your SQL server setting.

Application Name and **Workstation** are automatically filled in by the system. There is no need to change them.

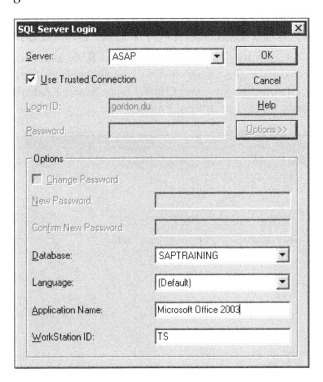

Click **OK** to close the **SQL Server logon** form. The screenshot is shown as follows:

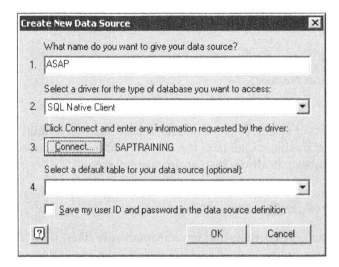

New data source added from the control panel

The previous steps are complete steps to add a new ODBC data source from Excel directly. You can get the data to a current Excel worksheet. However, there is a more professional way to do so directly from **ODBC Date Source Administrator** under **Administration Tools** from the **Control Panel**.

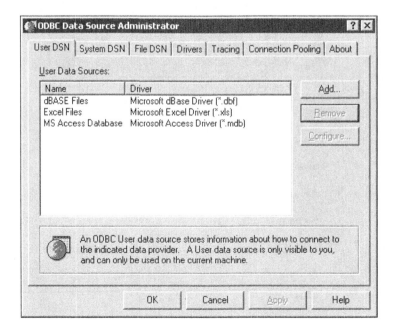

The first tab for this tool is **User DSN**. **DSN** is short form for **Data Source Name**. This is the tab that we are interested in. Click **Add**, and the **Create New Data Source** form pops up. You may find that much fewer drivers are available to set up a data source than from Excel directly. SQL Native Client may be just on top. Click **Finish**, and you can go to the next screen.

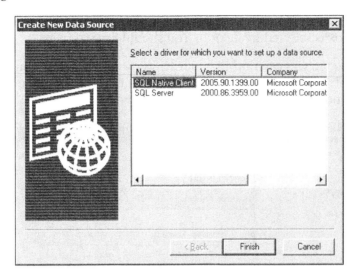

The process in the following few screenshots is almost identical to the one provided by Excel. The user interface is from SQL Server directly though.

You can have a bigger form for the same info required. The name, description, and server are filled in, as shown in the following screenshot:

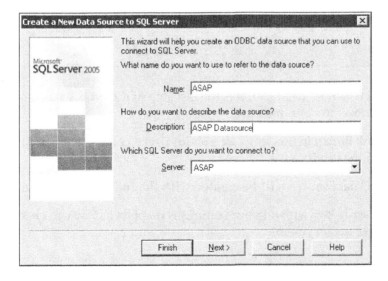

There is one more form apart from the previous example. You can select a more detailed way to choose how SQL Server should verify the authentication of the log in user ID. Default will be **With Integrated Windows authentication**. If you like, you can also select **With SQL Server authentication using a login user ID and password entered by the user**.

Connect to SQL Server to obtain default settings for the additional configuration options checkbox is selected by default. You should leave it there.

Click on **Next** again, you can find the following screenshot. Here, you can change the default database to SAP Business One database that you plan to create. All other options should not be changed to avoid incompatibility.

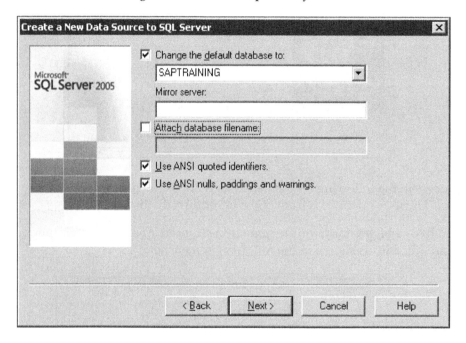

The next screen is more technical. It is the last step in the process. You can fine tune the way to connect to your database.

When you click **Finish** in this form, you should get a confirmation message window. A message on the header says:

A New ODBC data source will be created with the following configuration:

A big text message box with all your settings is displayed. You can check the setting to verify the connection detail.

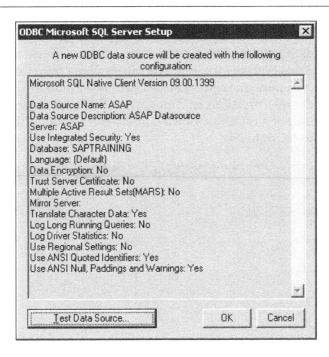

Click on the **Test Data Source...** button at the bottom of the previous message form; you can test data source immediately. If it is the correct setting, then you can get a successful message for it.

Query wizard for database query in Excel

We have spent a lot of time on getting the data source, and now we can come back to the main topic: Database query for Excel. We will continue from the first step in **New Database Query**. Assuming the correct data source is selected, you can go through Query Wizard under Microsoft Query. You get **Available tables and columns** in the left box. The table selected is OCRG. Expand and select all columns with the arrow key to send them to the right box.

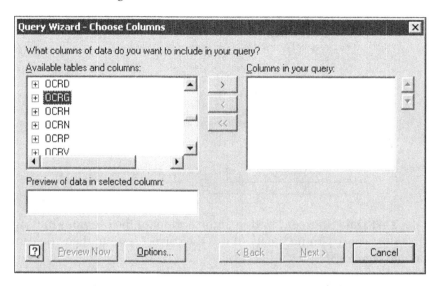

You can preview data in the selected column to confirm you are on the right track.

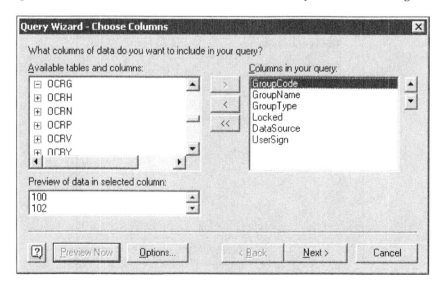

The **Next** screen is an option form to filter the data. You can use the given formula to add conditions to restrict the data. In the following example, **GroupCode< 102** is selected. You can use **And Or** to add more conditions to filter data.

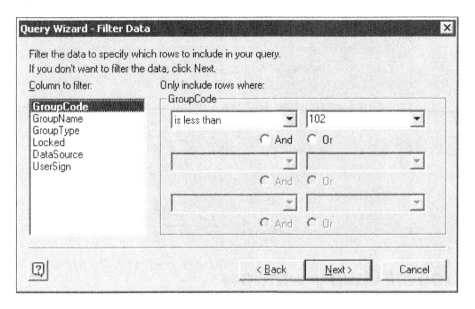

Sort order is the next form that the follows filter form. You can specify how you want your data sorted. It is also an optional form. Since we don't want to sort the data, just click **Next**.

You are now on the last form for Query Wizard — Finish. There are three options for you:

- Return Data to Microsoft Office Excel
- View data or edit query in Microsoft Query
- Create an OLAP Cube from this query

If you select the first option, you will return to Excel directly. This is for beginners only. The last option is beyond the topic of this book. The option in the middle is the right one. Let us go on this route to **View data and edit query in Microsoft Query**.

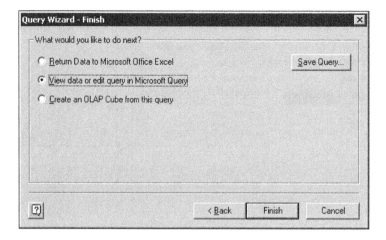

Microsoft Query window

You are now getting into the center function of the database query for Excel. You can view data and edit a query within this query window.

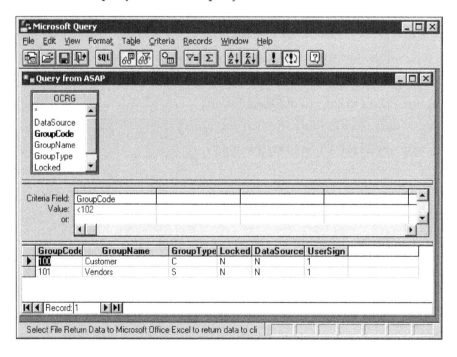

You can click the SQL icon in the middle of the toolbar to edit the SQL statement in the SQL form.

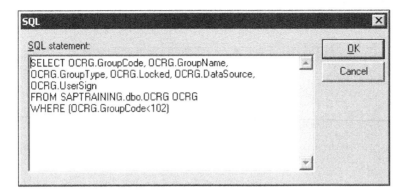

When everything looks fine to you, you can return data to Excel at any time. When you return, the system will ask you to select one cell for return. It is better to keep the first cell in column A. For better format, you can choose between A4 and A7. This is to give you enough space for the report header.

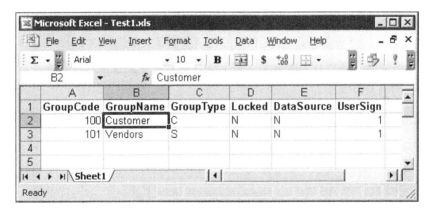

You have the option to edit the query by using the **Edit Query** function under the same menu tree. In order to get this function, your cursor must be inside the query result. One option for you is to open the SQL form and copy one of the entire tested queries directly. You can test the query under SAP Business One's Query Manager.

To choose this option, the database name and the characters of "dbo" must be added in front of the table name. This is required by Microsoft Query. In fact, even if your query does not include those parts being displayed, you can see it is automatically added after you close and reopen the SQL window.

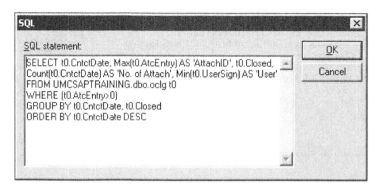

After copying the query, you can view the query result in the Microsoft Query window to decide if you need to further edit the query.

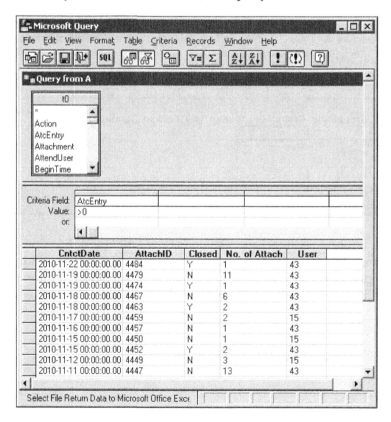

When you are satisfied with your result, you can return to the Excel worksheet. The query report is going to look different now.

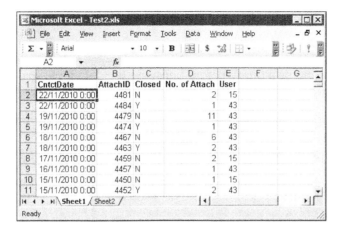

Under **Edit Query**, there is a **Data Range Property** menu item if your cursor is within the query result area.

One option under the bottom of the form is very useful. It is called **Fill down formulas in columns adjacent to data**. This option is not ticked by default. When you check this option, you will find you can extend the query capability. All formulas – directly beside the query – can grow automatically when the query result is changed.

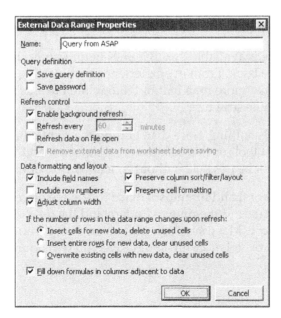

Avoiding pitfalls while building queries

There are many pitfalls when you begin to create new queries. You can find some of them by yourself. It would be better if you can avoid them before your start.

Here is a useful list of pitfalls I found that should be avoided:

- Starting to create a query before knowing the data table structure you are querying
- Creating a complicated logic inside your SQL query and not simplifying it
- Trying to do too many things in one query
- Relying solely on others' help and not doing trial runs on your own

These topics are discussed one by one.

Creating a query before knowing the data table structure

One of the most common problems for query writing is related to data structure. A new query learner tends to start building the query as soon as possible. However, that is not realistic without a good understanding of the data dictionary.

If you want to be good at query writing, the first thing to do is to understand the grammar of the query. That may only take a couple of hours. After that, the most important task is to know the database, tables, and the columns within the tables. It may need a month or more.

A good table reference is available through SDK help. This is already mentioned at the beginning of the book. From my experience in correcting query mistakes for many users, I found that more than half of them related to a lack of knowledge of SAP Business One's table structure.

Business Intelligence is nothing more than getting the right data at the right time. SQL Query is the right tool for this task to access database and to get the specific data you need. This may not be possible without a clear picture of the data.

Now, you will get my first and foremost advice to anyone interested in writing queries. You need to take out the time to understand the data and not be so eager to just start writing a query. Make sure you understand what you are going to query. One hour spent in a table relationship could save you two hours or more in writing a good query.

Complicating the logic instead of simplifying it

I often find some users that so quickly complicate a query beyond what is really needed. That may be necessary when you face very complex problems to be solved. To me, any query should never be too complicated.

My believe in query writing is: the simpler, the better. It is always possible to simplify the logic. If you can get the same thing done, you must select the least complicated way to achieve it. There are a few drawbacks for complicated queries as follows:

- Difficult to maintain
- Difficult to troubleshoot
- Difficult for others to understand
- Query will use more resources
- And so on……

The list can go on and on. To simplify the matter is only a habit. Whenever I have completed writing a query, I always check to see if it can be simplified or not. If I find a way to simplify it, I will definitely do it. In this way, I can more efficiently get the simplest query done in the shortest possible time. Some users are astonished by the speed with which I answered their question. A similar topic is discussed in *Chapter 1* already. It is emphasized it from a different angle.

Trying to do too many things in one query

This problem has the same root as the previous topic. Trying to do too many things in one query is the main reason most users have complicated queries. You should attempt to keep the results, and hence the query itself, to providing results in only one functional area.

A query is not there to be used for a complicated financial statement. A statement usually needs more than one query in one report. One query should focus on one function only. Use a maximum of two functions when one function is not good enough.

To check if your query is trying to show too many things should not be too difficult. Check how many tables are queried. If there are more than nine, that is most likely too many. And, without a doubt, it will be extremely difficult to change when the user requirements change in the future. If your query contains more than nine tables, then it is time to go back to the end-users to see if their requirements would be best addressed by Crystal Reports or by reducing the information they want from the SQL query.

My advice is to breakdown a complicated query into more than one small query. A small query can give you more pertinent information quickly and easily.

Relying on others' help only

It is understandable that we always try to get as much help as we can. Especially when you start to learn query, help requests are always more than welcome.

There is a line there though. You may ask help from time to time. But if you always rely on others' help, you may never learn how to write a correct query by yourself. There is absolutely no substitute for experience. Once you take on the task of writing an SQL query, you will always learn something—either the process of writing SQL query or the structure of the database and its associated tables. Going as far as you can will make it easier for others to help you also.

Learning SQL query is an ongoing process. The logical power can grow only if reasoning is from everyone's own point of view. The ability to reason logically can only grow and mature if you yourself try to execute a query and then take the next step to seek help from others. This will also aid in asking the correct question when you do ask for help.

Actually, one of the best ways to learn a SQL query is to help others with their questions and problems. I am certain one of the reasons that I have become an "expert" in SQL query for SAP Business One is that I was fortunate enough to have the opportunities to help all those other individuals who are walking the same path as you: writing SQL query so your company can make solid decisions with the data at hand in SAP Business One.

Summary

In this chapter, you have learned some of the more complicated query usages in detail. The first such usage is CASE expressions. You should know how to use each expression correctly and reasonably. Going through the more interesting topic of subqueries, you must learn when and where to use those subqueries. Pivot function is also a powerful function. Through the real case discussion, you can tell how much difference this function can make. The length of the query can be reduced by more than 50 percent from the ordinary query.

Database query for Excel is one of my favorite functions. Through this utility, you can get the power and convenience to link office documents with SAP Business One live data. You do not need to log in to the system to get the data you need.

There are so many other topics to discuss. However, every book must have its boundary and its ending. I hope this book can help you to study and create your own SQL query successfully for SAP Business One!

Appendix

Original transaction list by code

In SAP Business One, there are hundreds of different transactions everyday. A coding system is required to facilitate those business processes. You can find them when you look up **Journal Entries (JE)**; you can get the Origin code on the top of JE details. There is a drill-down arrow beside the code if the JE is not manually entered but automatically posted.

Here is the most often used code list for SAP Business One:

Code	Description	Origin Object
BC	Closing Balance	-3
BN	Bank Charge	-4
BT	BoE—Deposit to Paid	182
CN	A/R Credit Note	14
CP	Check for Payment	57
DD	Postdated Credit Voucher Deposit	76
DN	Delivery	15
DP	Down payment	25
DT	A/R Deposit	203
IF	Landed Costs	69
IM	Inventory Transfer	67
IN	A/R Invoice	13
JE	Manual Journal Entry	30
MR	Material Revaluation	162
OB	Opening Balance	-2

Code	Description	Origin Object
PC	A/P Credit Note	19
PD	Goods Receipt PO	20
PR	Goods Receipt	21
PS	Outgoing Payment	46
PU	A/P Invoice	18
PW	Production Order	202
RC	Incoming payment	24
RE	Return	16
RU	Payment Linked to Reconciled Transaction - Internal	-5
SI	Goods Receipt	59
SO	Goods Issue	60
ST	Stock Taking	58

Original transaction list by name

A similar list that can be checked by the transaction description:

Description	Code	Origin Object
A/P Credit Memo	PC	19
A/P Debit Memo	PU	18
A/P Down Payment Invoice	DT	203
A/P Invoice	PU	18
A/P Reserve Invoice	PU	18
A/R Bill	IN	13
A/R Credit Memo	CN	14
A/R Debit Memo	IN	13
A/R Down Payment Invoice	DT	203
A/R Exempt Bill	IN	13
A/R Export Invoice	IN	13
A/R Invoice	IN	13
A/R Invoice + Payment	IN	13
A/R Invoice Exempt	IN	13
A/R Reserve Invoice	IN	13
Bank Charge	BN	-5
Bill of Exchange – Deposit to Paid	BT	182

Description	Code	Origin Object
Check for Payment	CP	57
Closing Balance	BC	-3
Delivery	DN	15
Deposit	DP	25
Goods Issue	SO	60
Goods Receipt	SI	59
Goods Receipt PO	PD	20
Goods Return	PR	21
Incoming Payment	RC	24
Internal Invoice	PU	18
Inventory Posting	ST	58
Inventory Revaluation	MR	162
Inventory Transfer	IM	67
Issue for Production	SO	60
Landed Costs	IF	69
Manual Journal Entry	JE	30
Opening Balance	OB	-2
Outgoing Payments	PS	46
Payment Linked to Reconciled Transaction - Internal	RU	-5
Postdated Credit Voucher Deposit	DD	76
Production Order	PW	202
Receipt from Production	SI	59
Return	RE	16

This list has more lines than the first list. That is because the duplicated codes are allowed for the same object. You can find the codes through different call names. This is the purpose of the list.

Object codes and names

This is a complete list of the objects used in SAP Business One. For query purposes, especially for SBO_SP_TransactionNotification, this list is important.

Code	Name of objects	Description of objects
1	oChartOfAccounts	Chart of Accounts
2	oBusinessPartners	Business Partners
3	oBanks	Banks
4	oItems	Items
5	oVatGroups	Vat Groups
6	oPriceLists	Price Lists
7	oSpecialPrices	Special Prices
8	oItemProperties	Item Properties
10	oBusinessPartnerGroups	Business Partner Groups
12	oUsers	Users
13	oInvoices	Sales invoice document
14	oCreditNotes	Sales credit note document
15	oDeliveryNotes	Sales delivery note document
16	oReturns	Sales return document
17	oOrders	Sales order document
18	oPurchaseInvoices	Purchase invoice document
19	oPurchaseCreditNotes	Purchase credit note document
20	oPurchaseDeliveryNotes	Purchase delivery note document
21	oPurchaseReturns	Purchase return document
22	oPurchaseOrders	Purchase order document
23	oQuotations	Sales quotation document
24	oIncomingPayments	Payments
28	oJournalVouchers	Journal Vouchers
30	oJournalEntries	Manual Journal entry
31	oStockTakings	Stock Taking
33	oContacts	Activity
36	oCreditCards	Credit Cards
37	oCurrencyCodes	Currencies
40	oPaymentTermsTypes	Payment Terms Types
42	oBankPages	Bank Pages

Code	Name of objects	Description of objects
43	oManufacturers	Manufacturers
46	oVendorPayments	Payments to vendors
48	oLandedCostsCodes	Landed Costs Codes
49	oShippingTypes	Shipping Types
50	oLengthMeasures	Length Measures
51	oWeightMeasures	Weight Measures
52	oItemGroups	Item Groups
53	oSalesPersons	Sales Persons
56	oCustomsGroups	Customs Groups
57	oChecksforPayment	Checks for Payment
59	oInventoryGenEntry	Enter general items to the inventory
60	oInventoryGenExit	Exit general items from inventory
64	oWarehouses	Warehouses
65	oCommissionGroups	Commission Groups
66	oProductTrees	Product Trees (Bill of Materials)
67	oStockTransfer	Stock Transfer
68	oWorkOrders	Work Orders
70	oCreditPaymentMethods	Credit Payment Methods
71	oCreditCardPayments	Credit Card Payments
73	oAlternateCatNum	Alternate Category Number
77	oBudget	Budget
78	oBudgetDistribution	Budget Distribution
81	oMessages	Messages
91	oBudgetScenarios	Budget Scenarios
93	oUserDefaultGroups	User Default Groups
97	oSalesOpportunities	Sales Opportunities
101	oSalesStages	Sales Stages
103	oActivityTypes	Activity Types
104	oActivityLocations	Activity Locations
112	oDrafts	Draft document
116	oDeductionTaxHierarchies	Deduction Tax Hierarchies
117	oDeductionTaxGroups	Deduction Tax Groups
125	oAdditionalExpenses	Additional Expenses
126	oSalesTaxAuthorities	Sales Tax Authorities
127	oSalesTaxAuthoritiesTypes	Sales Tax Authorities Types

Code	Name of objects	Description of objects
128	oSalesTaxCodes	Sales Tax Codes
134	oQueryCategories	Query Categories
138	oFactoringIndicators	Factoring Indicators
140	oPaymentsDrafts	Payments
142	oAccountSegmentations	Account Segmentations
143	oAccountSegmentationCategories	Account Segmentation Categories
144	oWarehouseLocations	Warehouse Locations
145	oForms1099	Forms 1099
146	oInventoryCycles	Inventory Cycles
147	oWizardPaymentMethods	Wizard Payment Methods
150	oBPPriorities	Business Partner Priorities
151	oDunningLetters	Dunning Letters
152	oUserFields	User Fields MD
153	oUserTables	User Tables MD
156	oPickLists	Pick Lists
158	oPaymentRunExport	Payment Run Export
160	oUserQueries	User Queries
162	oMaterialRevaluation	Material Revaluation
163	oCorrectionPurchaseInvoice	Purchase invoice correction document
164	oCorrectionPurchaseInvoiceReversal	Reverse purchase invoice correction document
165	oCorrectionInvoice	Correction invoice document
166	oCorrectionInvoiceReversal	Reverse invoice correction document
170	oContractTemplates	Contract Templates
171	oEmployeesInfo	Employees Info
176	oCustomerEquipmentCards	Customer Equipment Cards
178	oWithholdingTaxCodes	Withholding Tax Codes
182	oBillOfExchangeTransactions	Bill of Exchange Transaction
189	oKnowledgeBaseSolutions	Knowledge Base Solutions
190	oServiceContracts	Service Contracts
191	oServiceCalls	Service Calls
193	oUserKeys	User Keys MD
194	oQueue	Queue
198	oSalesForecast	Sales Forecast
200	oTerritories	Territories

Code	Name of objects	Description of objects
201	oIndustries	Industries
202	oProductionOrders	Production Orders
203	oDownPayments	Sales down payment
204	oPurchaseDownPayments	Purchase down payment
205	oPackagesTypes	Packages Types
206	oUserObjectsMD	User Objects MD
211	oTeams	Teams
212	oRelationships	Relationships
214	oUserPermissionTree	User Permission Tree
217	oActivityStatus	Activity Status
218	oChooseFromList	Choose From List
219	oFormattedSearches	Formatted Searches
221	oAttachments2	Attachments detail
223	oUserLanguages	User Languages
224	oMultiLanguageTranslations	Multi Language Translations
229	oDynamicSystemStrings	Dynamic System Strings
231	oHouseBankAccounts	House Bank Accounts
247	oBusinessPlaces	Business Places
250	oLocalEra	Local Era
258	oNotaFiscalCFOP	Nota Fisca ICFOP
259	oNotaFiscalCST	Nota Fisca ICST
260	oNotaFiscalUsage	Nota Fisca Usage
261	oClosingDateProcedure	Closing Date Procedure
278	oBPFiscalRegistryID	BP Fiscal Registry ID
280	oSalesTaxInvoice	Sales tax invoice
281	oPurchaseTaxInvoice	Purchase tax invoice

Index

Symbols

'%[%2]%', parameter 91
$ values 190-193
[%0] variable 27
@list_of_cols_val_tab_del nvarchar(255),
     input parameter 260
@list_of_key_cols_tab_del nvarchar(255),
     input parameter 260
@num_of_cols_in_key int, input parameter
     260
@object_type nvarchar(20), input parameter
     260
!< operator 69
!> operator 69
< operator 69
<= operator 69
<>/!= operator 69
= operator 69
> operator 69
>= operator 69
@transaction_type nchar(1), input parameter
     260
_(underscore), wildcard character 72
[ ], wildcard character 72
[^], wildcard character 72
%, wildcard character 72

A

Account Segmentation Categories
     (oAccountSegmentationCategories)
     316
Account Segmentations
     (oAccountSegmentations) 316
active item list 122

ActiveX Data Objects (ADO) 242
Activity Locations (oActivityLocations) 315
Activity (oContacts) 314
Activity Status (oActivityStatus) 317
Activity Types (oActivityTypes) 315
Additional Expenses (oAdditionalExpenses)
     315
ADM 15
Administration. *See* ADM
alert
  A/R Invoice past due alert 137
  for invoice, without base document 137
  for sales order, special ship 138
  open sales opportunity alert 139, 140
  right alert, creating without duplicated lines
     136
  user query alert guide 140-143
  user query for 135
Alias (T0) 55
Alternate Category Number
     (oAlternateCatNumber) 315
Amount 32
A/P Credit Memo (PC) 312
A/P Credit Note (PC) 312
A/P Debit Memo (PU) 312
A/P Down Payment Invoice (DT) 312
A/P invoice document date, subquery
  displaying, for items 290
A/P Invoice (PU) 312
approval procedure
  approval stages, creating 161
  approval templates, creating 162
  creating, steps 160
  query, using for 159, 160
approval stages
  creating 161

column 12
command, crystal reports
    adding 245, 246
    fields, selecting from 247, 248
    working with 246, 247
Command function 246
Commission Groups (oCommissionGroups)
        315
Comp, computation options
    Amount 32
    Average 32
    Maximum 32
    Minimum 32
    Total Distinct Records 32
    Total Records 32
conditions, query wizard 32-34
consultant, SAP Business One 10
Contact Persons. *See* CPR
Contract Templates (oContractTemplates)
        316
Correction invoice document
        (oCorrectionInvoice) 316
COUNT(*) 78
COUNT() function 77
CPR 15
CRD 15
Create New Connection stage 244
Create Report button 226
Credit Card Payments
        (oCreditCardPayments) 315
Credit Cards (oCreditCards) 314
credit memo user check 110, 111
Credit Payment Methods
        (oCreditPaymentMethods) 315
Cross Join 63
crystal reports
    about 238, 239
    basic formatting 251-254
    command, adding to report 245, 246
    command, working with 246, 247
    creating 240
    fields, selecting from command 247, 248,
        249
    new database connection, creating 240-244
    records selection form, working with 249,
        250
    standard report wizard, working with 239

templates form, working with 249, 250
Currencies (oCurrencyCodes) 314
Customer Equipment Cards
        (oCustomerEquipmentCards) 316
Customs Groups (oCustomsGroups) 315

D

Database Owner (dbo) 55, 60
database query
    for Excel 294
    Microsoft Query window 304-307
    new data source, adding from control panel
        298-301
    new data source, adding within Excel 295-
        297
    new data source, creating 294
    query wizard 302, 303
Data Control Language. *See* DCL
Data Definition Language. *See* DDL
data dictionary 14
Data Manipulation Language. *See* DML
Data Manipulation Language (DML)
        commands 53
data source, database query
    adding, from control panel 298-301
    adding, with Excel 295-297
    creating 294
Data_type 81
Date 80
Date1 79
Date2 79
DATEADD() function 80
DATEDIFF() function 78, 79
date function
    about 91
    fixed date range, inputting 93
    months production balance 92
Datepart 78, 80
DATEPART() function 80, 81
DCL 13
DDL 13
Deduction Tax Groups
        (oDeductionTaxGroups) 315
Deduction Tax Hierarchies
        (oDeductionTaxHierarchies) 315
Delete Document? 235

UDF, populating from OITM in UDF on
    quotation 206
UDF value calling in BOM, to production
    order 213
UDF value, multiplying with system field
    value 213
warehouse in stock, commitment checks
    for 211
warehouse name, displaying beside
    warehouse code 208
foreign key, table links 18
Formatted Search . *See* **FMS**
Formatted Searches (oFormattedSearches)
    317
Forms 1099 (oForms 1099) 316
four variables
  in one query 89, 90
FROM clause
  about 58
  linked tables, group 61
  multiple tables, separated by commas 62
  single table 59, 60
Full Outer Join 68

G

General category 44
golden arrow 94
goods issue
  for none super user. blocking 277, 278
Goods Issue (SO) 312, 313
goods receipt
  item wise, subtotal 285, 286
goods receipt entry
  blocking 268, 270
goods receipt PO
  blocking 278
  within ten days 106, 107
Goods Receipt PO. *See* **PDN**
Goods Receipt PO (PD) 312, 313
Goods Receipt PO (PR) 312
Goods Receipt (SI) 312, 313
Goods Return (PR) 313
GROUP BY clause 72, 73
GROUP BY T1.ItemCode 101
GRPO
  blocking 272, 273

H

HAVING clause 73
HEM 15
House Bank Accounts
    (oHouseBankAccounts) 317

I

IF expressions 83
incoming payment
  about 131
  filtering 134, 135
  linking, with invoice 132
Incoming payment (RC) 312
Incoming Payment (RC) 313
Industries (oIndustries) 317
Inner Join
  about 63
  Key Columns 64
  syntax 63
IN operator 69, 71
Internal Invoice (PU) 313
INV 15
inventory count 123, 124
Inventory Cycles (oInventoryCycles) 316
Inventory Posting (ST) 313
Inventory Revaluation (MR) 313
inventory transactions
  queries for 120, 121
inventory transactions, queries for
  active item list 122
  item list completing, without transactions
    126-130
  item list completing, with
    transactions 126-130
  items undelivered, within 15 days 122
  price updates, queries 124, 125
  production orders list adding to, from sales
    order 126
  stock taking detail, finding 123, 124
  stock total, adding to queries 120, 121
  total, adding to query bottom 121, 122
Inventory Transfer (IM) 311, 313
invoice
  alert for, without base document 137
  blocking, GL account based 271, 272
  blocking, project based 271, 272

Maximum 32
Max(T1.Dscription) 101
Messages (oMessages) 315
Microsoft Query window, database query 304-307
middle part, query generator form 26, 27
MIN() function 77
Minimum 32
miscellaneous query, examples
about 145
service call related query 146
two text columns, concatenating 146
monthly sales
by geography 291, 292
Multi Language Translations (oMulti LanguageTranslations) 317

N

negative sign, FMS query 194
none cash outgoing payment approval 172, 173
Non-SAP Business One users 11
Nota Fisca lCFOP (oNotaFiscalCFOP) 317
NotaFiscalCST (oNota Fisca lCST) 317
Nota Fisca Usage (oNotaFiscaUsage) 317
notes
filtering by, from OCRD 103
NOT EXISTS operator 71

O

OCRD 30
OCST (State table) 26
OLE DB (ADO) 241
On Account outgoing payment approval 170
OPEN 89
Opening Balance (OB) 311, 313
open sales opportunity alert 139, 140
OPR 15
orange arrow
about 94
sales order updating alert, with drill down 96, 97
ORDER BY clause 74
ORDER BY SUM(T1.LineTotal) DESC 101
originator tab, approval templates 162, 163

OSLP 30
O tables 16
Outer Join
about 65
Left Outer Join 65, 66
Right Outer Join 66-68
Self-Join 68
outgoing payment
above 20,000, restricting 268
for specific BP, blocking 266, 267
Outgoing Payment (PS) 312
Outgoing Payments (PS) 313
over booking sales order
approval for 171, 172

P

Packages Types (oPackagesTypes) 317
Payment Linked to Reconciled Transaction - Internal (RU) 312, 313
Payment Run Export (oPaymentRunExport) 316
Payments (oIncomingPayments) 314
Payments (oPayments) 316
Payments to vendors (oVendorsPayments) 315
Payment Terms Types (oPaymentTermsTypes) 314
payment transactions
types, listing 133
PCH 15
PDN 15
Pick Lists (oPickLists) 316
pitfalls
avoiding, while building queries 308
logic, complicating 309
query, creating 308
Pivot
monthly sales, by geography 291-293
used, for simplifying cross tab style queries 291
planned quantity
versus in stock 125
POR 15
Postdated Credit Voucher Deposit (DD) 311, 313
Price Lists (oPriceLists) 314

right alert
  creating, without duplicated items 136, 137
Right Outer Join 66, 67
right part, query generator form 26, 27
RIN 15
row table 21
RPC 15

S

sales
  by states 115, 116
sales analysis report
  customized 108, 109
Sales credit note document (oCreditNotes)
      314
Sales Credit Notes. *See* RIN
Sales delivery note document
      (oDeliveryNotes) 314
sales documents
  blocking, dates based 275, 276
Sales down payment (oDownPayments) 317
sales employees name
  adding, to queries 104, 105
Sales Forecast (oSalesForecast) 316
Sales invoice document (oInvoices) 314
Sales Invoices. *See* INV
Sales Opportunities. *See* OPR
Sales Opportunities (oSalesOpportunities)
      315
sales order
  with PO 118-120
Sales order document (oOrders) 314
Sales Orders. *See* RDR
sales order updating alert
  with drill down 96, 97
sales per month
  average 109, 110
Sales Persons (oSalesPersons) 315
Sales Persons (Sales Employees). *See* SLP
sales quotation
  blocking, if no value in row level UDF 270,
      271
sales quotations. *See aslo* QUT
Sales quotation document (oQuotations)
      314

Sales return document (oReturns) 314
Sales Stages (oSalesStages) 315
sales summary
  reducing from two lines to one line 112-114
Sales Tax Authorities
      (oSalesTaxAuthorities) 315
Sales Tax Authorities Types (Sales
      TaxAuthoritiesTypes) 315
Sales Tax Codes (oSalesTaxCodes) 316
Sales tax invoice (oSalesTaxInvoice) 317
SAP Business One
  consultant 10
  database table references 14, 15
  developer 10
  end user 10
  naming conventions, for table 15
  Non-SAP Business One users 11
  query generator 24
  query wizard 28
  SQL queries, benefits 9, 10
  SQL query tools 23
  stored procedures 261
  system queries 36
  table links, examples 18
SAP Business One Database Tables
      Reference 14
SBO_SP_PostTransactionNotice 261
SBO_SP_PostTransactionSupport 261
SBO_SP_TransactionNotification 261
  about 257, 259
  maintaining 262
  menu, panels 262
  objects 263
  toolbar, panels 262
  working with 261
SBO_SP_TransactionSupport 261
searched CASE expression 82
securities
  handling, for query usage 149
Select All button 51
SELECT statement
  about 53
  clauses 57
  column name, descriptions 56
  complete database table columns, returning
      55

UNION clause 74
WHERE clause 68, 69
Stock Taking (oStockTakings) 314
Stock Taking (ST) 123, 124, 312
stock total
adding, to queries 120, 121
Stock Transfer (oStockTransfer) 315
Stock Transfers. *See* **WTR**
stored procedure. *See* **SP**
stored procedures, SAP Business One
SBO_SP_PostTransactionNotice 261
SBO_SP_PostTransactionSupport 261
SBO_SP_TransactionNotification 261
SBO_SP_TransactionSupport 261
Style 81
subquery
item groups 288
last A/P invoice document, showing 290
similar records, checking 289, 290
working with 287
YTD sales, for two years 288
subtotal
getting, from query 97
SUM() function 76
SUM(T1.LineTotal) 101
Superuser 45
system queries
about 24
benefits 36-39

T

T0.docdate >= [%0] and T0.docdate <= [%1]
101
T0.doctype = 'I' 101
table 11
table links
about 17
examples, with SAP business one 18
examples, with SAP Business One 18
foreign key 18
primary key 17
table links, examples
OCRD-Business Partner table and OSLP-
Sales Employee table 18
OITM-Items table and ITM1-Items Prices
table 18

OITT-Product Tree table and ITT1-Product
Tree Child Items 18
table naming convention, SAP Business
One
A tables 16
document header tables 16
document line tables 16
O tables 16
tables, examples 17
three letter words 15, 16
tables, examples
ADOC-Document History 17
OINM-Warehouse Journal 17
OJDT-Journal Entry 17
tables, query wizard
selecting, for report 29, 30
target table
versus base table 18,-21
tax code summary 114, 115
Teams (oTeams) 317
templates tab, QPLD 223
terms tab, approval templates
about 165
query, selecting for approval template 165-
168
Territories (oTerritories) 316
Tools menu 45
Tools | Queries | Query Wizard 28
TOP 5 T1.ItemCode 101
TOP clause 58
top N customers 131
total
adding, to query bottom 121, 122
Total Distinct Records 32
Total Records 32
Transtype
displaying, as code 282, 283
T-SQL 13
two text columns
concatenating 146

U

UDF
updating, by different dates 286
UDV. *See* **user-defined values**
UNION ALL clause

UNION clause 74
User Default Groups (oUserDefaultGroups)
    315
User Defined Field (UDF) 12, 46
User Defined Tables (UDT) 46
User Defined Table (UDT) 12
user-defined values
  $ values 190-193
  about 176
  and FMS 176
  existing values, searching 181-189
  FMS queries, running directly 194
  searching in 195-203
  values, retrieving 193
  working with 177-180
User Fields MD (oUserFields) 316
User Interface (UI) 35
User Keys MD (oUserKeys) 316
User Languages (oUserLanguages) 317
User Objects MD (oUserObjects MD) 317
User Permission Tree
    (oUserPermissionTree) 317
user queries
  creating 45, 46
  deleting 47
  saving 46
User Queries (oUserQueries) 316
user query alert guide 140-145
Users. *See* USR
Users (oUsers) 314
User Tables MD (oUserTables) 316
USR 16

V

variables
  defining, for queries 89

first 90, 91
last 90, 91
Vat Groups (oVatGroups) 314
Visible check 230

W

Warehouse Locations
    (oWarehouseLocations) 316
Warehouses (oWarehouses) 315
Weight Measures (oWeightMeasures) 315
WHERE clause 69, 250
wildcard character
  [ ] 72
  [^] 72
  % 72
  _(underscore) 72
Withholding Tax Codes
    (oWithholdingTaxCodes) 316
Wizard Payment Methods
    (oWizardPaymentMethods) 316
WOR 16
Work Orders (oWorkOrders) 315
WTR 16

X

X button 26

Y

YTD sales, subquery 288, 289

Thank you for buying
Mastering SQL Queries for
SAP Business One

About Packt Publishing

Packt, pronounced 'packed', published its first book "Mastering phpMyAdmin for Effective MySQL Management" in April 2004 and subsequently continued to specialize in publishing highly focused books on specific technologies and solutions.

Our books and publications share the experiences of your fellow IT professionals in adapting and customizing today's systems, applications, and frameworks. Our solution based books give you the knowledge and power to customize the software and technologies you're using to get the job done. Packt books are more specific and less general than the IT books you have seen in the past. Our unique business model allows us to bring you more focused information, giving you more of what you need to know, and less of what you don't.

Packt is a modern, yet unique publishing company, which focuses on producing quality, cutting-edge books for communities of developers, administrators, and newbies alike. For more information, please visit our website: www.packtpub.com.

About Packt Enterprise

In 2010, Packt launched two new brands, Packt Enterprise and Packt Open Source, in order to continue its focus on specialization. This book is part of the Packt Enterprise brand, home to books published on enterprise software – software created by major vendors, including (but not limited to) IBM, Microsoft and Oracle, often for use in other corporations. Its titles will offer information relevant to a range of users of this software, including administrators, developers, architects, and end users.

Writing for Packt

We welcome all inquiries from people who are interested in authoring. Book proposals should be sent to author@packtpub.com. If your book idea is still at an early stage and you would like to discuss it first before writing a formal book proposal, contact us; one of our commissioning editors will get in touch with you.

We're not just looking for published authors; if you have strong technical skills but no writing experience, our experienced editors can help you develop a writing career, or simply get some additional reward for your expertise.

SAP® Business ONE
Implementation

ISBN: 978-1-847196-38-5   Paperback: 320 pages

Bring the power of SAP Enterprise Resource Planning to your small-midsize business

1. Get SAP B1 up and running quickly, optimize your business, inventory, and manage your warehouse

2. Understand how to run reports and take advantage of real-time information

3. Complete an express implementation from start to finish

4. Real-world examples with step-by-step explanations

Learning SQL Server 2008
Reporting Services

ISBN: 978-1-847196-18-7   Paperback: 512 pages

A step-by-step guide to getting the most of Microsoft SQL Server Reporting Services 2008

1. Everything you need to create and deliver data-rich reports with SQL Server 2008 Reporting Services as quickly as possible

2. Packed with hands-on-examples to learn and improve your skills

3. Connect and report from databases, spreadsheets, XML Data, and more

Please check **www.PacktPub.com** for information on our titles

CPSIA information can be obtained at www.ICGtesting.com
Printed in the USA
LVOW03s1915190315

431273LV00005B/25/P